W0018143

SAGE DUPREE

— BOOK 1 —

Dirty Secrets

print ISBN: 978-1-09835-089-5
ebook ISBN: 978-1-09835-090-1

Contents

The Beginning

It was August 7th, 1999, and my birthday. One would have expected me to be happy but I was the furthest from that mood. I was 13 that day and becoming a teenager didn't live up to what I expected. Living on a Native American reservation at Saltwater was like being sentenced to life in a state prison. We were absent of the gun tower and warden, but it wasn't the best thing on earth. I was living in poverty in a crime-stricken area on the rez called the Pit. When you walked through it, you saw, single-wide trailer homes that were worn down and barely standing on the earth beneath them. Graffiti was scattered on different dwellings, telling the story of our life as Native American Indians. That was a sure sign of grief, drugs and gang activity. Alcoholism was the norm here and suicide among kids my age was popular and no different than being a drug dealer for the mafia. It felt more like hell. If only I could be open and tell my family about the pain that I'd endured since the age of nine perhaps my life would change. I often dreamt of becoming rich and famous, to move me and my family away from this hell. It was only that—just a dream. I put my singing ability to the back of my mind because I knew that I would never get the opportunity that people off the rez get to becoming famous. I was tired and getting ready to take my own life. I took the .38 from underneath my leg and I was about to put it to my head when I heard—

"CHEETAH!" I turned to see two of my friends from off the rez, making their way towards me. I was sitting near the Devil's Belly, which was nothing but open mountain and land. It extended so far out that at night, it looked like you were looking into a black hole out in space. So many people died in this place and many bodies were found unclaimed. Mitch and his brother Novi are black boys who lived on 89th, which was ten minutes away from the reservation. We met by accident. I was getting ready to fight with Novi, when his brother saved him and from that day, we have been cool. They introduced me to the neighborhood off the rez and I introduced them to rez life. "What you doing over here on your birthday?" Novi quizzed with a fixed grin on his face. He was always smiling about something.

"I'm just over here thinking." I had the gun hidden.

"Man, it's your birthday and you're over here by yourself looking at this scary shit?"

"This does look crazy," Mitch added. He scanned the Devil's Belly with suspicious eyes. "I wouldn't want to be caught over here at night."

"How did yawl find me?"

They pointed to my brother Marcus, who was standing off to the side, talking to a girl. He wasn't supposed to know that I was here. I tucked the .38 underneath the rock that I was sitting on and asked, "What yawl want?"

"We wanted to come and chill with you since it's your birthday."

"Yeah, get yo ass up and come chill with us!" Mitch said. He pulled me up and gave me a tight hug. "Happy Birthday B dog!"

I chuckled, not feeling it but it was cool that they showed up. "Thanks."

"C'mon Cheetah, they invited us to the block to hang out." Marcus said after the girl he was talking to walked away. He was always talking to girls and he was having sex and only a year older than me. I hoped nothing happened to the gun that I hid under the rock. It was stolen from my aunt. Nobody knew that I had it.

"What yawl doing on the block?"

"It's a surprise, I think you'll be happy. I'm glad that we found out." Mitch put his arm on my shoulder. I realized that he drove on the rez because when we got to my house, there was a black Audi parked in front of it. "Whose car is this?"

They exploded in laughter. "This is one of Mitch's G-rides, c'mon."

Marcus opened the back door pushing me in. He climbed in after me and I looked forward to my mom asking where we were going, but she was probably in the house laid out drunk, as usual. My dad was on the Air Force base, always gone, so my mom drank her life away. Mitch jumped behind the wheel and started the stolen car and he pulled off at top speed.

"Slow down, dog! The tribal police be out here fucking with folks, especially us." Marcus told him.

He slowed his speed and I was looking at everything that we passed, grateful to be leaving the reservation. It was hot out and the AC was on full blast in the car. I was wondering where Mitch has stolen this car from. They were always stealing. It was a way of life for them. Marcus fired up some weed in the back seat and he took a big hit and passed it to me. “Nah, I’m good.”

“Hit it bro, it’s your burfday—

I snatched it from him and hit it. I was coughing instantly and they thought it was funny. The coughing seemed to be nonstop as we came to a light exiting the reservation. I thought I was going to puke until Marcus passed me some water. “Drink this; it will stop you from coughing.”

I took a big swig of the water and he was right, it helped. I started feeling the euphoric effects and everything was good suddenly. We made it to 89th and it was filled with guys. They were all black and once I saw that, it gave me a sense of comfort because nobody looked at me mean. I felt the welcoming stares as we parked and got out of the car. Guys were going up to Mitch and greeting him with firm handshakes and love. He introduced Marcus and then they introduced me.

“It’s his birthday,” Mitch explained and one of the guys laughed and hugged me.

“Happy Birthday man, I’m Sneaky,” He stuck his hand out. I shook hands with him.

“Happy Birthday,” he said, digging in his pocket. He pulled out a hundred dollars.

“For me?”

“Yeah, dog! Happy Birthday! Here, take it!”

I took it and thanked him with a firm handshake to let him know that I wasn’t just a soft dude. I felt the vibes of the fellas here and it was different because on the rez, they made me feel like an outcast, especially since my dad is black and my mother is 100 percent Native American.

It was a totally different vibe here. Novi came over and put his arm around me. "See, bro, look at the love you're getting on the block dog. You need to be from my hood. Let me introduce you to the homies. This is Flip … this is Cal, yawl this is Cheetah, he's from the reservation, him and his brother over there," Novi pointed to Marcus who was on the other side of the lawn in front of the apartment building with guys his age. They were shooting dice and I was over here with the guys my age.

Sneaky came over and told me, "These dudes are the homies from the Nation. If you wanna be from the nation, all you gotta do is let me know." He said, "I got your back."

"Nigga, how you gone make him from the nation, that's my friend," Novi said.

"Shut up, dog, he's old enough to speak for himself, right?" Sneaky said making me laugh.

"Happy Birthday, Cheetah," Sneaky said. "I'm about to go over here and win some money," he said, leaving us alone to chill. "Aye, Cheetah, it's always some fine girls on this block, too. It's one girl that everybody's trying to get at but she won't let nobody hit," Novi said and his boys laughed. "You talking about Alia?" Cal said.

"Yep! Alia! If you see her don't talk to her because that's who I'm trying to link up with."

"Man, Cheetah she's FINE! Hella fine, she's dark skin with long hair and gray eyes. I've never seen a girl that fine in my life!"

"Yep and it's all her hair and her eyes too, nothing on her is fake," Flip added. He came and whispered to me. "Don't join this hood; stay solo. We can start a dance crew, no gangs!"

"Why you say that?" I asked him.

"Trust me, I know," he said. I nodded and stayed quiet while the fellas talked about different things, from females, to money to cars. It was far better than sitting on the rez about to commit suicide. A few moments later, I hear the guys singing happy birthday to me and Mitch walks up with a big cake in his arms. "Awwww shit!" I laughed. I wasn't expecting this.

"HAPPY BIRTHDAY DEAR CHEETAHHHHH HAPPY BIRTHDAY TO YOUUUUUU!" They all cheered and Mitch ran his finger across the whipped cream and wiped it across the tip of my nose. It was funny. "Awww, wow. Thanks."

"Cut me a piece, dog! I want some cake."

"Dog, you gotta be from the hood now," Sneaky said.

"If my brother's gonna be put on I need to be the one to do it," Marcus interrupted.

"You're from the Nation," I looked at my brother and they all laughed.

"Marcus been from the hood, dog!"

I had no idea that my brother was banging the nation. "Nah, Marcus, you can't put your brother on. Let him fight, Novi, and if he wins, he can be from the Nation."

"Aiight, aiight. Bet."

Novi had his shirt off like he was excited to fight me and little did he know, I have five brothers and they all taught me how to fight from getting my ass kicked by all of them. Not to mention the fights on the rez.

"Whup his ass, Cheetah!" Marcus pointed at me with warning eyes. I knew that I needed to win this fight. Mitch set the cake on top of the car and nobody touched it. I realized that this was already planned for me. Novi and I moved to the middle of the block and everybody was outside watching. We squared up. I wasn't scared. I remembered what I was taught and I used it on him. When he rushed up, I caught him in the mouth and he fell.

"OOOOOOOOOH, HOLD ON, BLOOD! HOLD ON!" Mitch yelled helping his brother up. He hollered something at him and Novi was pissed. I could see that he was embarrassed, too, but I put my guards back up after Mitch moved out of the way and we squared off again. We did some circular movements, swinging at each other but nothing connected and then I caught him again with another hard one to the face. He grabbed his eye and backed up.

"FUCK HIM UP, CHEETAH! DON'T STOP RUSH THAT FOOL!" Marcus pushed me in on him and he swung and I ducked just in time and I gave him more body blows until they stopped the fight.

"Cheetah's IN!" I heard Sneaky yell and he grabbed my arm and pulled it up in the air while the fellas gave me praise. Novi was mad. He went and sat down on the curb, nursing his eye. I felt bad because he's the homie and I didn't want to hurt him but I liked to fight. I took out my aggression with fights on the rez, so off the rez wasn't nothing!

"Aye, Cheetah, you can fight!" Cal said, giving me love with a firm handshake and a hug. Flip came to me with big smiles and a hug, as if he was glad that I won the fight, too. I wasn't trying to hurt Novi, but I had to defend myself because these guys didn't know me and I had to make a good impression. Marcus came to where I was standing, getting my wind back, he pulled me over to him and whispered, "Good job' li'l bro. Love you."

"Love you, too," I whispered back, glad that my brother was with me. I'm tall for my age, so people thought that I was older than thirteen. I still can't believe that I'm here in the hood being shown this much love. I appreciated it and it gave me a reason to keep living. A girl came downstairs from the apartment complex passing out paper plates and Mitch called us over to get pieces of the birthday cake. I looked at Novi, "You good?"

He nodded, but never looked at me. He wasn't good. I felt that from him. He was pissed that I beat him up in front of the homies like that. I felt kind of bad, but I went and sat down on the stairs alone to eat my cake. Chocolate is my favorite and I dunno how Mitch knew. Marcus came and sat beside me. "You happy about the cake? It was my idea!" he said.

"I knew it! You're the only that know I love chocolate, thank you. You paid for it, too?"

"Nah, Mitch owed me a favor so I told him to buy you that cake. I just wanted you to get off the rez since mom is at home drunk and only thinking of herself. I didn't want you to be sad."

"Where's Chepi?"

"Working with grandpa … he got you a present, too. I'm just glad that we were able to get off the rez and you could enjoy today."

"Yeah, me too. I just hope mom doesn't make me go back over Aunt Rowena's house now that I'm thirteen."

"She won't."

"I think Novi's mad." I told Marcus.

"He looks like it, huh? Oh well, it was a fair fight. His loss!" His pager went off and he took it from his hip. I finished my cake and Marcus asked Mitch if he could use the phone. "Aye bro, we might have to leave," He told me. I didn't want to leave. I was having too much fun.

"Oh shit! There's the pretty girls," Sneaky pointed. "That's Alia!" he boasted in a loud voice, and I was looking to see if she was as fine as they said she was. I'm picky and weird when it comes to pretty girls. It was NO pretty girls on the rez at all, maybe one or two, but that was it. The rest of them were super fat and out of shape and a majority of them were looking like the guys. "Aye Cheetah, there she is … maybe you got a shot. Novi likes Alia, but she ain't fucking with him." Sneaky whispers. He didn't want Alia with Novi.

They came across the street and I tossed my empty paper plate in the trashcan that was on the side of the building. "Come on, dog, lemme go introduce you," Sneaky said.

"Aye, dog, hold up," Novi caught up with us. He told me that he liked Alia and that he was going to put his bid in with her. I nodded. I didn't care, I was just trying to see what she looked like. She was with two light-skinned females and they were all smiles as we walked up. "Aye, ladies what's up," Sneaky spoke up. Novi said nothing. He was face to face with her and he didn't even open his mouth. When Alia turned towards me, my heart almost stopped. She was super pretty! Wow! I guess there is a such thing as beautiful. She's gorgeous! I looked at Novi, waiting for him to talk to her. He was quiet. He said nothing. "Hello," I spoke to her. She smiled at me.

"Hi, I'm Alia," She stuck her hand out and I grabbed it and shook it, getting butterflies all over my body it seemed. I never felt that from anybody. She touched my soul right then. Wow! Everything started moving in slow motion.

"Are you new on the block," her friend asked. I let her hand go and put it in my pocket. I didn't pay her friend any attention; she was more important to me. We were both staring each other down like we had seen a ghost.

"He's from the rez. This is my homie, Cheetah," Novi cut in. Alia stayed silent, but she was staring at me hard as if she forgot how to speak. She was checking me out, even the clothes that I was wearing and I took pride in how I dressed. Even with us being poor, I dressed as if I was a middle-class kid. Everything that I wore was matching and even down to my tennis shoes. I felt her vibe and she seemed cool. "Do you want to walk over here and get out of the sun," she finally spoke.

"Uh, um yeah … okay." I followed her and Novi stayed behind. He had an instant attitude.

"Wait, are you talking to Novi?" I asked in front of him just in case he thought I was trying to push up on his girl. I wasn't here for that and out of respect, I had to ask.

"Who me? Hell no!" she frowned. "I just know him and his brother Mitch. I'm not talking to him like that," she explained. I looked at him and shrugged and he waved us off and moved over to Sneaky and the other girls that she came with.

"So your name is Cheetah," she asked after we were away from everyone.

"Yeah … my nickname."

"What's your real name?"

"I don't tell people my real name."

"Oh … how come? Wait … don't tell me, you're ashamed of it because you're Native American?"

I laughed. "First of all, I'm not ashamed of my heritage. I'm proud to be Native, but I'm native and black, so I guess I got the best of both sides."

"Wow … I can't tell."

"You can't tell what?"

"I didn't know you were mixed with black."

"Yeah, my father is black. He's from Jamaica actually but he's in the military now."

"Oh cool … at least you know your parents. I don't know my mom or my dad."

"Oh, wow, I'm sorry to hear that, did they die or something?"

She looked sad once I pried into her personal life. Maybe I shouldn't have. "I dunno where my mom is and my dad either. I don't think they're dead. Just put it this way, I'm an orphan. Right now, I live with my aunt who treats me like crap. She treats my cousin like a queen because she's light skin, and that girl over there in the red shorts is my cousin."

"Oh really?" I nodded.

"Yeah that's my cousin Nikki and today she's nice to me, so I'm over here. I dunno how she might be towards me tomorrow."

Her cousin was looking our way and she didn't seem too nice with the way she was staring. "So, what's your story, are your mom and dad still together?"

I wished that I could really tell her my story, but it would've been too heavy for her. "Yeah, my mom and dad are still together, it's just that my dad is in the Air Force, so he's always gone and he only comes home twice a year."

"Wow, that sucks. I bet you miss him, huh?"

"Oh yeah, I do. He calls a lot. My mom, she stays drunk half the time so I don't really have a relationship with her. I hope you're not with anybody and they pull up and see us talking."

"I don't have a boyfriend," she replied and that was music to my ears because Novi was about to be angry with me. I liked this girl. She made me feel alive again. She was the most beautiful girl that I had ever seen in my life and I wanted to get to know her. After meeting her, my life changed. "Do you have a girlfriend? You are very handsome."

"Thank you and no I don't have a girlfriend."

"How old are you?"

"I just turned thirteen today."

She was all smiles. "Happy Birthday."

"Thank you."

"I'll be thirteen in October on Halloween. I'm compatible with Leos."

"Oh you believe in the zodiac stuff? It's all new to me."

"Really?" she laughed. "I read a lot and I'm into astrology. I'm in the 7th grade."

"Me too. I go to school on the rez but my dream is to go to PVA."

"Really? Me too! I'm into performing arts. I like to act and dance."

"I like to dance and sing," I admitted. Her eyes lit up.

"You sing?"

"Yeah I can sing!" I told her. "I wrote a whole bunch of songs, but I mean, I dunno if you'd like to hear 'em."

"I want to listen to them. Do you have them recorded?"

"I do. I have them on cassette tapes and I can bring them tomorrow if you want to hear some songs that I wrote."

"Oh my gosh, yes! We have so much in common. What else do you like to do?" She had me feeling as if I was on a different planet.

"I like music a lot. One day I wanna start my own group and become famous."

"Have you applied at PVA? It's hard getting in that school, but I heard that if you're good, you can do it and you being from the Native reservation, you should be able to get in easily."

"I wish. I don't even know how to apply."

"I'll help you. Give me your number," she said. "Wait, I have to find a pen." She got up and left me on the benches in the apartment building where Novi lives and then here comes Marcus. "Bro, we have to go. Chepi said that Mom is worried about us. She called the tribal cops."

"What? Awww man. Okay, hold on, lemme give her the number."

"Who?"

"Alia!"

He smiled. "You're talking to her? I thought that was Novi's girl?"

"Nope! She said that she wasn't going with him!"

Marcus found it funny and when I looked over at the front of the apartment complex, Novi was mean mugging me with lowered angry eyes.

Alia came running back with the pen and she had paper, "What's your number?" I gave her the number.

Marcus gave me dap with a closed fist against my fist. "That's right, baby bro, handle that shit," He laughed.

We left the block at a quarter to seven. We had Mitch stop the car at the rez entrance and we decided to walk because he was driving a stolen car and he would've gone to jail on the rez if the cops found out. "Good looking out, Mitch, we'll see you tomorrow, dog," Marcus shook hands with him, and I climbed out of the back. Novi didn't ride with us to go home; he was mad, and Mitch admitted that he was pissed that I took his girl. Oh well! She told me straight up in front of him that she wasn't with him, so what was I supposed to do? As we're walking home, Marcus asked me what I was doing over at the Devil's Belly. "I was just sitting and thinking, bro."

"About what? Nobody goes over there, man."

"I know, but I wanted to get away," I told him. I wasn't about to tell him that I had planned to off myself. I kept that hidden. I wished that I could tell him what had been going on with me, but I had to keep it all a secret. "Don't go over there anymore, bro, do you hear me? It's dangerous over there and it's on sacred ground."

"I know."

"Don't let me catch you over there anymore, Cheetah. I swear, we're going to have it out if I do."

"All right, bro, I hear you! I won't go over there anymore," I told him, just to shut him up.

Once we made it to our block, there were three tribal cop cars outside. "THERE THEY ARE!" I heard my mom and we got rushed by two cops. We were thrown to the ground. "Wait a minute, don't hurt them!" Mom yelled. "They're okay!"

"Step back ma'am!"

"We didn't DO NOTHING!" Marcus yelled and they lifted me up and lifted my brother up and another cop hit him in the stomach with the flashlight hard, bending him over making him fall to his knees. I started crying. "LEAVE MY BROTHER ALONE! WE DIDN'T DO NOTHING!" I yelled. My mom was crying and my other brothers came outside, wondering why we were in handcuffs. They put me in the backseat of a patrol car and Marcus was put in the other car in front of me. Why we were getting arrested when we were both minors and didn't commit no crime? One of the cops was talking to my mom and I heard her slur, "They're just kids!"

I was driven away from the house with a tribal cop in the car alone. "I'm innocent. I didn't do anything wrong," I said and the cop looked at me through his rearview once we got away from the house. The look in his eyes was sinister, something that you would only see in a movie. "You listen to me, you fucking nigger! As soon you turn eighteen, I'm going to put a bullet in your head!"

"Why?"

"Because I don't like the looks of you! You think because you're passing for a Native American that you can get away with stuff? You ain't sovereign, BOY! I'm gonna kill you because I know you're going to grow up to be a FUCK UP just like your brother Marcus! We don't like your kind around here!"

"Where are you taking me?" I asked because the police station wasn't this way. We were driving on a dark road and I was scared that he was going to take me to the Devil's Belly and leave me there in the dark. If he did, I was going to find that gun and shoot myself. Fuck it! "I asked you where you're taking me?"

"Shut the fuck up and ride, nigger boy!"

When we pulled up at my aunt Rowena's house, I was pissed. She was in the front yard with a glass in her hand and I knew that it was gin she was drinking. My whole mood changed and I felt that misery return. She was the reason why I was going to kill myself. I hate her! "Take me to jail!" I told the cop. He laughed.

"Niggers don't get choices!" He pulled in the driveway and she was standing there smiling and put a thumbs up. He climbed out of the car, If I wasn't in handcuffs, I would've jumped out and ran but I had no choice but to sit there. It was dark outside and hot. The patrol car was still running and he went to Rowena and hugged her and they were talking like they were buddies. Why wasn't he like this to my mom? Where did they take Marcus? Tears ran down my face. I didn't want to be here! I felt that once I turned thirteen that it would be the end of dealing with this. The cop came to the car and opened the back door, grabbing me out. He turned me around and took out his keys. He leaned in my ear, "You remember what I said, boy. Today is just your thirteenth birthday, you got five more years to enjoy life!"

He took the cuffs off and shoved me towards Rowena and I almost fell. He went back to his car and I wanted to run, but I didn't. I walked up to her and she grabbed me, "You scared me half to death boy, get your ass in here." She grabbed my arm tight and pulled me towards her house.

"I wanna go home. Call my mom," I cried. She took me in her mini mansion and slammed the front door shut. "You ain't going no fucking where! You're going to stay here and fuck me like a man! Get out of those clothes!"

"Rowena, please! I'm begging you! I don't wanna do this anymore!" She walked over to me and stood in my face. "Do you want your dad to die?"

"NO! Just let me go and I'll see that we move off the rez."

She was laughing. "How in the hell are you going to move off the rez? You guys don't have any money! I'm the one with all the money and the power! Get out of those clothes, Cheetah!"

"Aunt Ro—

"NOW! I don't wanna hear any more of your whining."

I wanted to fight her, but if I did, I would have to kill her and if I killed her, I was going to have to end my life, too. I was picturing images of me killing her in my head and seeing blood everywhere.

"HURRY UP CHEETAH!"

I stripped out of my clothes, feeling numb. I was naked like she had always wanted me to be, ever since the age of nine. The first time anything happened, it was on my ninth birthday. She had this massive party for me and I was happy because she had favored me out of my siblings, always buying me whatever I wanted, giving me whatever I wanted and being so nice to me. I cherished her and loved her for it, but later when I turned nine, I found out why she had been so nice. On my ninth birthday, she had me come to her house for a gift allegedly and upon my arrival, there was no surprise gift, she was upstairs in the bedroom stark naked, waving me over to the bed to fondle her naked body. I was in shock and she told me that if I said a word to anybody that she would have my dad killed. My dad means everything to me, so of course I kept quiet about it and now that I'm 13, I'm filled with rage and anger. I pictured myself killing her as she gave me oral sex. This is what she's been doing to me since the age of nine. She puts her mouth on my penis and sucks until I ejaculate. She makes me go down on her, too. I left my body again and went with the program because if I didn't, who's to say what would happen to my dad. With her money and power, she could have my dad murdered and make it look like an accident. I was having dreams that my dad was found dead in a car and in some of my dreams he would be in a bad car accident. It woke me up in hysterics and Marcus and Chepi would have to calm me down, telling me that I was only dreaming. She instilled fear in me at a young age, but now my fear was turning into rage. After I was finish pleasing her, she lay there calm now, looking at me with those fake loving eyes. "I know you like music, Cheetah. What do you want to do with your music?"

Get away from you! "What do you mean?"

"I want to know what it is about music that you like so much? Do you think that you can be a famous singer one day?"

"I dunno."

"Wrong answer, Cheetah!"

"What do you mean?"

"I want you to say that you will be a famous singer and everyone will love your music and you will be known all over the world. SAY IT!" she snapped and I repeated what she said.

“Good job! Now if you keep what just happened between me and you, I will get you exactly what you want … do you want that?”

“Yes!”

“How badly do you want it?”

“I want it bad!”

“Okay, what do you need?”

“Ummm, I need studio equipment for my brother Cochise and I need CDs to make mixed tapes.”

“Find out what type of studio equipment you need and I will get it for you. What else do you need?”

“I need layout cards of pictures of me.”

“That’s not a problem. I’ll get all of that for you, Cheetah, but you better keep your mouth closed about what’s going on between me and you, do you understand?”

“I wanna go to PVA, too.”

“Slow down! If you want to get into PVA you have to do more than go down on me,” she said, cutting her eyes at me. What the fuck else did she expect me to do? “Get on top of me,” she whispered and I rolled over and got on top of her. She grabbed me and started massaging my private parts. I was uncomfortable and I closed my eyes and took myself somewhere else and she put me inside of her and started schooling me on what to do with her. She wrapped her grown up legs around my waist and once I got the hang of what I was supposed to do, I did, giving her the feeling that she wanted. She rolled me over and sat on me, bouncing up and down on me. I closed my eyes trying to escape through my mind and it wasn’t easy. This was wrong and she knew that it was wrong. This woman is my mom’s sister. She screamed out loud and fell over on top of me and I wanted to throw her across the room but I held myself in check. I had to think about the music. What if she was lying about getting me this stuff? Time would tell. "Will you really get me the stuff that I need?"

"Yes, Cheetah! I said that I would, right?"

I nodded and she rolled off me. She went to the bathroom and a few moments later came out of the bathroom with a warm wet soapy towel. "Happy Birthday, young man. Clean yourself up and I'm going to have Rick take you home."

When I walked in the house, my mom was on the sofa, sloppy drunk and passed out asleep with an empty gallon bottle of where her wine was. I stood looking at her, wondering how long she'd been passed out like this. The house was quiet. I went to the doorway of the hall looking at the bedroom that I shared with two of my brothers, Chepi and Marcus. The door was closed and music was going. Elina snuck up behind me, "Did the cops let you go?"

I put a finger to my lips, "Yeah … go back to bed."

"Are you okay?"

"Yeah, I'm cool," I said, taking her back to her room.

"Mommy's drunk again."

"I know … get in the bed."

"I'm hungry," she whispered.

"Come on," She followed me to the kitchen. She started crying.

"Shhhh, Elina stop crying."

"I thought they were going to keep you in jail. They beat Marcus up. He's got a swollen lip."

“Is he in the room?”

She nodded that he was. “You want a peanut butter and jelly sandwich?” I asked her.

“Yes, please.” I made her a sandwich, wondering why my mom didn’t feed my sister. It pissed me off. She knew how to make her own food but she wanted me to make it for her. My sister was scared of everything, even her own shadow. I took care of my baby sister because she was innocent and last year this time Rowena threatened to touch her if I didn’t have sex with her, so I did. She always had something over me to make me do things with her. I took my sister back to the room and she climbed in bed eating her sandwich and chips. “Cheetah, don’t leave me.”

“I’m going to take a shower.”

“Okay. Will you come back in here with me until I go to sleep, I’m scared.”

“I’ll be back, Elina. Leave the light and television on.”

“K.”

I closed her in the room and went back to the living room. “MOM! MOM?” I called her and she grunted and rolled over. I went over and shook her. “Mom!”

“What?! I’m tired, leave me alone!”

“It’s me! Cheetah! I’m home!”

“Okay, good, go to bed sweetheart, Mommy loves you,” she slurred and I smacked my lips and went to the bathroom. I closed the door and locked myself in there, wishing that I could die, but if I did that, who would Elina have? I was so miserable. I turned on the water and let it get hot before I climbed in. I took my hair down from the braid and let it fall down my back. I let the water run over my face and hair, trying to wash away what happened to me tonight. I scrubbed myself until my skin burned. If only I could wash away the pain that I was feeling, too. I needed music to take me away from this life that I was living. I stayed in the shower for an hour until I realized that my little sister needed me, so I hurried out, wrapping the towel around my waist. I went to my sister's room and saw that she was asleep. I turned the light out but left the television going and I closed her door before I headed to my room. I sat on my bed, which was across from Chepi and Marcus who shared a bunkbed. Chepi slept on top and Marcus was on the bottom because he smoked a lot of weed and had access to the window to open and close to blow the smoke out. I laid across my bed staring up at the ceiling. I didn't know how my life was going to turn out, but that pretty girl with the gray eyes crossed my mind and it made me feel so much better. I got up from my bed and slipped into my boxers and went to the closet and grabbed the box of cassette tapes from it. I sorted through it to see which ones I wanted her to have. I wrote a lot of my songs when I was depressed and going through a lot with Rowena. I used the music as a way of escape. A lot of the songs wrote themselves; all I did was recite them. We knew a guy that lived off the rez, a white boy named Danny who had a music studio. We would go to his house and record. Cochise learned a lot about mixing and mastering and making beats with Danny. Danny ended up moving overseas last year, which killed all of our music efforts, so now it was back to the drawing board. I hoped that Rowena was serious about buying me the equipment that I needed. She claimed that she would talk to Cochise and find out what he needed and make it happen, but that was yet to be seen.

The next morning, I was up at 6 a.m. before any of my siblings, and even my mom was still asleep. I walked over to the Devil's Belly to see if that gun was still there. I made sure that I took a way where I knew the tribal cops wouldn't be pulling up on me, catching me out this early, especially that one cop, Redclaw. He meant what he said about killing me when I turned eighteen; I felt that he meant that. Maybe I could kill him first or someone else on the rez could kill his ass. He didn't like me because of my father being black. He called me a nigger and I would never forget what he said. I made it to Devil's Belly and went to the rock that I had sat at yesterday and voila! I found the gun! It was Rowena's gun. She never brought anything up to me about her gun being missing. She pulled it on me a few times forcing me to have sex with her, but I had it now and I was going to use it to my advantage.

I made it back to the house and took the gun and put it behind the shed. I buried it there. I went back inside and my sister was up. "Where did you go, Cheetah?"

"I just stepped out. Braid my hair for me."

"Okay. Some girl called for you."

"Really, what she say?"

"She just said that she was going to call you back."

"Did she leave her number?"

"No."

"Aww damn. Okay, braid my hair."

Elina was good at braiding hair because she had so many dolls that my grandma gave her and she would always practice braiding hair with the dolls. She knew how to French braid too, but I only wanted two plaits. She was hooking my hair up when the cordless phone rang. "Oooh it's Dad. Hello," she answered.

"Let me talk to him," I told her.

"Hi Dad," she smiled. I was hoping he would come home. I hated that he was gone so much and maybe Rowena would think twice about having me at her house once my dad came home to stay. "Yeah, his birthday was boring. He left," my sister said in the phone. "Okay, hold on. Dad wants you." I took the phone.

"Hey Dad?"

"Hey Son, how was your birthday? I'm sorry I missed you yesterday, I called and they said you were out with your brother."

"Yeah, we went off the rez to hang out with a few friends."

"Off the rez, Son? Did you tell your mom?"

"No, she was drunk, like always. She's always drinking, Dad. When are you coming home?"

"I'll be home next month for thirty days. I sure do miss you guys, especially you. Are you still doing music?"

"No, because Danny moved, so we don't have nowhere to do music."

"Well, I'mma see if I could get a loan to get your equipment."

"No, Dad, don't do that. I'mma see if I can come up with something."

"Like what? You let me handle it, Son, I wanna see you do something positive instead of hanging out. Where do your friends live?"

"Oh, on 89th."

"89th? That's a bad area son, those little fools from the Soowhoop Nation are over there."

"I know, Dad, but it's cool."

"No, it's not cool. A lot of those guys have been getting shot and killed on that block. You better be careful. Where's your mom?"

"Hold on, Dad," I said, getting up and going to find my mom, who was in the kitchen, washing dishes.

"Who is that?"

"Your husband," I told her being a jerk because she was being grouchy like always when she didn't have wine.

She snatched the phone, "Hey Raymond."

I went back to my sister and she finished my hair. "Where are you going, Cheetah?"

"I'm going on the block. Don't tell Mom, aiight? I'll buy you something."

"What will you buy me? Get me some chips and a burrito."

"I'll do it, just make sure Mom don't find out."

"Okay … are you and that girl going out?"

"Nope, she's just a friend for now."

"Oh … is she pretty?"

I nodded, "Really pretty. Her name is Alia. She's dark like dad."

"Oh … you better be careful, Cheetah."

"Don't worry, I'll be aiight," I said, going into my room. Marcus was up and dressed, looking better than he did when I saw him in the bed last night. The swelling on his lip had gone down, but there was still a scab over it where it had been busted.

"You wanna go with me to the block, Cheetah? I hit up Mitch and they got his mom's car this time. They had to scrap the other one."

"Yeah, I wanna go," I said, grabbing the cassette tapes.

"Yawl better be careful over there. It's a lot of thugs on that block," Chepi warned us.

"It's fine girls over there, too," Marcus told him. His eyes lit up.

Chepi decided to roll with us this time on the block and I was happy about that. Out of all of my brothers, he's my favorite. I haven't told him what was going on with Rowena because I didn't want him to try to kill her and end up in prison. I know how Chepi is. When guys on the rez fucked with me, he was always ready to throw down. I wanted to make a clean getaway with Rowena without involving any of my family members.

"Aye, Cheetah, Mitch mentioned as he drove. "Novi is mad that you are talking to Alia, dog, he ain't even mad at about the fight no more. He's mad about the girl."

"Awww, my bad. She said that she wasn't with anybody."

"She's beautiful man … you're lucky she's talking to you, she wouldn't talk to NOBODY on the block until you came."

"That's what's up," I laughed, glad that she wasn't talking to nobody else over there.

"Is she over there now?"

"Nah, not yet, but they'll be out. Yawl wanna run a game of Madden," Mitch asked my brothers. They were always down to play any type of sports be it in the streets or on a video game, they didn't mind. I was looking out of the window wondering where Alia was and if she would be coming out on the block. We pulled in the building and Mitch parked in the back where his mom's car belonged. I was the first to get out and the guys were hanging out on the benches this time because of the heat.

"SUP CHEETAH!" Sneaky was the first to speak. He was really cool. I went over to him and gave him love.

"You enjoy your birthday yesterday?"

"I did until we got home. The cops were waiting for us."

"They beat my ass," Marcus admitted. "Cheetah, why didn't they fuck you up? I hope you aint snitching."

"Hell no. Redclaw said he was going to kill me when I turned eighteen."

"Fuck that faggot, he ain't gone do shit," Marcus said and the guys laughed.

"Damn the police is bad on the rez too huh?"

"Yep."

"Yeah, they don't like blacks either. He was calling me all kinds of niggers."

"Me too," Marcus admitted and told me that they dropped him off by the Devil's Belly after they beat him up and he had to walk home. "Luckily I knew my way," he added.

"I'm glad you all right bro," I admitted.

"Aye yawl there they go. Look at Cheetah," Sneaky grinned. He leaned in my ear.

"You better get at her bro, she's a baddie."

"I know," I admitted.

She was smiling when she and her friends walked up. The cousin wasn't with her; she was with another light chick and a Mexican girl.

Chepi hit my arm, "Introduce me, bro, to the Latina chick," he recited. I took Chepi over and introduced him to Alia and she introduced us to her best friend, Marisol.

"Did you bring the tapes?"

"I did," I went in my shirt pocket and pulled out the four tapes.

"Thank you ... oh my God, I can't wait to hear it."

"Yeah, let me know what you think."

"I called you."

"My sister told me, I'm sorry I didn't have a number to call you back."

"Yeah, my aunt trips out about me giving the number out, but I'm going to call you tonight because she's not going to be home."

"Okay, good. I can't wait to talk to you. So what did you do yesterday after we left?"

"Nothing, just went back to the house and grabbed a good book to read. I'm reading this book called, 'The Coldest Winter Ever.'"

"Oh, is it good?"

"It's so good, I'm trying not to go through it so fast, but it's really good," she explained.

I was checking her out, from head to toe, she smelled great and her eyes were so pretty, it was hard not to stare at her. Her toes were done a pretty red and her feet looked perfect. I never thought I would get caught up over a girl at thirteen, but she made me feel good inside. She made me want to stay alive and see her every single day. Her friend Marisol took us to her car and Chepi went with us. She had a cassette player in her whip. I climbed in the back with Alia and her friend was in the front with my brother Chepi, while Mitch, Marcus and the other fellas went inside to play Madden. Marisol turned on the engine and put the A.C. on because it was so damn hot. Arizona gets so hot; it's record breaking temperatures out here. Once the A.C. was kicked up, it was comfort for us all. Alia handed her the first cassette, Mindless Love. She put it on and I was a little shy at first, but I calmed down once the music started. *One day I wanna know what real love feels like…what it's like to hold you…to love you all night long…*

Alia looked at me with a big smile. Her eyes filled with tears as I was singing on the tape. She lifted her arm and I saw chill bumps. "Oh my God."

"Is this you," her friend Marisol looked back at me.

"Yes, that's my brother," Chepi explained. "He can sing, huh?"

"Oh yes! Wow!"

"This is so beautiful," Alia said. "Can I have that tape?"

"Yeah, you can have it," I told her. I felt good that she liked my music enough to ask if she could keep it.

"Turn it up Marisol," Alia recited and Marisol cranked the volume. Alia was blushing and she looked at me and I looked in her eyes.

"You really like it?"

"Are you kidding me? YES! You're going to be famous one day, you keep singing like that, yes. You remind me of Tevin Campbell."

"Oh my God, everybody says that. I'm Cheetah, I'm not Tevin Campbell."

"Not like that but the way your voice sounds."

"I think he sounds better than Tevin."

"Thank you, Marisol."

"I think you sound better than him, too, but you're going to be famous, Cheetah."

I didn't like for her to call me by my nickname. I was going to tell her my real name, but I wanted to get to know her better first. I wanted to make sure that she wasn't like the other girls, being deceptive. Marisol played the other tapes and Alia was amazed and addicted to my music. She was silent now, looking at me with different eyes. "Why are you so quiet now?"

"I dunno, I'm just thinking. You're going to be famous one day and then you might not wanna talk to me anymore … plus you're really handsome…a lot of girls are going to want to be with you."

"What makes you feel like that? I'm not famous and we don't know if I will be famous, I just brought the tapes over for you to listen to. Where did all this come from?"

She chuckled as if she was embarrassed. She became serious. "I dunno, I love your voice. I just know that one day if you continue with this music that you will be a major artist and I can fill out the application for you to get in PVA. Do you want me to?"

"Yes! Can you do that for me, please?"

"Yeah, I need your name and address."

"If I tell you my real name, you're going to have to be my girl," The thought of her being my girl made me smile.

"Okay."

"I'm serious, I'm not just saying this and when I'm not on the block I want you to be at home. Not talking to Novi or nobody else."

"I won't be."

"So you're my girlfriend from this day forward?"

"Yes."

We shook hands on it. "Can I have a kiss?" She laughed and then she leaned over and kissed me on the lips. It was fast and easy.

"I like that kiss." I made her laugh again.

"Why do you laugh?"

"Because, I was nervous, and I never kissed a boy before."

"So, I'm your first kiss ever?"

"Yes," she admitted. "What's your real name?"

"It's Anthony, Anthony Featherstone. I got my mom's last name because we're part Native American. My dad wanted us to have her name to keep us sovereign."

"That's cool, wow…you have a beautiful name and Anthony fits you. Antonio por vida."

"What does that mean?"

"It means Anthony for life. I speak Spanish. My family is from Belize."

"Really? Wow, so you speak more than one language, huh? I speak Apache and Navajo."

"So you're trilingual?"

"Yep, but I haven't spoken Navajo in so long, my grandmother is Apache and she speaks it more than any other language so I understand that more."

"Does she live on the rez too?"

"Yeah."

"You're lucky."

"Lucky?" I laughed. "Ain't nothing lucky about living on the rez. It's fucked up on the reservation."

"What is it like there?"

"What do you see in your head?"

"I see beautiful green grass with nice houses and beautiful mountains and teepees."

She made my brother Chepi laugh in the front seat. "I'm not trying to be in you guys' conversation but it's nothing like that on the rez. Tell her, Cheetah."

"Nah, it's a lot of crime and poor people. It's nothing like how it is out here. You guys got real houses and we got trailer homes that we live in and a lot of drug addicts and it's just not cool."

"Wow. I still wanna visit one day."

Chepi and I looked at each other. I didn't want her seeing where I lived. It wasn't a place to bring a pretty girl, especially her.

"Can I visit you one day?"

"I dunno, we'll see."

She had me write down my information and she told me that she was going to do the application for PVA because she had computer access and A.O.L. with email. PVA is a rich white school so they had access to better technology. I had no clue how to use a computer but she did. She was going to make sure that my application for admission was accepted for next year. That would be cool if I got in. "I'm going to make sure that I put that you live on the reservation because you might get in faster that way."

"PVA is private tho," Chepi added. "It's going to be hard, bro, because you're going to need a scholarship."

"If he can sing, that's what they're looking for."

"Sing? He can dance, too. My brother is bad with dancing and singing," Chepi boasted. I didn't want to brag, but let him tell it. He had Alia mesmerized.

"You know who else can dance? Flip. Have you ever seen Flip dance?"

"Nah, I didn't know he can dance."

"Yes, he applied at PVA, too," Alia informed me and that was good to know that someone from the block applied, too. That meant that I had to get closer to him and I remembered him telling me not to get involved with Mitch and Novi because they were trouble. He told me this yesterday and I never forgot it. Novi came to the car right as I was thinking about them and he wanted to get in, but Marisol didn't want too many people in her parents' car, so we climbed out and walked back across the street. Novi was a little green about us leaving him.

He leaned in my ear, "Aye bro, you wanna go on a lick with us to make some money?"

"When?"

"This weekend? It's a lot of money involved. Thousands?"

"Hell yeah, I wanna go."

"You down to use a gun," he whispered.

"Are you serious, yeah!"

He was smiling, "Aiight, we're on then."

"Does Marcus know?"

"Yep, he's in on it. It's his lick, him and Mitch."

"Oh I'm in too," I said, making sure that Alia didn't hear what we were talking about. I think Novi just wanted to see if I would be down enough to do something crazy and I was, my life was on the edge anyway. We went back to the benches and sat under the shade and she was telling Flip that I could sing and dance.

"Word? You sing too dog?"

"Yep." He told me to hang out. He went back inside of the complex. It wasn't long before he came back with his boombox, challenging me on what dance moves I could do. He didn't want to hear me sing, he wanted to see if he could outdance me.

I ended up dancing with Flip for the remainder of our time we were on the block. We danced and drew a crowd of other girls to watch as we put on a mini performance. I enjoyed this more than hanging out. Chepi was ready for us to head back to rez and somehow, he talked Marisol into driving us back. They liked each other and I was glad that they hit it off and he's my big brother, so I had to leave when he left. Alia rode with us. I didn't want her to see the rez, but Chepi didn't care if Marisol saw where we lived. To me it was embarrassing because she's such a beautiful girl and I didn't want her to see what shambles we were living in. Our house was kept clean on the outside and inside, but it's just the area that we lived in that was kept a mess. People dumped trash near our alleyway and a lot of stray animals hung out over near our house. I wasn't happy about her coming but I had no choice. She slipped her number in my hand and told me to only call her late at night because her aunt would have a fit if she knew that Alia had given the house number out to a boy.

"Are you going to call me tonight?" I asked her after we pulled up in front of my house. She was looking at the area. "This is your house?"

"Yep, this is where we live."

"Wow, this is cool. Do you have your own room?"

"No, it's a lot of us," I said, when Steven came out on the porch looking at us with curious eyes. My mom came out; she was drunk. "CHEETAH, GET YOUR ASS IN HERE RIGHT NOW!"

"Awww man, I gotta go, I'll see you okay," I leaned over and kissed her quickly before my mom saw us. I hurried out of the backseat and went in through the back.

My mom was yelling so loud. She was embarrassing me. "Where the fuck have you guys been?"

"MOM relax, we only went to a friend's house so Cheetah could shop his music."

"Rowena's gun is missing. Does any one of you fuckers know where it is?"

"NO!" I was the first to spill out.

"She just left here…and I hope you guys don't have her gun."

"Why would we have her gun, Mom? Maybe she misplaced it," Chepi added and I went to the room to get changed into something comfortable because it was hot.

Cochise came in my room, "Cheetah, c'mere bro, you gotta see this," he whispered looking like he was excited about something. I changed into my sling shot and basketball shorts and followed him out in the backyard. We went in the shed and my eyes popped out. I felt like I had hit the lottery.

"WOW, when did you get all this?"

"This morning, Rowena had it delivered. We got our own studio bro! Now we can make music and you don't have to leave the rez no more. Look at this! We got pop filters and compressors; we got everything that the white boy had and more, bro. WHOOOOO!" he shouted and my other brothers came in the shed looking in shock. Cochise had set everything up as if we were in a real professional studio.

"Look at this, we got the soundproof booth over here, see that shit? The white boys helped me set everything up."

"I see! This is amazing!" I admitted. He even had a portable A.C. blowing in to keep it cool because our shed used to be hotter than it was outside and Rowena spent a ton money on all of this equipment. She kept her word which meant that I had to keep mine and keep her secret hidden. Damn! She bought the stuff like she said. Cochise got behind the keyboard and started playing and smiling hard.

"This is dope," Chepi admitted. "Now Cheetah you can make music, bro, and stay out of the streets."

"I need some money tho," I told him.

I was making music with my brother and Rowena walked in while I was in my notebook trying to write a new song. She killed the vibe quickly. She wanted to talk to me outside. My heart was racing and I hoped she didn't want me to leave with her. "I'll be back, Cochise."

"Take your time, bro," he said, behind the mixing board. He was happy and satisfied that he had his own music machine in this shed.

I went out to the Mercedes that was idling in front of the house. She went to the driver side, "Get in," she said. I climbed in the passenger's seat and she looked at me, "Did you take my gun?"

"No! I didn't take it," I lied. If I had told her that I took it, she would've been pissed.

"Cheetah, I reported the gun stolen, so if you took it and you do anything with it, you're going to jail, do you understand me?"

"I understand but I didn't take it." We held a stare for a long time. She knew that I was lying but how can she prove it?

"I want you to ride with me somewhere," she said and we pulled off. My mom was in the doorway as I looked from the window. She didn't trip; she didn't have a problem with me being with her sister but she had a problem with me going anywhere else. She freaked out. Rowena reached over and started feeling on my dick. I just looked at her and let her know that I wasn't happy with what she was doing. "I want a baby," she said. She turned away from my block and we pulled off on a road not too far and she put the car in park and looked at me. "I want a kid, I want you to get me pregnant."

"What? A baby? I don't want kids right now; I'm way too young."

"I know but I want your kid and if you give me a baby, I'll leave you alone. I promise."

"That's a lot to ask. I'm young; I don't want responsibility like that. I want to make it in the music business."

"And you can. If you let me help you, I can get you a record deal just like that," she snapped her finger. "I know a lot of people, Cheetah, and I can make things happen for you."

"I wanna go to PVA. They have a good performing arts program there and I read up on that school; they made a lot of celebrities come out of that school."

"Okay … if you want to go, I can help you."

"My friend is going to help me."

"What friend? It better not be no goddamn girl!"

"It's just a friend."

"I can help you. I have more pull than your fucking friend!" She was being bossy again and I wasn't going to argue with her. She did have a lot of power with people on the reservation. I wasn't sure how it was for her off the rez, because PVA was in Paradise Valley, a rich white area where the school was tucked away. How would she pull this off? "Let me help you Cheetah! Give me a baby and I'll give you what you want."

"I don't want a baby."

"I do … you don't have to take care of it; I can do everything for it."

"Yeah you're saying that now but what happens if you get pregnant and then you want me there, I don't want to be with you like that."

"Do you have a girlfriend?" she asked. I started to say yes, but something told me to tell her no, so I denied it.

"I don't want a girlfriend, I want the music." She was happy to hear that.

"Let me get you in PVA. I promise I'll get you in and after I get you in, you give me what I want, deal?"

I looked at her. "Will you stop coming to my house and messing with me if I make this happen for you?"

"YES! I promise. I'll even give you money."

"How much?"

"As much as you want, but you better give me what I want if you want your dad and sister to be safe. You know what kind of influence I have with the cops. I'm not making no more deals."

"I don't want your money, because I don't want you to think you can own me. I would rather make my own money. Just get me into PVA and I'll do the rest."

She grabbed my face and said, "I can make your sister do what you're doing."

"Please don't." She leaned in trying to kiss me and I kept my mouth closed tight. Uggh! It was disgusting. She fell back. "I love you, Cheetah."

I didn't reply to her at all. She took her hand and dug into my basketball shorts. She pulled out my penis and smiled at me. She leaned over and went down on me and I didn't stop her like I wanted to. I was just looking around, nervously wondering why she was doing this to me right here out in the open. She's crazy. I wanted her to stop and I couldn't control what my body was doing; my body was responding the way she wanted. "Your cock tastes so good," she said, turning my stomach. I wanted to vomit all over her, but I made myself go away like I did all of the other times that she molested me. I didn't want her touching my sister or having nothing happen to my dad. What other choices did I have? She tried to make it seem like I had a choice when I didn't. I'm just a kid and she was treating me like a grown ass man. "I want you to come in my mouth, baby."

"I can't."

"You better or else I'll have your sister right in my bed tonight."

"Okay, I will." I gave in and closed my eyes to force myself to enjoy it. I had to go into a make-believe world and picture another girl doing what she was doing. It wasn't long before I ejaculated like she wanted. "Mmmmm," She continued sucking but I started feeling ticklish all over. She made my entire anatomy disappear down her throat. I couldn't even see myself. "Okay can you please stop?" I said squirming as she touched me. My entire body was tingling and I never felt like this before. It wasn't supposed to feel good.

She brought me back home and I hurried out of her car feeling so dirty and violated. "Cheetah," she yelled. I stopped at the shed looking at her. "Remember what I said."

"Yep!" I went in the shed, disgusted and angry. I took it out on my notebook and made music with my brother. I went in the booth after I finished the song that I wrote and before I put on my headphones to record, I broke down crying.

I heard the door open, "What's wrong, Cheetah? CHEETAH? What the fuck man, why are you crying? What did she say to you?"

"Nothing! It's nothing!" I said.

"Oh so now you're going to lie to me? She said something to you. What the fuck did she say?"

"She thought I stole her gun," I said. I told him that because I didn't want him to keep bugging me about what else was going on. I wanted to spill out my heart and tell everything but I didn't want my dad or sister to be hurt. They didn't deserve it.

"She came over banging on mom, too. I don't really like her, but I'm glad that she looked out for us with this music equipment. You need to go hard on your music, bro, so we can get the fuck away from her. You hear me?" he said, hugging me. "Don't cry."

I tried to suck it up as much as possible and he separated from me and I saw Chepi standing in the studio looking in curiosity. I grabbed the headphones. He was asking Cochise why I was crying. "He'll be all right, just some bullshit Rowena's accusing him of stealing her gun, bro," he told Chepi and I was glad that it was that instead of what it really was.

I opened my notebook and looked at the song that I wrote. I closed my eyes and put my heart into the song. *Everybody's asking if you are real… if you exist at all… if you can take away the pain that we feel. Why do we have to die, when we fight to live…we don't understand, the love that you have to give. Sometimes you punish us just to make us see the real…you bring it to our attention that it's you that we must seek. But I'm wondering if you're real because my heart and soul is weak.*

The next day was like a fog to me because I had so much on my mind. My mom was complaining to my dad early in the morning over the phone about money for school clothes. We were going to be going back to school next month and she was needing money, but I'm sure most of the money was going to be spent on liquor. We have no rent to pay on the reservation; the only thing that we needed money for was food and utilities and cable for television. We didn't really have a lot of bills but still my mom complained. Marcus was up and getting dressed. I wanted to go with him today to get this money that Novi was on about. I figured if we could come up on that money in the hood that we could purchase our own school clothes. I wanted to make sure that my little sister would be good with clothes, too. She said that last year the girls were teasing her because she had holes in her shoes and I didn't like that. I wanted Elina to be straight. I had money on my mind and a mission to accomplish. I had talked to Alia the previous night, but only briefly because her cousin was in her ear about needing to use the phone. It sucked because she was going through her own problems and I had my own.

I went out to the backyard and behind the shed and dug up the .38. Something told me to bring it just in case. I hoped that I didn't have to use it. We were meeting Mitch and Novi at the rez entrance so that way they didn't have to come on the rez in a g-ride. That was big of Marcus to make them meet us outside.

"C'mon Cheetah, you ready?"

"Where you going, Cheetah?" Cochise asked. "We need to finish this song, bro."

"I'mma finish it when we get back."

"Where yawl going?" Chepi asked.

"We'll be right back, bro," Marcus said but Chepi followed us outside.

"Where the fuck yawl going and you're taking Cheetah, Marcus, and not me?"

Chepi ended up going with us. We met up with Mitch, and Novi was in the backseat smiling and looking weird. Mitch drove and on the way he asked if we had a gun. He said that the gun he had didn't work. Shit! I had the .38 "I got one," I said and Marcus and Chepi looked at me in disbelief. I pulled out the .38 and showed it to Mitch. "Can I use it, bro? We need it where we're going."

"What am I gonna use?"

"Just be the lookout, you can sit in the car with Novi until we get back."

"I got my own shit," Marcus admitted and Chepi had a .22. They all had guns and I didn't now.

"I'mma drive by the block really quick and see if we can find some more iron," Mitch said, turning down 89th.

"Aww shit, there's Sneaky. Let's see if he got a strap we can use." We pulled up on Sneaky, and Mitch asked if he had a strap that we could hold.

"Man, yawl asking for my burner and I only got one on me right now."

"We'll bring it right back, Cheetah needs it."

He looked at me. "Aiight, bring it back, dog." he said, leaning in the car and giving me his 9-millimeter. It was clean. We drove away from the block and I told Mitch to give me back the .38 and take the 9 but he was adamant about keeping the .38 because he said that it left no shell casings. Welp, I was assed out. I didn't know where we were going, but it wasn't too far from the block.

"These white boys over here have hella meth and money; they're always showing off and they keep the money out like it's no big deal," I heard Mitch telling my brother Marcus. "Okay so we just go in there and take the shit or what? Do you know if they have guns?"

The white boys were so relaxed; they didn't have guns around for nobody just in case. We all got out and Novi got in the driver's seat. "Nigga keep this car on just in case," Mitch warned him.

"Okay," he nodded. Mitch gave me a mask for my face and he gave Marcus and Chepi masks too. We all slipped them on before we got to the trailer. It was two cars and a motorcycle sitting in front of the trailer. Mitch listened at the door first and heard females inside. They were having sex. Mitch waved us on and he did something with the door lock and it opened; we went right in and drew our guns out.

"GIVE IT UP, MOTHERFUCKER!" I heard Chepi. They were fast and I had my gun aimed ready to shoot, I was aiming directly at the white boy near the door.

"GET ON THE FLOOR!" I yelled and he was on the floor.

"Please, man, I have kids!" he screamed. I saw a bag filled with hundreds. I grabbed that bag quickly and Mitch was going through the cabinets going off asking where the drugs were. He ended up shooting the white girl. Oh my God! This was getting real just that fast. I didn't expect no one to get shot but Mitch was ruthless and wanted that money! "WHERE'S THE REST OF THE FUCKING SHIT?"

"It's UNDER THE MATTRESS!" the other white boy yelled and Mitch hit him with the gun and he passed out and Marcus threw the mattress up and they grabbed all of the drugs and guns that were under the mattress. It was so perfect. I was a nervous wreck but I felt numb! After they got the drugs, I hit the other white boy hard in the back of the head and he passed out and the other white girl was screaming until Marcus knocked her out. Mitch had shot her in the leg but she was bleeding a lot. The blood was gushing out; it was crazy. We got up out of there in a hurry and ran straight to the car where Novi was parked. We jumped in the car and Novi drove off.

"SLOW DOWN ASSHOLE, you gone get us caught," Mitch yelled. Novi was being stupid, he couldn't drive.

"Pull over, man! Dumb ass!" Mitch yelled. We were out of the masks. My heart was thumping as Mitch jumped in the driver's seat.

I was looking out of the back window and no cars were coming after us. It was still early in the morning. Mitch drove us to another location where there was another car that we all climbed into. Mitch was wiping off the steering wheel, but he forgot the door handles. I told him but he didn't give a damn. I followed Marcus and Chepi's lead, I didn't touch nothing without covering my hands. We got into a Jeep and Mitch drove.

When we got to the block, Mitch told Novi to keep everything quiet about the lick. "I swear to God man, you bet not talk, I know how you like to open your mouth."

I climbed out of the backseat after I gave Marcus the bag of money. I went straight to the front of the building and looked for Sneaky. I saw him gambling with a fat dude who looked like E-40. I walked up. "Sup man, you got my shit?" Sneaky asked.

"Yeah, thanks."

"Where you coming from with that heat, youngster?" The big dude asked.

"This is the big homie, G.B.; this is Cheetah. He's down and he's cool; he just got put on day before yesterday," Sneaky told him.

"Whuuut. How old are you?" G.B. asked.

"I'm old enough," I said and he laughed.

"What you about sixteen, seventeen?" I guess he figured that because of my height so I ran with it and told him I was sixteen.

"C'mere li'l youngster," he waved me over. I went to see what he wanted, with my mind on the money. "What you doing gang banging man? You're a pretty boy; you don't need to be out here gang banging, where do you live?"

"I live on the reservation."

"I thought so. You're Native American and all of America is yours; you don't need to be out here doing no fucking gang banging."

"Aye dog, he can sing and dance," Sneaky told him. "I told Razz about him and I let Razz listen to the tape you did, Cheetah," Sneaky was looking out for me and I was honored by that. "My big brother is in the game."

"I know, I've heard of Razzmatazz; he's a dope rapper. I didn't know that was your brother."

"Yep ... he told me that he's going to be back in town next week, so make sure you're on the block."

"Man, I heard your tape and if you singing, you need to fuck with us and not these niggaz," G.B. said. "Gimmie your number, you gotta phone?"

"I don't have a phone but I will," I said.

"Yeah, hurry up and get one ... Sneaky, write my number down and give it to the youngster," G.B. ordered and Sneaky went to the Mercedes that was pimped out; it was nice with rims and music bumping from it. This was G.B's car and he was dressed like he had some money with big diamonds on his fingers. "Man, I got a connection to some label owners," G.B. said. "If you're serious about music, we could link up."

"Okay," I said when Marcus came out whistling for me, waving me over.

Sneaky gave me G.B's number.

"Call me, Cheetah. Make sure you keep my number."

"Aiight, nice meeting you," I shook his hand.

I ran back over to Marcus. “Here, bro, who was that you were talking to. Ain’t that G.B?”

“Yep, you know him?”

“Hell yeah, dude is paid. He knows a lot of cats in the music industry. What he say?”

“He gave me his number. I need to get a cell phone.”

“Well, you just made five thousand dollars. We all split the money and got five thousand apiece.”

“Oooh, I need that, I can go shopping and get a phone.”

I went with Marcus up to Mitch’s house and got my money handed to me, a fat wad of hundreds. I was happy about that. He gave me some blue and pink pills too. “You can sell these and make some more money.”

“What the fuck is this?”

“It’s E pills. You don’t want ‘em? Let me have ‘em,” Marcus said.

“How much can I make?”

“You can make another five thousand off those easily.”

“I’mma keep em then,” I smiled and stuffed them in my pocket.

“Aye, Mitch, lemme get my gun back!”

“Nah, Cheetah, let him keep it, you can’t take that back on the rez, bro,” Marcus informed me with a frown. “He shot somebody with it.”

“Yep, forget that gun bro, it’s a wrap,” Chepi added in agreement.

Marcus’s pager went off. “We out bro, good looking.” He shook Mitch’s hand.

“We’re leaving?” I looked in surprise, I wanted to see Alia, but I guess we couldn’t.

Mike and Steven had come and got us in my mom's truck. On the drive, Marcus tapped my arm, "That was Rowena's gun huh?" I just looked at him with a grin. He shook his head. We stopped by the mall and I bought some clothes for myself and my sister. I was into Jordan's so I bought myself a few pair of those to rock with my outfits when school started. I made sure that I found my sister some nice shoes, too, so that way she wouldn't be teased and she could be happy. I spent close to three grand on us in the mall. We had about a month's worth of gear and I caught a lot of sales. I still had two thousand dollars in my pocket so we went to the Sprint store and I got myself a Nokia phone. We all got phones. I even got my sister a phone and my brother opened a Sprint account and put us all on his plan. Steven warned me not to lose my phone or let anybody use it. He was the only one with I.D. and so he made it happen for us. We all pitched in and bought his phone so that we could have the phones in the first place and he asked where we got all this money from. Chepi lied and told him that we sold some of my mixed tapes.

"Cheetah, your music is moving like that?"

"Yep," I nodded.

"Well, shit, you need to let me be your manager then! If it's moving like that, because you guys spent a lot of money in the mall today."

"Let me make more music and you can be my manager."

We left the mall with Marcus on his phone, I didn't want to call Alia because of what she said about her aunt being mean, but I did store G.B.'s number in my phone. I sent him a text message letting him know that this was my new number and that if he wanted to hear my music that he was going to have to talk to Steven first.

I rode home feeling rich and I only had two thousand dollars on me. I wished that I had Alia's number. It hit me, I should've bought her a ring, just for the sake of her being my girl. I wanted her to have a token of us being together. I missed her and wished that I could've seen her today.

That Monday evening when we got home, my sister was outside with her friend, which was the only friend she had. She lived down the road from us. "Cheetah, what did you buy me?"

"Come and see," I said, bringing the bags in. She bid farewell to her friend and followed me in the house. My mom was passed out on the sofa yet again, drunk.

"Mom was drinking today?"

"Yep, Aunt Rowena came by looking for you, too, and she got mom drunk and gave her a lot of money then she left."

I shook my head. I gave Elina the bags with her stuff in it. She went crazy when she saw her new clothes and shoes. "Oh my God, Cheetah, this is so nice. I get to be hooked up for school." She went through all of her things and loved her shoes; she tried her shoes on. "Ooooh, these are so nice, I can't wait! I bet they won't have nothing to say about me now. I'm going to be looking good," she cheesed. I even bought her sandals to wear until it got cold.

"Here, I got you a phone, too. Don't be giving your number out to no boys; it's only for you to call us if you need us," I told her. "It's Steven's account so make sure you're not doing anything silly."

"Oooh, I got a cell phone?" she was happy about that too, and I felt like a big brother with some responsibility. "Mom's going to be so happy; Dad sent her money through Western Union, too." She got money from my dad and my aunt.

"How much?"

"She didn't say but she's all happy. I bet she's going to lie and tell daddy that she bought us all these clothes."

"Oh well … let her buy you more clothes," I whispered and went to my room sorting out my things. Marcus was happy about his new gear and so was Chepi. Chepi was on his new cell phone talking to Marisol.

I called Alia after I settled in. It was late as she asked and she answered the phone. "How are you?" I whispered. My brothers were asleep and I didn't want to wake them by talking loud.

"I'm good, I missed you today, I heard you were on the block."

"Who told you?"

"My cousin. She was bragging that she saw you."

"I didn't see her, she's lying. I was only there briefly because we had some stuff to do. I didn't see her."

"Oh. I was hurt because I thought you didn't want to see me today. I turned in your application at PVA."

"Oh you did? Thank you. Why do you sound so sad?"

"Because I'm miserable over here. My aunt said some mean things to me. I'm starving. She made me go to bed without food and I haven't ate anything, I'm so hungry," Her voice trembled.

"Really? That's not right. Why did she do that?"

"Because my cousin told her that I was talking to you and she doesn't want me seeing any boys. She's really mean to me, Anthony,"

Alia whispered in tears and it was hard to hear her cry. I felt sorry for her. "She's always calling me ugly and saying that I'm so black, I can't change my color."

"You're beautiful, don't listen to her. I'm going to make sure that I bring you food tomorrow, okay? I promise. I'm going buy you stuff so you can eat."

"Thank you … uh oh, I have to go, she's coming, bye." She hung up quickly and I felt bad that she was going through that with her aunt. She was getting abused by her aunt, but through violence and I was being abused through sex. We had so much in common. She called me back to my surprise and I was happy that she did.

"You okay?"

"Not really, I'm so hungry, my stomach is hurting."

"Damn. I'm going to get my brother to bring me over there to bring you some food."

She was silently crying. I could hear her.

"I just wanna get away from here. I wanna run away."

"But that's not a good idea. Where would you go?"

"I dunno, anywhere but here. I hate her, she beats me up bad. The last time she almost broke my arm."

"Okay, listen, I'm going to talk to my brother and we're going to get you food, what do you want?"

"Anything. I'm so hungry, anything, but you should to come to the side window. Write down the address," she said, and I grabbed a pencil and took down the address. It was on 91st street, not far from the block.

"Okay, we're on our way."

"Thank you."

I went to my brother Steven. He was still awake in the room. Cochise was still in the studio working on mixing and mastering the music we made together. I was just hoping that we could get a record deal. Steven was listening to my music. I tapped his shoulder and he snatched the earbuds out of his ear. "Wassup?"

"I need you, bro."

"For what? It's after eleven o'clock Cheetah and I'm listening to your songs."

"I know but I really need a big favor right now, please, I'll pay you a hundred dollars."

"What's going on, Cheetah?"

"My girlfriend is hungry. She doesn't have food and I wanna get her something to eat."

"Are you serious? Where does she live?"

I gave him the address. He looked at it and held his hand out for the money and I gave him the hundred dollars. He went in the living room and snuck my mom's keys from her purse. I snuck out of the house in a hurry. He unlocked the truck from the alarm switch on the key and I climbed in, glad that we were able to come to Alia's rescue. I called her phone again. "Hello?" she whispered.

"Hey … I'm on my way, what do you want?"

"Anything it doesn't matter."

"Okay, we're going to stop by McDonald's."

"Okay, a Big Mac meal, with a large drink."

"Okay, I'll be right there."

"Okay, thank you Anthony so much."

Steven drove me to the nearby McDonalds on 87th. I ordered her food and told them to make it fresh. I was going to give her some money so she could buy herself food just in case her aunt did her that way again. I wish she could live with us.

We got her food and headed to 91st. I was looking for the house and Steven pointed it out. "There it is," I said, hoping that we weren't caught. I went up to the window and tapped on it. A few seconds later she looked out and smiled, opening the window in a hurry. I handed her the food and the money. She grabbed the bag quickly and closed the window. I ran back to the truck and jumped in and waited a few minutes until the light went out in the house. I called the phone and she answered. "Thank you so much," she said, sounding like she was eating. "Oh my God, this is so good."

"You're welcome. Did count the money?"

"Yes, thank you."

"I hope you're not being used," Steven said and I covered the phone so she didn't hear him. He was on some big brother shit and Alia is not like that. She was moaning from the taste of the food.

"Oh my God, I feel so much better thank you. My stomach was so hungry, thank you Anthony."

"You're welcome. I'mma get you a ring," I whispered and Steven shook his head.

"You need to be concentrating on your music, I like your stuff," he cut in.

"I'mma call you when I get home, Alia, okay? Keep the phone by you."

"Okay, I will."

"How old is she, Cheetah?"

"She's my age and she's not using me. Why were you talking so loud? She could hear you."

"So, what? I'm protective of you because you're my little brother and these girls are not any good for you, especially if you make it big with music. That's important right now. If I'm going to be your manager, I want to get you right."

I was stressed out by the time I got back home with Steven. He was on my head about Alia and he didn't even know her like I did. We just met and he was griping about me having a girlfriend and being so young. I felt like she needed me and she appreciated me bringing her the food. I didn't want to go to bed knowing that I left the girl hungry and alone. I learned to keep quiet about Alia after that night. Steven put the keys back into my mom's purse and I went back to my room and quietly got out of my clothes and into my sleep clothes and climbed in my bed quietly dialing Alia's number.

"Hello?" she whispered answering on the first ring.

"Are you full now?"

"Yes, I am, I feel so much better, my headache went away. Thank you so much, Anthony. I wish I could repay you for this."

"You can, by just being loyal to me and not hurting me."

"Never! I will be loyal. Thank you for the money. I just have to find a way to get to the store so that I can buy food and put it underneath my clothes in the closet. I don't have my own room. She has an extra room for me to sleep in but she said that she didn't want me in there. I have to sleep in the den on the sofa and my clothes are in the closet in the hallway, so I will have to sneak the stuff in there."

"Wow! Why is she so mean to you?"

"I dunno. She's been like that for a long time and I can't wait to turn 18 to get away from her. She treats my cousin like gold, because she's light skin and sometimes my cousin is mean to me. Like today she was mean because I told her that I was your girlfriend and she said, 'Why did he pick you instead of me?'"

I couldn't believe the things that Alia was telling me about her family. They were some evil people and it made me think about all the evil that Rowena had put me through. "Don't worry, you won't have to deal with this for too much longer."

"I just wish that I knew where my mom was. She told me that my mom was deported and that she didn't want me, but I think she's lying. I hope she's lying."

"She probably is. Don't listen to her. From now on I want you to think about me and focus on us and how I will work hard to get you out of that house okay?"

"Okay. I really like you and I just hope that we can stay together."

"We will. We're young but I promise you that I will never leave you, Alia. I want you to promise me that no matter what, you will be here with me."

"I promise. I want you to promise me that you will never leave me for another girl, not even when you become rich and famous from your singing." We were laughing but I made her the promise. Who knew what the future held, but I liked how it sounded right now. The conversation with her made me feel alive and whole again. I felt like I was living a normal life as a teenager now instead of growing up so fast after being robbed of my innocence. She made me smile and she made my heart beat for a purpose now and all I wanted to do was rescue her and make her happy as well. We talked until we both fell asleep on the phone.

The next morning, I woke up with Alia on my mind, wondering if she was okay after our conversation the previous night. I was worrying about her a lot but I tried not to let it control my mood.

Steven came in my bedroom looking at me with excitement in his eyes. "Good morning, young buck. Guess what?"

"What?"

"I got some info on how to send your demo out to Prestige record label."

"Okay."

"Okay? Cheetah, do you know what that means?"

"What does it mean?"

"If they like your demo, you can get a record deal. I want to get you some local shows so people can get to know you and we need to start shopping your music around so that people will know who you are. I need you to focus, Cheetah, and really want to do this music stuff because if you want it, I will help you. That song, 'I hope that God is Listening,' that's a good track. I think that you can get this off as a hit."

"You think so?"

"Yes."

"I wanna start a group. My homie Flip can dance and I just need two more people that can dance to start my own group."

"Yes but can they sing like you?"

"I dunno about that, but they can dance."

"Okay, so why don't you start your group and you be the lead? We can do that."

"Let me call my boy." I called Flip. We had exchanged numbers after I found out that he could dance and we had come up with a nice routine together on the block the day before yesterday. I was feeling his energy too; he was cool.

"Hello?" he answered.

"Wassup man? This is Cheetah."

"Aww what's up, I was just talking about you dog … where you at?"

"I'm at home, but I was wondering if you wanted to start up a group?"

"Hell yeah! Awww wow, I was just talking to my boy Smoke about you man, he can dance too, Smoke and Jap, he's Asian but he can dance too and they both go to PVA."

"Really? Wow, yawl wanna come by?"

"On the rez? Hell yeah … aye Jap, Cheetah wants us to come over."

"That's cool," I heard the dude in the background.

"Aiight, Cheetah, tell me how to get there."

I gave him directions and he told me that he was on his way. I was excited because this was the first time that I had ever thought about having a group when it came to music. If I could get these guys to be a part of a group with me, that would be another thing to keep hope alive for me. This would be something to look forward to and it would keep me happy besides Alia. I went to Steven and let him know that the guys were coming over.

"Okay cool, now you said that they could dance, right?"

"Yep. I know Flip can dance, I haven't seen the other guys."

"Okay, listen I'm going to check them out and I hope they can sing. If not, you'll be the lead and we can figure something out with them, but I'm not going to worry right now because I know it will work out."

"I hope so," I whispered. Elina came in my room showing me how her new outfit looked on her. "That looks nice. Did you show Mom?"

"Nope, not yet. I don't wanna hear her mouth. You like it?"

"Yeah, you look nice."

She was happy. "Yayy, I can't wait for school to start. Thank you, Cheetah."

"You're welcome."

I went and took a shower and got dressed. After I was dressed, I went out to the back and told my brother Cochise that the guys were coming over. I told him that I wanted to start a new group.

"That's what's up, Cheetah. Will you be the lead singer?"

"I dunno, hopefully."

"I'm sure you will be. I haven't heard anybody sound as good as you yet."

"They go to PVA, bro, that's cool huh?"

"OH yeah, that means they're getting taught by the best."

"Yep. I hope I can get in; Alia did my application for me."

"Just stay positive, Cheetah, you'll get in."

I sat and chilled with my big brother, listening to what he was doing in the studio and I did a lot of thinking about how things would turn out with me starting my own singing group. I did what Cochise told me to do, visualize it.

Flip and the crew showed up. Jap was chill; he had a nice vibe about him that I liked and he wasn't the type of Asian dude that made me feel uncomfortable; in fact, he was honored to be on the rez and he let it be known that he had never been on the reservation before. Steven came out and met the guys. Smoke was cool, too; he had a nice vibe to him. He was the whitewashed type that even sounded like a white boy when he talked. He wore his hair in blond dreadlocks and they fit him.

"Let me see what yawl got," Steven said and Flip was all for it, unloading his boombox from the car. He put in a CD and they got in position and as the music played, we watched them unload a tight dance routine for us. Steven was all smiles and my mom even came out on the porch watching them. She never said anything but she liked it I could tell.

"What you think, Steven?" I asked.

"They're great, which one of you guys can sing?"

They all raised their hands. "I sing a little bit," Flip added. "I'm not as good as them but I can hold a note."

"That's perfect. What do you guys think of the name Battlecats?"

"Nah," I laughed. "That's corny, bro."

"I got an idea, how bout Sun Gods."

"Uh uh, nah, that sounds too spiritual."

"How 'bout Eleven?" I said.

"Just plain Eleven? That's dope," Flip agreed with me.

"I like that, too," Steven agreed. "Okay, so you guys will be called Eleven, and tomorrow I want you guys to be here at twelve noon to do a photoshoot. I'm going to take you to a spot where you guys can do some images and then get your name out there. Cheetah, I want you to work on a song for the group and help them put it together."

"That's easy, I can do that," I agreed.

"Let's put a dance routine together," Flip suggested. I could tell that he was good at choreographing and so was I, but I let him take the lead. He was looking for some music to put something together and I suggested that we use a song that I wrote so that way we could rehearse it and learn the song at the same time.

"Great idea, Cheetah." I took them in the shed and introduced them to my brother Cochise. They were in love with the studio. "We can practice in here, it's so hot outside."

"Yep." I nodded. "This is perfect in here; we have privacy and we can stay cool."

I sat and started writing. Steven wanted to hear the guys sing and I kept writing until I heard Jap singing. He sounded pretty good; Smoke and Flip were okay, but not as good as Jap. It was going to take work, but I liked how they sounded.

"Cheetah can you help them with harmonies?" Cochise asked.

"You already know that's my thing," I told him. "Yeah, I can help."

"I'm learning from school, too," Jap agreed. "I'm taking vocal lessons at PVA."

"That's what's up, I got it natural. I'm praying to get in PVA tho; you're lucky."

"I'll give you a reference if you need one," Jap offered. We shook on that and I was grateful. "What's your real name?" I asked Jap.

"David, but everybody calls me Jap."

"I'm Anthony but I go by Cheetah, I prefer Cheetah," I told him.

"Cool."

Everything seemed like it was coming together. Novi hit my phone, but I didn't answer. I wasn't going to answer because I was doing what I love for once until Rowena showed up again, throwing me off. It ruined my moment of joy. I played it cool and went outside to see her parked in the driveway looking at me with sinister eyes. I climbed in the passenger seat.

"What now?"

"What do you mean 'what now?' Are you happy about the studio set up that I made happen for you?"

"Yes! But you show up here when we agreed for you not to come anymore."

She laughed. "Do you think I'm not going to get my return on my investment? Cheetah, I want a baby."

I sighed. "I don't even know if I can make babies."

"You can … you cum when I go down on you and you've reached puberty, so you can get me pregnant."

"Do I have to do it right now? I'm busy and my friends are here. Can I please just have a moment of enjoyment?"

I looked in her eyes and she was frustrated with me, but she closed her eyes and said, "Fine … but I'll be here later tonight to collect on my interest."

I grabbed the door handle and she grabbed my other hand, "Wait."

I sat back frustrated from her touching me. She went in her purse and pulled out a wad of cash. "Here, put this in your pocket."

"What is this for?"

"It's for you to have, because your mom is a drunk and she doesn't seem to be responsible enough to take you clothes shopping for school and I want you to look decent when you go to school this year."

"Oh," I replied, taking the money and stuffing it in my pocket. The bulge was sticking out from my jeans. "Cheetah, don't forget about me tonight."

"I won't," I climbed out of the car irritated by the fact that I had to go and have sex with her again. I felt like I had made a deal with the devil. If I changed my mind and didn't do it then she would take everything away from me and I wouldn't have the opportunity to do any music. Not to mention, her hurting my sister and my dad. My opportunity to leave this reservation would be destroyed. I didn't want any kids right now. I was just a kid myself and she was expecting me to do things as if I was a grown up. My life was hard. I went back inside and tried to cure myself of the bad feelings that I had. I had to hide them and keep this dirty secret from the surface. I sat back in my space while the guys practiced with the dance routines. I catch on easy, so it wasn't a big deal for me to learn later. I was writing and trying to get a good song out of the beat that my brother made.

"Aye, Cheetah, your brother makes dope beats, dog," Flip admitted.

"I know he does. He's going to make us famous."

Flip was all smiles and he had the vision in his eyes just like I did. David came over to me and showed me a logo that he made for our group name, "Eleven." It was dragons and swords that were so dope. I fell in love with it and vowed to make this my first tattoo once I got old enough to have one without my mother complaining. After I made the song. I sang it for the guys and gave them their vocals on what they needed to do and how it was supposed to sound. It was a dance track called, "Eleven Eleven." I felt that this song was going to make it big and hopefully we could see some results out of this group. Once I taught the guys how to sing what they were supposed to sing, my mom came in the studio. It was late and she wanted me to wrap it up. Damn. I wanted to finish it, but now I had to face Rowena and deal with that and when we left the shed, she was parked in front of the house waiting for me. DAMN!

I was back at Rowena's house, fixated on the time for me to be done and leave. I felt so disgusted. I was naked, and she was devouring my flesh with her mouth as if I was no relation to her. I felt sick and alone, inside I was screaming for help. Nobody heard my cries and she climbed on top of me, straddling my innocence. She was moaning so loudly that it was drowning out my escape. My body responded as if it were best friends with her and I was an outcast, starving for control. It was a feeling that I hadn't felt before; it was good and bad. I didn't want to reach orgasm, but my body was fighting against me and I felt myself pulsating inside of her without any approval. I felt her muscles tightening around my penis and it was an odd feeling, I didn't understand it. I was upset, wanting back what was mine, but she had it, crying out that she was reaching orgasm, but I couldn't care less. I just wanted to be free. She was happy now, smiling as she rolled off me, giving me space. I turned on my side and in tears I was silent. I didn't want to live anymore, but that little bit of humanity that I had left, told me to hang on. I hated her! I hated this moment and I just wanted to escape this moment.

"I love you, Cheetah," she whispered, but I didn't hear her with my heart. I remained silent and she rubbed my chest. "You're going to be so great when you get older. You're handsome now, but when you reach manhood, the women are going to fall at your feet. You will be successful in your music because I'm going to help you. If I become pregnant, Cheetah, I'm going to make sure that I help you. I've already contacted the principal of PVA to get you in there. It might not happen overnight, but he knows that you sing and he owes me a favor. I'm going to get you in there as soon as you hit 9th grade. You will be a student, so make sure you don't get into trouble, make sure that you keep your grades up, so that way I'll have that to back me up about you."

"I wanna go home," I whispered. She looked at me.

"I know … thank you for tonight. I think it worked." I hoped that it didn't.

I was quiet on the ride home. It was dark, hot and lonely. I felt like I didn't really accomplish anything that I wanted. "Cheetah, you will see how important you will be to the world. Keep doing your music," she said but inside I was boiling with anger. As soon as she pulled up to the house, I got out of the car in a hurry and slammed the door shut. I rushed inside and my mom was up. She was sober, and she ran out to speak to Rowena and I went straight to the bathroom, closed myself in and locked the door, starting the shower. I emptied my pants pockets and put my phone on the counter. Alia called, but I let the phone ring. I was in no mood to talk to her, although I needed to, I ignored the call.

After a good cry and a hot long shower, I was okay. Not perfect but okay. I went to my room and luckily my brothers were asleep and I decided to call Alia, in hopes that she wouldn't be upset about me ignoring her earlier. "Hello?" she responded.

"Hey."

"Hey, are you okay? I didn't wake you up did I?"

"Nah, I was in the shower when you called."

"Oh. How are you?"

"Okay," I said.

"You don't sound too convincing, what's wrong?"

"I don't really wanna talk about it. I'm cool. I'm in a music group with Flip, Smoke and David."

"I don't know the other guys but I know Flip."

"Where you on the block today?"

"No, I'm grounded. Nicole was there. I didn't go anywhere; I stayed here and cleaned all day. I had to wash everybody's clothes and they treat me like a savage. I feel worse than Cinderella."

"Don't worry, it will be over soon."

"So what's the name of the group?"

"Eleven."

"That's great, you should be happy."

"Yeah, tomorrow we're doing a photoshoot so we could have layout cards to pass out, but we need to work on more music so we can have material to sell or give to the people, you know?"

"I'll help you, just let me know what I need to do."

"I just need you to be my girl and stay as pure as you are, Alia. I know you're pure because I saw it when I first looked at you."

She chuckled a little and said, "Yes, I never had sex like my cousin. She's already having sex, but she's older than me. I'm scared to do that. I want to wait until I get married."

"That's good, I'm glad that you're thinking like that. I like that about you. You're perfect and I'm going to get you a ring. A promise ring that I'll marry you when we get older."

"Awww thank you, Cheetah."

"Don't call me Cheetah anymore. From now on, I want you to call me by my real name."

"Okay. I'm sorry, Anthony. I'll do that from now on."

"No need to be sorry, just stay perfect like you are."

September 17

I'm Alia Duarte. I'm not even sure if this is my last name, but I was told that I'm a Duarte because of me being a ward of the court. My life has been hell on earth and since my mother's deportation, I haven't known anything called love until I met Anthony Featherstone, also known as Cheetah. Today is my first day of school and I have nothing new to wear like my cousin Nicole. She is dressed like a millionaire's daughter and looks the part and here I am in her old hand-me-downs from last year. I'm feeling so ashamed and I know the kids are going to laugh at me because the jeans that I am wearing are old and have holes in the knees. I try my best to make the outfits look decent, but it's not enough. I feel horrible looking. My aunt came to the den, looking me up and down. She slams my dollar and fifty cents on the table and says, "Hurry up, ugly, before you miss the bus."

Uncle came and looked at me with sad eyes. He never says anything. He acted like he's afraid of her. He looked as she left him standing there and he went in his wallet and gave me five dollars. "Have a good day, okay?"

"Thank you." I took the money and the dollar fifty that she left me. At school is where I could eat the best because I was starving at home.

"Come on, James!" My aunt yelled at her husband. He was looking at me as he left and there was something in his eyes; he wanted to say something, but he left.

Nicole came to the doorway, "Your bus is here, get out!" She rushed me, being mean to me. "Too bad Cheetah don't go to your school. He would be laughing at what you got on, you look stupid."

"You gave me these clothes, cousin."

"Oh well, so what," she pushed me outside and slammed the door in my face. I wanted to cry, but I turned and saw the bus and hurried to it, keeping my head held high. Marisol wasn't on this bus; she had her parents' car, and she drove to school. Her family had money so they gave her the best of everything and she didn't have to go through the pain and suffering I did. I dunno why my aunt hated me so much. I tried everything that I could to get her to like me but it didn't matter what I did, she didn't like me. I heard the kids laughing and whispering and saw those eyes on me as I made my way to the back of the bus and sat down, tuning them out. They were giggling. I heard, "*You see those holes in her jeans, and it's the first day of school, HAHAHAHAHAHAHAHA.*"

I looked at my astrology book and tuned them out. It was the only way to survive being a victim of mean junior high school kids. They were all talking to each other and I was alone, I didn't have friends. I wasn't very popular with the girls like my cousin Nicole. Everybody knew her. Her best friend, Megan, had driven to the house to pick her up. She was in high school already, ninth grade, and I was still going to

Maricopa Junior high. I'm glad that Anthony didn't go to school here to see me in these clothes. He dressed really nice and every time I saw him, he was dressed nice, from head to toe, and during the summer, Nicole was nice to me and allowed me to borrow her nice clothes, as long as I was helping her with the chores around the house. She was very nice until I met Cheetah and then it all changed. Even her best friend, Megan, was rolling her eyes at me and they treated me bad, when they were both already seeing other guys. Why did they have a problem with me seeing Cheetah?

The bus arrived at the school and all of the kids were hanging out. I waited for everybody to get off the bus before I slid off to fall into invisibility. When I stepped off, Marisol was waiting for me and her mouth dropped open when she saw my outfit. "Oh my God, what happened to your new clothes?"

"I don't have any, my aunt didn't buy me any."

Marisol grabbed my hand and we snuck off campus and she drove me to her house which was about twenty minutes from the school.

"We're going to be late."

"Oh well, that's okay, I don't want you getting laughed at. You can wear some of my stuff."

"Thank you, Marisol, you didn't have to do that, I'm going to have to give it back before school is out."

"NO! You can have it. My mom will buy me more clothes." I was so ashamed of what I was wearing and what if Cheetah's friends saw me before we left the school? I'm sure they would've been laughing at me too. We pulled up at Marisol's place, and she lived in a gated community in a beautiful two-story home with a three-car garage.

Her house is what I had always dreamed of living in once I left my aunt. I wanted to make sure to do well so that I could get a great job and buy a home like this one day. “C’mon,” Marisol said, getting out of her car. I followed her to the front porch. She opened the door and disarmed the house alarm. We went up her stairs to her room. She had a beautiful house, everything was brand new and her room was a dream room, with a queen-size canopy bed that was high off the floor; her carpet was the color of oatmeal and so clean. I had never had a bed, so I went straight to it and sat down on it once we arrived in her room. She opened her walk-in closet and waved me over. I got up and went to her closet, floored by the garments inside. “Here, what do you want to wear? Pick out what you want.”

“Really?”

“Yes, hurry,” she said. Her stuff still had tags on it. I grabbed a Guess denim shirt and the jeans that were on the hanger to match.

“This?”

“Yeah,” she snatched it from me and tore off the tag. “Here, go in my bathroom,” She said and I rushed in there and took off the clothes that Nicole passed down to me and slipped into the new outfit that my best friend let me wear. It was a perfect fit and I felt so cute now. I smiled at myself in the mirror. I couldn’t believe that I looked decent for a change. I went out and showed Marisol how I looked. “You look fantastic, now here, put these on to match.” She threw her white Guess tennis shoes out to me.

“Marisol, those are brand-spanking new, I can’t—

“YES, you can, take them, hurry up.”

"Oh my God," I laughed and grabbed the shoes and went to the bed and put them on. I was so grateful for this. She had a bag filled with clothes sitting next to me. "You can wear those to school, so you can feel confident. You're my best friend and I want to see you looking great, too."

"Thank you so much, Marisol."

"No problem. C'mon, let's go," she said after I had the shoes on. We hurried out of the house and back to the car. I felt so much better and I smiled all the way to the school. We made it back to the school just when the second bell had rung, so we ran to our first period class and made it on time. I went to my seat and sat down next to one of the girls that was in my first period. She always dressed nice, her name was Eunice. "You look cute, Alia …I like your outfit."

"Thank you, you look cute, too."

She smiled big and thanked me. I felt so much better. I couldn't wait to see Nicole during Nutrition; this was going to bust her bubble to see me looking better than she was today. I had on name brand clothing with the shoes and she was dressed in an outfit from Ross.

During Nutrition I ran into Novi, who was staring me down hard. "Hey, sexy mama, hi you doing?"

"I'm good, Novi, how are you?"

"I'm great now that I see the most beautiful girl in Maricopa."

"Stop it, have you talked to Cheetah?"

"I talk to my boy all the time," he said when Marisol met us at the benches. I pulled out my fruit that I bought from the money that Anthony gave me, and we sat down to eat. I didn't want to spend my money that Uncle gave me because I wanted to save it for a rainy day. "So what's up with your number, Alia?"

"I can't give you my number and besides, I go with Cheetah, that's my boyfriend."

"Oh word? Yawl together? He didn't tell me that!"

"Ask him."

"I will," he said. "You should be with me. I can protect you. He can't since he's on the rez and you're not. I heard he had other girls anyway."

"Stop lying, no he doesn't."

He laughed with his friends standing by him. "You think Cheetah is a one girl guy? Think again." He and his friends laughed and walked away.

"Don't listen to him," Marisol whispered.

Megan and Nicole walked up. "What the fuck?"

Nicole looked at me. "I'mma tell my mama, where you steal that outfit from?"

"I didn't steal anything!"

"Yes you did, you wasn't wearing that before, where the clothes that I gave you?"

"In my backpack, in my locker."

"I think she looks cute. Stand up, Alia, let me see your outfit," Megan said and I stood up and turned and showed it off. "OOOH SHIT she got on Guess tennis, too."

"I'mma tell!" Nicole warned.

"Oh well, I didn't want to wear your clothes, they were old and dirty."

"Yeah and she deserves to look nice," Marisol added.

"Nobody asked you, stay out of family business, bitch!" Nicole said to her. Megan started laughing and they gave each other a high five and walked away. Nicole was mad and I was afraid to go home now. "I'm going to get in big trouble for this, Marisol, I have to give these back to you after school."

"No you don't, you can keep those and the other clothes that I gave you, don't worry about it."

"She's going to lie to my aunt and tell her that I stole these clothes."

"Well I know that you didn't and if you need me to tell her that I gave them to you, then I will."

Marisol's cell phone rang and she reached in her purse to retrieve it and she looked at it, a big smile came across her face. "It's Cheetah's brother Chepi. Hello!" She had the phone to her ear. "I'm good, how are you? I'm eating breakfast with Alia. Oh yeah she's right here. Okay, hold on, Cheetah wants to talk to you."

"Oooh," I took the phone. "Hello?"

"Hey sweetheart, what's up?"

"Heyyy ... where are you?"

"I'm at school, I just wanted to say hi to you and I had my brother call your best friend. So, you good?"

"Yeah, except your friend tried to talk to me, he told me that you had other girls and he was saying that I should be with him but I told him that he was a liar."

“What friend?”

“Novi?”

“Oh for real? He said that I had other girls?”

“Yes.”

“He’s lying and I’ll see him when I get out of school … don’t talk to him anymore.”

“I won’t.”

“Matter fact, meet me on the block today, can you do that? What time do you get out of school?”

“I get out at two-thirty.”

“Okay, meet on the block at three.”

“Okay, I’ll see you then.”

I gave Marisol the phone, wondering how I was going to do that if I had no ride over there. Marisol talked to Chepi for a while and after her phone call, I asked if she would take me over there. She agreed to do it because Chepi wanted to see her, too.

I went through the first day of school with flying colors and it turned out better than it started off on the bus. I didn’t have to ride the bus home; I rode with Marisol because we were going to stop on the block. The bus usually dropped me off at the pickup point at three-thirty but since Marisol was driving, it gave us a head start and I would be able to see Anthony by three. I was excited about seeing him; I missed his face and I wanted to at least have contact with him before going home and dealing with the evil that I lived with. Nicole was acting funny all day today after she saw how nice I looked in the changed clothing. She wanted me to get laughed at today, but it didn’t turn out that way. The universe had my best interest.

We pulled up on 89th and made a turn to the left so that we could park in front of the apartment complex. I looked at my watch. It was two minutes before the hour and a truck pulled up behind us with music jamming from the inside. I looked back and saw Anthony and his brother Chepi. They climbed out of the car and came to Marisol's car; Cheetah had this fixed grin on his face. He's so cute! I can't even explain how gorgeous he is, and he looks like a Native Indian that you would see on television. His hair is long and beautiful in two neat braids on each side and he had on a beaded headband, representing his Native American heritage. I felt like the luckiest girl on the planet. He was dressed nice. I climbed from the front seat and met him outside of the car. Chepi got in the front and closed the door and I hugged Anthony. He had a tight grip on me. "You look beautiful," he whispered in my ear.

"Thank you. You look handsome yourself."

"Thanks. Let's get in the car, it's hot."

"I know it is," I agreed, and we climbed in the backseat. He gave me a look as if he had something to tell me. "What?" I laughed and he laughed and told me to close my eyes. I closed my eyes and then I felt his lips against mine. We kissed and I opened my eyes laughing.

"No, no, close them," he told me.

"Okay," I closed my eyes again and he grabbed my left hand and took my finger next to my pinky and I felt something cold slide on my finger. I opened my eyes and gasped at the beautiful gold nugget ring that he placed on my finger. "Wow, this is beautiful. Thank you."

"Let me see," Marisol turned and looked over the seat. "That's pretty."

"It is, I'm about to cry," I frowned as the tears filled my eyes.

"No, please don't cry. Don't cry," he said. "I bought this for you as a promise ring. Don't ever take it off."

"Never!" I whispered, wiping the tears from my face. "Thank you so much. This is beautiful, Anthony. Nobody ever got me anything the beautiful before."

"No?"

"No."

"They treat my best friend like shit," Marisol said. "She needs to get out of that house."

"Yeah, this morning, I went to school with holes in my jeans and Marisol was nice enough to give me this outfit and these shoes," I told him. "I'm going to get in trouble if I don't get home by four." I looked at my watch and time was moving fast, it was already three-thirty. "I don't wanna leave."

"I don't want you to leave either. Don't worry, Alia, you will be happy one day. You won't have to deal with that bullshit for too much longer. We started a group and I'm going to do music and get rich so we can all be happy."

"Yep," Chepi said. "My brother makes great music."

"I know he does. Nicole stole my cassettes; she gave some to her friend Megan, too."

"I'll get you some new music, don't worry," he told me and I was happy, so happy at this moment being with him. I looked at my ring again and it fit my hand so perfect. "How did you know my ring size?"

“I didn’t, I just guessed. I got lucky,” he said, laughing with his brother. I saw a crowd of guys walking from the corner. “Is that Novi?” Anthony said, craning his neck. “That’s him, huh Chepi?”

“I think so, yep that’s him.”

“C’mon man, I wanna get at him.”

“Nooo, wait till I leave.”

“No, I need to get at him right now; he tried to make me look like a cheater and I’m not like that.”

I was nervous about Novi and Anthony getting into it. I should’ve kept quiet, but it was too late. He walked up with the other guys and Anthony confronted him. “Man, I didn’t tell her that, she’s lying!”

“I’m not lying, Novi, you did say that he had other girls.”

“I was just playing with her Cheetah!”

“I already beat your ass before; I’ll do it again.”

“No, Anthony, don’t please,” I begged. Novi feared him and I didn’t realize it until I saw the look on his face and the fact that he tried to lie his way out of it. I felt sorry for him and the other guys were laughing at him; they wanted to see a fight. “I should beat your ass,” Anthony told him.

“I swear to God, Cheetah, I didn’t know she was your girl.”

“Yeah, she’s my girl and you see this ring on her finger, that solidifies it, so don’t let me find out that any of yawl been trying to get at her! She’s off limits!” he said and those guys were silent. Wow! He had them all scared of him. “C’mon let’s go.”

“I’m sorry, Cheetah,” Novi shouted and Anthony climbed in the backseat of the car.

I looked at the time. "I have to go."

"I know, gimmie a kiss," he ordered and I leaned in and kissed him three times. He smiled; he has a beautiful smile and his teeth are white and perfect. "Can I see you tomorrow?"

"Yes."

"Okay, I'll see you tomorrow," he said, climbing out of the backseat. I climbed out behind him and Chepi got out of the car. "Aye, NOVI, hold up!" Anthony yelled and Novi stopped walking with his friends and headed back towards us. I felt bad. I climbed in the front seat and Marisol started the car and drove me towards the house.

"Did you see the look on Novi's face? He was scared, huh?" Marisol made me laugh, but it wasn't funny. We laughed until we turned down my street and I saw my aunt and Nicole standing outside talking to Megan; they were all looking at me like I was in big trouble.

"Uh oh. I'm scared," I whispered.

"Here, I'll tell her that I gave you the clothes," Marisol said, turning off the engine. She got out of the car. "Hi, Miss Olivia."

"Hi, Marisol, how are you?"

"I'm fine, I just wanted you to know that I gave Alia these clothes."

"Okay, that's fine, but next time, run it by me first and before you drive her home, I need you to call me, okay?"

"Okay, I'm sorry."

I climbed out of the car scared to death. I took my time walking by them and Nicole flinched at me making me jump in fear. They started laughing and I rushed in the house. I felt so bad and I hated it here. I headed to the closet to put the clothes in, when I heard my aunt yell my name. "Yes, Auntie!"

"Come here right now," I put the clothes in the closet and made sure that my food that I bought was still intact and it was; they knew nothing about that. I went to see what she wanted. She was standing in the living room with Nicole and Megan. "Come and stand right here in front of me!" she ordered. Nicole and Megan were looking at me with suspicious expressions.

"Yes, Auntie?"

"You think you're slick, seeing that boy on 89th. I drove by and saw you standing out there hugging him, you little fast ass tramp!" SLAP! SLAP! She backhanded me and then slapped me again with a forward palm, leaving the whole left side of my face stinging.

"Auntie, I didn't do anything with him!"

"Is that your boyfriend?"

"NO, he's just a friend."

"She's lying, Mom, that's her boyfriend, she was over there with him. They're having sex too," Nicole lied.

"NO AUNTI, that's not true!" I cried and she punched me hard in the mouth. I saw a flash of light and I grabbed my mouth, making sure she didn't see the ring on my left hand.

"You whore! You're ugly I don't see how any boy would see anything in you. You black monkey looking bitch!" I tried to go around her but she grabbed my hair and started punching on me in my head and going crazy on me like I was a girl off the street that she was fighting. She was giving me hard blows in my face, back and head until Uncle walked in.

"WHAT THE FUCK ARE YOU DOING, OLIVIA? HAVE YOUR LOST YOUR GODDAMN MIND? LET HER GO!"

“NO! She’s a whore!” She held on tight to my hair and I was trying to free myself.

“I SAID LET HER GO RIGHT FUCKING NOW!” he grabbed her hand and I was free.

“Have you lost your mind? What in the hell is wrong with you punching her like that? HUH?”

“SHUT UP, JAMES! You don’t know what she’s out here doing!”

“It doesn’t matter. You’re beating on a child!” he shouted and I was so glad that he came home in my defense. He finally stood up to her. He told Megan to leave and she looked at me with a smirk on her face as if she hated me. The look she had told me that she wanted to be the one to beat on me like my aunt had done. Perhaps they were outside plotting this for me when I wasn’t here. I don’t know why they hated me so much. I couldn’t understand what I ever did to make them hate me the way that they did. I ran to the bathroom and locked myself inside, crying and wishing that Anthony could come and take me away from this crazy bitch! I looked in the mirror at my face; my lip was swollen. I looked like one of those big ugly fish that one would find in the deepest part of the ocean. My face looked like someone that I didn’t know. I looked horrible and it made me cry harder. I turned my face to the right and saw her palm print on my skin. I even saw the little defined lines of her palm prints. The skin that she claims to be so ugly because of the melanin. I couldn’t go to school like this tomorrow. I turned on the cold water and ran it across my face when Olivia opened the door. Her eyes were wide like she was on drugs and her lips were turned inward showing all of her teeth, even the ones that she didn’t have.

"You better NOT leave any blood on my furniture! You ugly black bitch!"

Uncle came and shoved her away from the door and she threw something at him and he told her, "You missed, you crazy bitch!"

"FUCK YOU, JAMES! WHO YOU CALLIN A BITCH, ASSHOLE!" she didn't like that he called her the names that she was calling me.

"Come on let's go," he said, grabbing my hand.

"Where the hell are you taking her?"

"Away from you! You're crazy!" he shouted.

"Uncle, let me get my clothes please," I pulled away from him.

"You ain't getting shit outta here!" she tried to block me from going to the closet. "YOU UGLY BITCH," she shouted with spittle hitting my face. I was disgusted by her, but Uncle pushed her out of the way and told me to get my stuff. She was trying to get past him but he held her out of the way, shouting for me to get my things and hurry up. I took my food and rushed it in the bag, too, just so I could have it and they wouldn't go through my things.

"You're so stupid, James, taking this black bitch out of MY HOUSE! You better not bring her back either! WHORE!" she shouted at me. She tried to swing on me again but she missed and I could hear her grunting.

I was crying as we left the house. She was cursing us out through the front window and the neighbors heard her. Miss Angel was out in the front yard watering her grass and she looked at me in surprise.

"Are you okay, Alia?"

"Mind your own business ANGEL, you nosey fat bitch! That's your problem, you're always in my FUCKING business! GO IN THE HOUSE!"

"How are you, James?" she said, ignoring my auntie.

"I'm okay, now that I'm getting the hell away from her," he said and I was in the front seat, relieved. He got in the car and my aunt ran outside, trying to get behind the car so Uncle couldn't back out but he was backing up anyway but slowly and she was hitting the back window. She was really going off, telling him to stop driving before he hit her. She was lucky that I wasn't behind the wheel, I would've run her over. Miss Angel went over and pushed her out of the way and Uncle backed out in a hurry and drove down the street. My heart was racing, and I was so happy to get away from here. "Do you have somewhere to stay tonight, Alia? I don't want you going back there. Can you call your friend Marisol?"

"Yes," I said, and he took out his cell phone. I thought he was going to drive around for a while but when he asked me if I could stay somewhere, I called Marisol. She answered on the first ring. "Hey, can I come and spend the night? My aunt beat me up." I said, holding back tears.

"Oh my God! Yes, hold on, let me tell my mom," she said and she started telling her mother what happened in Spanish. It was embarrassing to have to face them with my appearance looking this way, but Marisol was my best friend and like a sister to me. She'd seen me at my worst before, but never her mom. "My mom said yes, you can stay. Do you need me to come and get you?"

"No, my uncle is bringing me."

"Okay, good. Come on."

“Thank you so much,” I frowned in tears.

“You know I love you; we’ll be here waiting,” she said and I felt as if Marisol was a guardian angel sent from heaven. I remember my third-grade teacher, Mrs. Alpine, used to always say that God takes care of babies and fools and I guess I’m a fool now because I should’ve run away a long time ago.

“Thank you, Uncle, for taking me and helping me.”

“Alia! I’m sorry that I didn’t help you sooner. I’m getting tired of Olivia and the way she treats you is unacceptable. I’ll be done with medical school soon and when I’m done, I will leave her for good.” He looked so sad and I could see in his eyes that he wasn’t happy with Aunt Olivia. I thought he only stayed quiet out of love, but he did it because he didn’t have anywhere else to go while he was in medical school, so he was stuck like me.

When we made it to Marisol’s house, he reached in his pocket and took out his wallet. “Here, this is two hundred dollars. If I had more, I would give it to you, but you can use that to get food or give it to them,” he said.

“Thank you, Uncle.” I took the money and tucked it with the money that Anthony had given me and what I already had. Marisol came outside and her mom came with her. “I want you to meet her mom, Uncle.” I introduced them and Marisol and I went inside.

She saw my face and started crying, hugging me. “Why did she hit you like that?”

“She hates me.” I said and we both cried together. “I don’t wanna go back there.”

"I'm going to ask my mom if you can live with us. You don't deserve this. You can sleep in my bed; I'll lay on the day bed," she said, sitting on it and I sat on her bed. This would be my first time ever sleeping at her house because my aunt never let me spend the night here. Marisol had been allowed to spend the night at my house but only once, when Olivia was in a good mood. I was relieved to be here, and I got up and went to the window and saw my uncle backing out of the driveway. He drove down the street. "I'm so glad to be here. I don't want to go to school with my face looking like this."

"I'm going to ask my mom if we can stay home tomorrow," she said and we heard her mom coming up the stairs. I sat back on the bed and kept quiet and her mom came in and gasped when she saw how my face looked. It was so humiliating.

"Mija, why did she do that to your face?"

"I dunno. She hates me."

"You can stay here as long as you want, okay? Don't worry about food and clothes, I will make sure that you are okay. She needs to be in jail, that woman!"

"Mom, can she live with us?"

"Sweetheart, I dunno, we have to talk to the courts, we can't just take her, but she can stay here this week if she wants. As long as her aunt doesn't call the police."

"I think she will, too." I whispered, looking at Marisol. I know how dirty my aunt can play and she was getting money from the state for me. She didn't want to lose that extra thousand dollars that she was spending on herself and my cousin Nicole. I didn't see a dime of that money and I needed clothes, shoes, and I wasn't getting any of that.

“I’m going to pray for you,” Marisol’s mom said, rubbing my face. Marisol asked her mom if we could stay home tomorrow because of me being embarrassed about the swollen lip. “Okay, but only tomorrow,” she said and I was glad, I was going to get a break from everything and not have to see Nicole tomorrow. Maybe I could see Anthony. Hopefully her mom would let her use the car and we could go on the reservation and see Anthony. I was going to call him once Marisol’s mom left us alone; I needed to tell him what happened. I took a shower and changed into something comfortable and I wished that I could stay here because it was peaceful and I didn’t have to worry about getting beat up or talked about. I could eat dinner without being starved.

Once I was out of the shower, Marisol grabbed her clothes for a shower. She has a cell phone and I didn’t have one like Nicole did. I had nothing.

“Marisol can I borrow your phone to call Cheetah?”

“Yes, go ahead, you don’t have to ask.”

“Yes, I do,” I grinned and she went in the bathroom leaving me alone and I dialed Anthony’s number.

“Hello?” He answered with music in the background.

“Hey.”

“Hey, I was just thinking about you, I called you but some crazy ass lady answered the phone and told me not to call anymore.”

“Uh oh, that was my aunt. She beat me up,” I told him.

“Whuuut? When?”

“Today, when I got home from school. My cousin Nicole lied on me and told her that me and you were having sex and she punched me in the face really hard, gave me a fat lip and slapped me. She was beating the crap out of me until my uncle saved me. I'm at Marisol's house right now."

"Shit! I'm sorry. Why would your cousin lie on you like that? That's fucked up! Are you talking about the light skinned chick?"

"Yes, her! She's a big liar!"

"That's messed up. Are you okay, do you need food or anything?"

"No, I'm safe and I'm at Marisol's."

"Good. I'm glad that you're over there. I wanna come over there and see you. Is that cool? I can get my brother to bring me."

"I don't want you to see me like this, my lip is swollen."

"So what? I wanna see you! Can I come over?"

"Let me ask Marisol if you can. I think she won't mind but I dunno," I said, knocking on the bathroom door.

"Come in," she yelled. I only cracked the door and poked my head in.

"Hey, Marisol, Cheetah wants to come and see me, make sure that I'm okay."

"He can come over, tell him to bring his brother Chepi."

I smiled. "Okay…" I closed the door. "Hello?"

"Yeah, what she say?"

"She said you can come, bring Chepi," he laughed and agreed.

I was excited and happy again. I kept the ice pack over my lip because I didn't want him to see my lip so huge and it was huge. It was embarrassing and I really didn't want him to see me this way, but if this was the only time that I could see him without repercussions, then great. I really wanted to see him. Marisol had made lemonade and put mint leaves inside and had it looking so delicious. Her mom had agreed to allow them to come over if we stayed in the den where she could chaperone us. Her mom was so cool. I wished that I did live here. At least I would have a normal life and not feel like I was living in a prison. I loved it here and I was going to talk to my uncle to see if I could stay here because living in the house with Aunt Olivia was misery.

The doorbell rang. I looked at Marisol, nervous, too ashamed to go to the door, so she did the honors while I sat in the corner of the sectional in the den. I heard their voices and I was so scared. Marisol's mom was looking and smiling and I heard Anthony speak to her. I heard Chepi. "She's in the den," Marisol said and I put the ice pack back over my lip and turned towards the television. Anthony came in the den, looking very handsome and dressed nice, he was holding some roses.

"Oh my God, thank youuuu, awwww, you didn't have to do that," I said, taking the flowers. He was looking at my face but I didn't want him to see my lip. "Thank you, Anthony."

"You're welcome, lemme see."

"Nooo." I chuckled, giving Marisol's mom the flowers to put in a vase for me.

I looked at Anthony and he was whispering, "Come here, lemme see." I took the ice down and he frowned, looking serious. "She needs to be arrested for that."

"That's what I said," Marisol's mom said as she put water in a nice vase. I turned away crying again, feeling like shit after he saw my face.

"Don't cry." Marisol said, hugging me. It made me cry harder because of the embarrassment for one and the fact that I felt so unwanted. I was so ashamed and felt unloved. I am so lonely and I just wanted a better life. Anthony was pissed, I could see the look in his eyes. He looked at his brother and Chepi was looking at me.

"Why did she do that to you?"

"Because my cousin lied on me about your brother. She said that we were sleeping together."

Chepi looked at his brother and Anthony shook his head. He grabbed my hand and took me to the sofa and we sat together. "Don't worry, I'mma get you away from her, aiight?"

"How? The only way to do that is to go to court."

He nodded. "I'mma think of something. She's not going to be hitting you like that anymore."

"She wouldn't have if my cousin hadn't lied and she cursed me out really bad. They treat me like an animal."

"I know," he sighed and looked straight ahead without words. I felt him looking at me and then we made eye contact after I covered my lip again. "Why can't you stay here?"

"Because she has to have a court order, that's what she told me," I whispered.

"Why can't she get one?"

I shrugged. "I dunno. It'll be hard."

"You know what," Marisol's mother said, bringing us lemonade. "You should call the cops on her and maybe they will take you out of her house."

"But could she stay here?" Anthony asked her. Marisol's mother shrugged.

"I would love to have her stay here but since she's a minor, it would be up to the courts."

"They'll probably send me to a foster home and I don't wanna go there." We were back at Ground zero.

I was in tears again. "Don't worry, you're not going to keep going through this. They're just jealous because you're pretty that's all."

"That's what I think too, she's so beautiful and they have always been mean to her. Mom can she stay with us please," Marisol begged her mom. She was almost in tears too. Anthony looked like he was pissed off. He was pouting and looking like how I felt. I just wanted to be happy and I thought about running away and just coming over here and hiding out until I turned 18.

Bittersweet Fall

It's October 30th. It's a day before my girlfriend's birthday and I still hadn't talked to her since she's been back home with that wicked aunt. I wanted to put a few slugs in her for punching my girl in the face like that. I swear I wanted to punch on her. If there wasn't such a thing as jail, I would've smashed on her. I wanted to smash on my own aunt, but I couldn't do that either. We were both going through the most and that's what made me fall deep in love with her. I've been going hard on my music and me and the group have been doing local shows around town, which made my life a lot less complicated. My brother Steven has been doing a phenomenal job keeping us busy. We weren't making as much money like we wanted to, but it was giving us more exposure to the people in the city. Steven was also working on getting us airplay on LIVE 105 FM radio station as well as sending our demo off to record labels for a possible record deal. People on the rez didn't support us because we were doing music that they weren't really interested in. They weren't into the R&B and Hip Hop and that's what we were delivering. The girls on the rez were going crazy and yes they were interested but the guys on the rez were on hater shit, not really giving us leverage to share our music and dance skills. I trained Flip, Smoke and Jap on vocals and they were doing far better than they were getting taught at PVA. The sound they had was good enough to give us great harmonies.

Today I was off from the music and looking forward to spending time with Alia before her birthday tomorrow. I bought her some nice gifts, a Tiffany bracelet, a pair of diamond earrings and two outfits from Macy's. I was going to go on the block and see about getting Marisol to get her out so that I could give her the gifts and spend some time with her. I was just waiting for Chepi to come out of the shower so we could head on over to 89th. The music was keeping me out of trouble, but Rowena was still on me with the sex thing. I was fucking her damn near every night since she offered to leave me alone if I got her pregnant. The sex was good, but it wasn't the right thing to do. In between having sex with her and doing music, I was trying to escape the pain of it. I went out on the porch to get some air and wait for my brother.

"Hey, Cheetah," Elina's friend spoke, they were out on the porch on an iPad that her friend had.

"Hello," I spoke trying to be nice, but I could feel that she liked me. I wasn't interested. I didn't really like girls my age, except Alia. She's mature for her age and beautiful. She's the only girl that I had my eyes set on to be honest. I was dying to see Alia. I missed her a lot.

"Where you going, brother?"

"Why are you being nosey?"

"Because, I see you dressed up nice. You're going to see that girl, huh?" she smiled.

“Maybe.”

“Yeeees, you’re going. How come I can’t meet her?”

“You will one day.”

Rowena pulled up. Oh my God! She was the last person that I wanted to see.

“Aunt Rowena’s here, MOM!” Elina yelled and Rowena climbed out of the car, with something in her hand, a bag. It looked like some liquor. My mom came out on the porch.

“Heyyyy, sister.” She ran down the steps and met Rowena in the yard hugging her.

Rowena looked at me over her shoulder and winked. She handed Mom the bag.

“Thank youuuu, you’re such a life saver,” Mom said. Of course she was a life saver, bringing liquor to her, stuff to keep her high and out of her mind.

Suddenly they were tight. Rowena gave my mom some money, I saw her slip the money in her hand and then she said, “Can I talk to your son for a moment before I come in?”

“Yeah, Cheetah, go see what she wants,” she said, going inside to get her drink on. That’s all she cared about. I went to the car and climbed in the passenger’s seat waiting for her to come and harass me again. My mom didn’t even realize what this woman had been doing to me all of these years.

“What now?” I said once she was in the car. “I got somewhere to go, I can’t leave witchu.”

“I’m here to show you this,” she smiled and reached over me and into the glovebox. She pulled out paper and gave it to me.

"What's this?"

"Read it … by the way, you smell and look delicious!" I rolled my eyes and sighed,

"Thanks."

I read the paperwork and didn't realize what it meant. "What does this mean?"

"I'm pregnant, Cheetah! We finally did it," she grabbed my face, kissing me and I pushed her away. It was horrible news for me. I wasn't about happy about it at all. I didn't think I could make babies, I was just fucking and doing the boy thing.

"Wow! So does this mean you're going to leave me alone? We don't have to have sex no more, right?"

"Yes, I'll leave you alone … but I just have to tell you that I taught you well and you're great in bed!" she laughed. "I'm so happy. Thank you."

"What about PVA? I thought you were going to help me, I knew I wouldn't get in."

"Cheetah, I told you that I would help you. I talked to the principal, he hasn't gotten back to me yet. How are your grades?"

"They're good. I've been in school every day. I'm working hard in school," I looked in her eyes.

"I heard that you guys are doing great with the music group, too. That's awesome. I'm going to call him again and get him to reach out."

"Yeah, right, you got what you wanted. I just don't want my family finding out and I want to be free."

"You are free. I won't say anything. This is our secret."

"Can I go now?"

"Gosh, why are you so in a rush? And who are you so dressed up and smelling good for? Look at you, you look so gorgeous, Cheetah, I'm sure it's a girl, right?"

"Maybe."

"I don't wanna see her."

"You won't, don't worry about that."

"I knew it was a girl. Is she your age?"

"Yes. She's perfect."

She rolled her eyes and I knew she was jealous but it wasn't going to stop me from being with Alia. I grabbed the door handle.

"Wait."

"For what?"

"Why are you so mean?"

"Because, I'm getting ready to leave," I told her, seeing Chepi come out of the house. I felt cocky around Chepi.

"Okay, we'll talk later."

Right! I wasn't planning on talking to her no more. She just spoiled my day, and hopefully Alia could make it better.

My sister's friend was staring at me hard with a lustful smile, "Bye, Cheetah."

"Bye," I said and hopped in the front seat of the truck with Chepi.

Chepi and I rode down the dirt road to the exit and I saw that dirty cop on the way out. He gave me a mean mug and I wanted to flip him off but I just readjusted my seat and paid him no attention. "That bastard is following us. It's okay cuz I got my driver's license."

I was looking at him in the side mirror and he made a left and went down another way. I was glad about that. I can't stand that asshole and I remembered him saying that he was going to kill me when I turned 18. Once we turned off the rez, I did a lot of thinking. I had a lot on my mind and thinking back on everything that I had been through, not to mention the way that Novi has been acting, it's been a lot for me to deal with. I realized that maybe he's not my friend.

"Aye, bro, what you think about Novi? You think he's my friend, you think he got my back?"

"Novi is jealous of you! You got the girl he likes and not to mention talent that he doesn't have. He's a hater."

"Yeah? I wonder why. I thought we were cool. I've always been loyal to him."

"Yeah, but Mitch is more of a friend than he is. Novi doesn't have your best interest, bro, not like Mitch does. I think Novi is holding some animosity because you beat his ass on your birthday."

"Nah—

"Yeah, bro, I'm telling you, Cheetah, ever since that day he's been a dick! Marcus told me that he's been whispering bullshit about you."

"Like what?"

"Just hater shit, that you think you're all that, little shit that he will never tell you in your face. You just need to watch him."

"I ain't worried about Novi. I know he does like Alia but she's not into him and she told him to his face that she wasn't with him the day that we met so it was all fair."

"Yeah, but just be careful, Cheetah."

"Ahhh, I ain't worried about him," I waved him off as we turned on the block. Everybody was hanging out. I sent a text message to Marisol and told her that I was pulling up on the block. I pulled the bag from the backseat. "Dang, bro, how may gifts did you get her?"

"Just four."

"Damn. You must be in love," He laughed as we parked. Novi, Flip and Cal came up to the car. I heard Sneaky's cool ass whistle. I climbed out of the front seat and threw my arms up with a big smile.

"CHEEEETTTTTAAAAAAAH!" Sneaky howled, making it a funny moment.

"Sup man," I gave Cal and Flip love. I looked at Novi; he was sizing me up.

"Damn, new Jordans, this nigga stay fresh in new Jay's, those are dope, Cheetah."

"Thanks," we finally shook hands and I could see what my brother was talking about; he was hesitant on the greeting. He stared me down while I gave Sneaky love. Sneaky stayed fresh, too, especially having a rich brother. "Aye, Cheetah my brother Razz heard your demo."

"Yeah? What he say? Did he like it?"

"He loved it. G.B. is on his way over here, too, I'm about to text him right now and let him know you're over here. How long you gone be over here?"

"I dunno, I'm not sure, I'm waiting on my girl."

"There they go," Novi pointed them out, he was smiling big. I got jealous, but I kept it under control. I hated that he liked her now that I had feelings for her. I didn't think it would happen this fast but in two months, it did. She climbed out of Marisol's front seat with a big grin on her face and she looked sexy and fine. All the guys were checking her out. I went and greeted her with a hug and a kiss.

"Wassup, you look beautiful."

"Thank you, you look nice, too, and you smell so good, what's the name of that cologne?"

"Cool water."

"Mmm, it smells good on you," she said, hugging me and sniffing my neck making us both laugh.

"Come 'ere, I got you gifts for your birthday. What are you doing tomorrow?"

"Uuuuh, don't knoowww, my aunt Olivia is not doing anything for me, but I think Marisol and her mom and dad are buying me a cake, that's if I get to go out. I hate that it falls on a Saturday and Halloween so it's going to be a lot of trick or treaters out."

"It's all good," I said, going in the front seat and pulling out the bag and giving it to her. She grabbed it and looked in. Marisol parked and Chepi went over to the passenger's side and climbed in the car. I told Alia to get in the truck. We climbed in the backseat and she opened up her first gift of the Tiffany bracelet.

"OOOOOOH, this is so beautiful," she looked at me with tears in her gray eyes. "So pretty, oh my God, thank you."

"You're welcome, let me help you put it on."

I clamped it on her wrist and it looked nice on her. She opened the other gifts, with a grin on her face. She's so pretty, one couldn't stop staring at her.

"OOOOH earrings, diamonds, these are real too, oh shit!" she chuckled. She removed her hoops quickly and tossed them out of the window making me laugh. I helped her with her earrings. "Oh my God, Anthony, thank you so much, babe," she hugged me. I asked for another kiss and I sucked on her lips this time, glad that she allowed me to do it.

"Mmmm. Thank you."

"You're welcome ... open the other ones." I took the other gifts out of the bag and she was happy.

"I never got anything like this before. I'm so happy, thank you so much," she whispered, opening up her other gifts with the outfits from Macy's. I bought her an ankle-length dress; it was black with spaghetti straps and lace over the front area. I bought her a two-piece pink pants set. She was very happy about what I got her. "You went all out for me, huh?"

"Yep, of course. I hope you can go out with me tomorrow, that would be nice. I wanna take you to the movies."

"I'd have to sneak out and then get my ass kicked."

"No, I don't want you to go through that. I didn't know you were back over there. I want you to be safe."

"Yeah. I had to go back home because she threatened to call the cops on Marisol's mom. I'm going to have to let Marisol hold my stuff so it will be safe. You make me so happy."

"You make me happy, too. I wish I could see you every day. I miss you all the time."

"I miss you too. I start worrying and thinking about all of the girls on you." She made me blush.

"Nah, I'm with you so you ain't gotta worry about that."

"I know but I do. You're my first boyfriend. I know one girl that likes you, my cousin's best friend; she likes you."

"I don't care about that, I like you. I'm falling in love with you."

She looked in my eyes and her eyes were so gray that they looked see-through. "I loved you from the first time we met, believe it or not. I never saw anybody as handsome as you. A lot of these guys have tried to talk to me, but when I met you, I was like, wow!" she smiled. I believed her because she was innocent and nothing like the girls that I've seen and been around when we did the shows. I had so many girls trying to talk to me when we went out to do the gigs, but I wasn't interested. I can't lie and say that I wasn't checking them out, I was, but none of them topped Alia.

I held on to her hand and she was rocking the ring that I gave her. "What are you going to do tomorrow?" she asked me.

"I wanna come and see you, but I dunno. I need to get you a phone so we can keep in touch."

"I know. Nicole hogs up the phone every night and it's hard for me to call you. She claims that your brother is her boyfriend now, so she stays on the phone with him a lot."

"So she's with Marcus?"

"Allegedly."

I held Alia's hand and just the touch of her skin was comforting. I got butterflies from touching her and when she swept her thumb across the back of my hand, chills cascaded down my skin like bubbles being blown from a bottle. She was amazing.

"I wish this day could never end," I whispered.

"I know. Me too … but I have to get going in thirty minutes," she said glancing at her watch.

"I'mma get you a phone and I'm going to call you for your birthday tomorrow."

"Okay. I hope they let me talk to you."

After Alia left, GB came on the block. Marisol had hung out with Chepi and I was on the block with the fellas while they spent time together. Naturally I was missing Alia, but Nicole came and got her quickly and was jealous once she discovered her being with me. I was glad that Alia gave Marisol her gifts first so that she could have them and not have them taken.

G.B. climbed out of his Mercedes and walked over to the benches where we were sitting. "Aye, Cheetah, wassup, young Magic?" I laughed and greeted him with a firm handshake. He reminded me of Sedrick the entertainer because he was heavy and dark like him, except G.B. was a thug in his style of dress.

"You always come up with those crazy ass names," Sneaky told him making us laugh.

"Wassup, Zeenbye," he called Sneaky and we were dying laughing.

"Zeenbye, man c'mon now," Sneaky was hilarious. He looked at me and shook his head. "You hear this fool, calling me some ole weirdo ass name?"

"Cheetah, lemme holler at you for a minute, playa." I walked over to the Benz with him. Sneaky came with us. "Young blood I heard your demo and I was impressed. I saw the video footage of the show that you guys did, too. Steven is your manager right?"

"Yeah and he's my brother."

"Yeah, I talked to him on AOL and he told me that you guys were trying to get a record deal but I'mma be frank with you Cheetah, you need to be solo."

"Solo? Man I got Flip, Smoke and David with me, dog, they're good at what they do."

"Yes, they can dance. They're great dancers but you got it all, Cheetah."

"Yeup, Cheetah, you're the shit by yourself, bro, you're a package deal," Sneaky agreed with him as if they had been talking about this before I came on the block. "I'm not knocking your boys' dance skills, they can dance but you need to be a solo artist! You don't need to split no money in a group. You can stand alone," G.B. said. "Another thing too, stop fucking with Novi. He ain't nothing but trouble, him and Mitch!"

"I told him the same thing," Sneaky added, which he did tell me that but I wasn't listening. It's crazy because my brother Chepi said the same thing. "Novi don't want shit outta life and he's jealous of you Cheetah."

Sneaky and I looked at each other in the eye. "I'm not just saying it, I know he's jealous and he wants your girl."

"Ooooh," G.B. snickered. "Watch him, Cheetah! Negroes like that will get you caught up. They're always stealing shit; him and Mitch are always taking shit from people and they will rob anybody, they don't give a fuck! Trust me I been knowing them niggaz since they were knee high to a duck and they're known for being jackers."

"I didn't know that."

"Cheetah, you might have some street cred when it comes to those hands but these niggaz are ruthless and you don't need to be caught up with them and trying to do music, too. Now I can plug you in with some decent artists and you can collab or put together your own demo by yourself and I can get it in the right hands," G.B. said.

"Wow, okay."

"What you mean 'wow,' tell this man, Sneaky."

"Aye, G.B. got the plug, dog."

"I believe him, it's just I don't wanna leave my boys, Flip and the crew behind."

"Keep 'em as your back-up dancers, they can dance! But not the singing part."

"Oh, okay," I nodded. "I gotchu." I was still feeling a little sketchy about leaving my boys behind. I can't do them like that.

"Here, holler at me, give my email to Steven and tell him to send me an MP3 of your demo, make sure you get me some tight songs on there, Cheetah and I'mma get you plugged in."

He was serious and I believe this is the reason why he came on the block was for me. "Cheetah, you got a big future ahead of you if you stay away from these haters. Don't discuss nothing that I just talked to you about with those niggaz, keep this to yourself."

"Okay."

"I'mma get outta here. Sneaky, keep him outta trouble will you!?"

"I will," he said and G.B. gave me a firm hug and his phone was ringing. He walked around to the driver's side of his Benz and jumped in answering his phone. I should've known that I was the reason why he was over here.

"Cheetah, you should come to my house and play me in some Madden," Sneaky offered.

"Aiight, lemme see what my brother is about to do, I'll come through," I told him and we headed back over to the guys.

"What was he talking about Cheetah," Novi asked.

"Nothing much, just sports and shit," I said and Flip and the other fellas gave me a curious look. I felt bad lying to them but I couldn't tell them what he told me; it wouldn't be right.

I ended up at Sneaky's house and we chilled for a few hours and I met his brother Razz, who I had admired and looked up to because he was one of the dopest rappers in the industry. Meeting him was like meeting Tupac. It was unbelievable and it gave me the drive to really go hard with my music. I sang two songs for him and he was impressed, telling me to get him a demo tape. I was excited and I couldn't wait to get home to let Steven know that I had hooked up with the rapper. He gave me his business card and I couldn't stop looking at it. "Cheetah, you're going to blow up, watch and see brother. I have faith in you. All you need to do is cut Novi off, leave them dudes alone on that block."

"Everybody's telling me to cut him off. I've been knowing him for a long time. He's all right."

"I'm telling you Cheetah, leave that nigga alone." Chepi replied.

We pulled in the driveway and my mom had music going loud. "Damn, Mom must be drunk again," Chepi said after we pulled up. It was after 8 o'clock and she was probably going to bitch because I was supposed to be home before it got dark, but I was with Chepi so it wasn't a big deal. It was the weekend now anyway. We walked in the house and Mom had her glass of wine dancing and looking like she was happy. "What you so happy about, Mom?"

"Your dad will be here in an hour; he's taking his leave."

"For real?" I smiled. I was happy to hear that. He missed my birthday but he sent me money, which was I was grateful for. I missed him.

"Yes, he will be here soon." She was excited and had the house looking and smelling good. She wasn't passed out on the sofa like usual, not this time. Elina came from her room,

"Cheetah, Dad's on the way home."

"Yeah I know, mom just told me, are you happy?"

She was grinning from ear to ear. "Yes! I get some money." I laughed and pushed her by the head like I always do.

I went and hung out in the garage with Cochise and I told him what G.B. had said.

"Aye, Cheetah, he's right. You do need to be solo."

"I don't know about that, bro. I love my group."

"I know you do, but you stand great on your own and that's what you need to be a great artist. Don't get me wrong, I like the group, but you're more talented than they are. You can sing, write your own songs and you dance. You have the looks; you got it, Cheetah."

Damn, even Cochise agreed with everybody else. "All you need to do is cut ties with Novi; he's trouble. All he wants to do is gang bang."

"But Flip, Smoke and David are not like that."

"No, I like those guys, but Novi, fuck no! He's trouble and I don't trust him in the studio bro, you can't bring him here."

"I won't."

"Speaking of that, now that I think about it, I'm going to get the insurance paperwork from Rowena, she said she put insurance on this stuff just in case. I don't trust that dude and I know you think he's your friend but it's something about him."

"He's a pussy, he's not nothing to fear. I beat his ass already."

"I heard, but I don't trust him."

I sat back thinking about what everybody had said about him and it made me wonder if they were just saying that because Novi's always talking loud and being loud, maybe that's what it is, but who knows? I know he can't win with me in a fight. I didn't trust him around Alia either, so maybe everybody was right.

I saw the white Range Rover pull into the driveway and I ran outside and greeted my dad with a hard hug. It brought tears to my eyes. He was home finally. I was so happy that he was home that it made me emotional and when we separated, I dried my eyes quickly and my brothers came outside. "How are you son? Huh?"

"I'm good, Dad, I'm glad you're home."

"Me too, I'm sorry I missed your birthday. Did you get the money I sent you?"

"Yes sir, thank you. I missed you," I said, hugging him again. I wanted to break down and cry but I held it in, my other brothers came over and hugged him. Boy, was it good to see him finally.

"Wow, you guys are amazing. I'm so happy to be home," he said, looking at all of us with a grand smile. He was dressed in his Air Force fatigues and they were starched to a Tee, perfect and his boots were shining like glass and all of his stripes on his arms stood out with the darkened blue star in the middle of his arm. I was proud of my dad.

He looked handsome in his uniform and he looked important. We followed him inside and when my mom turned and saw him, she screamed and laughed running to his arms jumping in them and wrapping her legs around him, kissing him and crying. She did the unthinkable. I hadn't seen her this happy in a long time and I think all of her drinking and being drunk had to do with my dad not being home. It was hard for all of us. Elina was crying and being a brat. She was glad that Dad was home, too; we all were happy.

We ended up going out to eat at a place called Sharkey's. It's a five-star restaurant in Phoenix. They served the best seafood and my dad had a lot of money on him; he was willing to spend and this place was expensive. One plate was forty dollars so you know it was going up and I thought to myself once I got famous that this would be a regular place for my family to eat.

My dad was supportive of me doing the music stuff. He came to a few of our shows and after seeing us perform, he agreed with G.B. and my brothers about me going solo. My father's opinion mattered the most to me and it made me feel good to hear him tell me that he was proud of me and happy to see me doing what I loved. For the first time ever, my mom even came to see us perform and I was happy about that. We didn't have a big crowd but it was over fifty people there to see us do our thing and Steven was still out networking and making sure that our name was out there.

My dad wanted me to stay on the rez and stay into the music and school and I was doing that, but missing Alia at the same time. I was trying to call her but the phone was always busy or I got voicemail. Steven ended up making me a Friendster account and I added her on there and we sent emails back and forth to each other. I was sending her pictures of our shows and keeping her up to date with what was going on. I still hadn't found the time to get her a phone but I had that on my to-do list. Right now, I wanted to spend as much time as I could with my dad. I was hanging with him a lot and going fishing with him, and when we weren't hanging out, I was in school or the studio doing music. My schedule was busy and it was a good thing because it kept my mind off of the wrong thing.

After I was done in the studio with the music, I went to take a shower and got a ring tone from my messenger. I opened my phone and checked and had a picture message from a number that I didn't recognize. Maybe it was Alia and she was sending me a picture to let me know that she had a new phone. I opened the message and a picture began downloading in my phone. Once it was done, it gave a beep. I looked at the image and it was a picture of Megan, dressed in a lace bra and panties and she was showing off her body. "Damn!" I whispered in surprise once I saw the image. I took the phone in the room and showed Marcus. "Dayyyum bro, who is that?"

"Megan, your girl's best friend."

"Lemme see."

I showed him again and he laughed. "Damn, bro, you getting at her, too?"

"Nah man, I dunno how she got my number."

He laughed, "Yeah right, you gone hit that or what, I would, especially getting pictures like that, tell her to send you a skin flick," He laughed and I was laughing too. Chepi came in the room.

"What yawl laughing about?" I showed him the image.

"Ooooh, who is that?"

"That's Nicole's best friend, bro, she's trying to knock Cheetah," Marcus laughed.

I was typing in the phone asking how she got my number. She wrote back, sending her number and telling me to call her. I went in the bathroom with the shower running and I called her. "Hello?" she answered with music playing in the background.

"What's up, is this Megan?"

"Yes, hi, Cheetah, how are you?"

"I'm good, how did you get my number?"

"I have my ways."

"Well I know you didn't get it from me, so how did you get it?"

"Novi gave me your number. Don't tell him that I told you." Why did this fool give this girl my phone number? I never asked him to do that and he never bothered to call me and ask if it was okay to give my number out. I can't lie, she looked hella sexy in the pictures.

"I won't tell him, you look sexy in the pictures tho … you got more, naked ones?" I laughed.

"Yep, you want to see 'em? Don't be showing nobody."

"Yeah, send 'em." I was holding back a laugh. If she sent the pictures, I was going to show my brother.

"Lemme call you back."

"Aiight, I'm about to hop in the shower, so give me like fifteen minutes," I told her and she agreed and I climbed in the shower, feeling like a grown man with a girl sending me pictures like that. I took my shower thinking about Alia. I would've been pissed if she had called a dude and did some shit like that. I would've wanted to kill her ass.

She's a good girl, stuff like this don't come from her. She's the type that you could make your wife. Megan sparked me to write a song called, "Anything Chick." Cochise had a dope beat that he produced that evening and this title was perfect for the song. ***She's the easy breezy type. Gave it up on the first night...she's all on my dick sending skin flicks ... giving all that pussy to your boys losing friendships...oooooo-hhh, she's a anything chick.*** The hook was in my head and I hurried out of the shower after I washed up and dried off, singing the hook in my head over and over. I hurried to my room and wrote down the lyrics for the hook. I was going to write the rest of the song later, but I wanted the hook to be down first so I wouldn't forget. I sang the hook out to my brothers and they were screaming about how dope it was.

"Megan must've sparked that one," Marcus laughed, giving me dap and she sent the other picture through.

"Oooh, shit nigga, look," I laughed as I pulled up the naked picture of her, showing all her ass and pussy. She had a pretty pussy and it was wet. She had baby oil on her butt cheeks.

"Daayyyyym, look at this shit, bro," I laughed.

"OOOOOO DAYYYYUM Cheetah, hahahahahahahaha, you gone hit that?"

"I dunno, should I?"

"Hell yeah, nigga, she's sending it to you, dog!"

"Lemme see," Chepi was nosy. I let him see the naked coochie shot.

It was funny how she sent me those shots and then she called. I took the call out of the room so my brothers wouldn't be in my conversation. "Wassup?"

"Did you get them?"

"Yeah I got 'em. So what's up, why you send me those naked ass and pussy shots?"

"You asked for them, duhhh."

"I know but … what does that mean? You must wanna give it up, huh?"

"To you, hell yeah! I wouldn't have sent them if I didn't."

"Oh right," I said making her laugh. "So when can this happen?"

"When do you want it to happen?"

"Shit, don't tempt me, I want it to happen tonight." I said making her laugh.

"I can come over there. I can use my mom's car and come and see you."

"For real? Right now?"

"Yes! Of course, Cheetah."

"Well if you do that, I don't want you telling my girl."

"This could be between us. Nobody has to know."

"Okay, well fuck it, come over," I said, hard and ready for her. I hung up with her and looked at the pictures again. I heard my mom and dad in the room getting busy. I laughed because they were loud and banging the walls. I guess everybody was having sex tonight. That shit was crazy. I went back in the room and told my brothers, "She's coming over here tonight to gimmie some."

"Cheetah's getting his first piece of ass HAHAHAHAHAHAH."

I let em laugh, but it wasn't my first piece. If they only knew.

Megan showed up at nearly eleven o'clock. She was driving an all-white Mercedes. It was clean and she was by herself looking fly. I didn't know she had it like that where she could get her mom's whip and come to the rez; that's what's up. I had her pull to the back and my brothers looked out of the window laughing. She didn't see them looking at her.

"Cheetah, you better strap it up bro," Chepi warned me.

"I'm not gone fuck; I just want some head," I said making them laugh. They found me comical tonight but I was dead serious and not thinking about penetration with a girl that I didn't have any feelings for.

I went out to meet her and climbed in the passenger's seat and she fired up a blunt, and had the music going. "You got your license," I asked her.

"Yeah, I'm sixteen, why?"

"Oh okay because the tribal cops be out at night around here and I'm just making sure, if they stop you and you don't have your license, they will take your car and impound it."

"Oh, I have my license, I had it since I was fifteen."

"That's what's up. I'm thirteen, did you know that?"

"I know how old you are, you're still fine and sexy and plus you don't look your age."

"I know I get that a lot … so how old do I look?" I asked wondering how she would respond.

"You look my age, I thought you were sixteen until Novi told me your real age."

"That nigga talk too much. What else he say about me?"

She was laughing, "He's a little jealous of you."

"Why you say that?"

"I could just tell. I used to talk to him a long time ago, when we were thirteen but I outgrew him. You look way way better than him," she whispered and then she said, "You look better than all of those niggaz over there," she exploded in laughter. She was actually cool to chill around and she passed me the blunt. "You won't get in trouble, will you?"

"Nah, my parents are in the house, just keep the music down," I told her.

"Oh, okay," she whispered turning the music down some. I hit the blunt a few times and then passed it to her. "Why don't you back up and let's go over there," I pointed towards the pit area, where the guys hung out during the day. Since it was late, nobody was out and it was dark enough for us to smoke and do what we wanted. She drove over to the area and was looking around with questions in her mind. "You lived on this reservation all of your life?"

"Nooo, of course," I chuckled. "I was born and raised here just like the rest of my brothers and sister."

"How many brothers do you have?"

"I have five brothers and one sister. She's the youngest out of all of us and then I'm the youngest out of the boys."

"Ooh, how cool is that and they're all Indian?"

"We're all mixed yep."

"Your mom and dad did a good job with you. I think I met Marcus; I didn't meet the one with Marisol."

"That's Chepi, that's my tight brother."

"Yeah, you are some nice-looking guys."

"Thank you. So, what's up? Do you like to give oral sex?"

"Hell yeah! You gone let me give it to you?"

"Yeah, but I want you to keep this between me and you. If this gets back to my girl, I will never speak to you again and I'll deny it ever happened."

"I promise that I won't tell nobody!"

"Not even Novi, cos that motherfucker talks too much and I will beat his ass if it gets back to my girl."

"You must like her a lot huh?"

"I do, that's why I don't want her to know."

"You might break up with her after I do what I do to you. I'm good at what I do."

"I doubt that. You're not her."

"Well let me see it," she said looking at me with smiling eyes. I unzipped my jeans and pulled it out. "Dayyyyyum, you're packing like a grown ass man, shit!" she said making me laugh. "Are you sure you're 13? Gotdamn! How many inches is that?"

"Don't worry about it, put your mouth on it like you said you was gone do."

I let the seat back and she did the honors and went down on me. I can't lie, it felt so good. I thought I had died and gone to heaven because she knew what she was doing. I was used to this but with it coming from a girl that I didn't know was natural and it made the moment more pleasurable. I will never forget this. I released and she kept going, which had me clinching the door and my eyes went crossed for a few moments. "AHHHHH DAYYYUM," I pushed her back and laughed. She backed up wiping her mouth. "Can I ride it?"

"You got condoms?"

"Yes," she said going in her purse. She pulled out a magnum and the gold glistened in the night and I took it and slipped it on. "Come on," I said, getting hard again for her. She was out of her panties fast and smiling, taking off her blouse. When she straddled me, I put her titties in my mouth, she had some nice juicy jugs and I held them in my mouth gripping her ass while she rode me fast and I pounded her from the bottom and then I felt the warmth of her wetness.

"Oh shit, hold up," I said "Stop," I told her and she kept going and screamed out my name. "Fuck hop up, I think it broke," I said. She was warm and her pussy was juicy and wet. She climbed up and the condom had broken.

"FUCK!" I looked in shock. I was irritated that the condom broke, I was trying to hit that shit, but oh well, it wasn't meant.

"You wanna go to the store and get more?"

"Nah, I'm good. I gotta go." I told her. "You can pull back up to the side of the house."

She pulled up and looked at me like she was sad. "Aye just don't say shit and keep this between us aiight?"

"I will," she grinned.

After I was back in the house my brothers were laughing. "Did you hit, bro?"

"Yeah but the fucking condom broke."

"Awww shit, you didn't nut in her did you?"

"Nah," I said, glad that I didn't.

"Did she give you head?"

"Hell yeah, that was the first thing she did," I said, grabbing my pajamas and headed to the bathroom. "You better hope she don't open her mouth to your girl man. Females are fucked up like that, especially if you gave her some good pipe."

Winter Madness

I was in my sixth period class moving around in my seat because I was uncomfortable. My dick was feeling weird, it kept tingling and stinging at the tip. I dunno why and I couldn't talk to my mom about it. I didn't know what this was. It was my dad's last week here and I was going to miss him once he left. I was going to need to talk to him about this issue because it had been bothering me for the past few days. We were getting ready to start our winter break for the holiday and Thanksgiving was right around the corner. I raised my hand to get a hall pass to go to the bathroom. I went up and asked for the pass. "Here you go, Cheetah, and on the way stop by the office. The principal wants to talk to you."

"For what?"

"I dunno, sweetheart, but I don't think you're in trouble," Miss Sunny smiled.

I hurried out of the class down the hall. I was not looking forward to the bathroom break. I rushed in the boys' bathroom and went into the stall and closed the door and locked it. I pulled out my dick and looked down at it. It was red at the tip and some white stuff was oozing out of the tip. I held it there and when I peed it felt like someone put a match to my dick. "Ssssss awwwwww shit," I frowned in pain. Oh my God. I felt like I was pissing flames out of my dick. My dick started to throb. I had to go home, there was no way I could sit in class like this. I flushed the toilet and then I grabbed some tissue after the toilet was flushed and I hurried to the sink, turning on the cold water since nobody was in there and I put the tissue under it and ran back to the stall, putting the cold tissue on my dick head. It soothed the burning. "Oh my God." I whispered. I saw the white stuff oozing out again, I didn't know what that was. I left the bathroom heading to the office and I took out my phone and called my house.

"Hello," my dad answered as if he was waiting for me to call. Tears filled my eyes. "Dad, I think something is wrong with me."

"Why what's going on, Cheetah?"

"I dunno, my penis is burning when I use the bathroom."

"Oh shit ... are you having sex, Son?"

"I did a few days ago with this girl and we used a condom but it broke."

"Oh my God ... okay ... I'm on my way up there to get you."

"Okay, I'll be in the office," I said, wiping my tears. I didn't care who saw me crying, my shit was hurting and I didn't like how I was feeling. I'd never experienced anything like this in my life. I was glad that my dad was still on leave. My mom would've probably flipped out and I didn't need that right now. My dad sounded like he knew what was going on. He stayed calm and that helped me. Mr. Acorn comes out and saw me sitting in the office with my head down."

"Cheetah, are you okay?"

"No, I don't feel good," I told him. "My father is on his way to pick me up."

"Okay, did you fill out an attendance slip?"

"Yes sir."

"Okay good … well I have good news for you. The principal at PVA called and said that they want to meet with you and your parents for a possible acceptance."

"Really? Are you serious? I smiled. My dad walked in. "There's my dad. Dad, guess what?"

"What, Son?"

"They wanna meet with us at PVA; that's the school that I was telling you about."

"Oh yeah? That's great, Son," he said shaking the principal's hand. Mr. Acorn explained what we needed to do and we needed to go up there tomorrow or next week. I was so glad that my dad was here for that. My dick was keeping me from being as excited as I would've been; I was uncomfortable. We left the school with the paperwork from PVA and I was excited but scared at the same time. "Dad, what do you think is wrong with me?" I asked after we got in the car.

"The bitch you had sex with gave you something."

"What do you mean, Dad? Is that bad?"

"It's not good! I'mma take you to the E.R. so you can get a shot in the ass and some pills. You'll be all right in a few days. You can't trust no female out here, Son. You have to stay protected at all times. These bitches are filthy and they will make your dick fall off if you're not careful."

I started crying, I was scared. “Is my dick gone fall off, Dad?” He laughed.

“No! That’s just a figure of speech. Suck it up and relax. You gone be all right. What kind of pain are you having right now?”

“My penis is burning especially when I use the bathroom and now my stomach is cramping a little bit,” I felt nauseated. He passed me a bag. I was so scared, I think that’s why I felt sick. By the time we made it to the E.R. I was puking in the bag. “Oh my God dad, I’m sick!” I sighed, barely catching my breath.

“You’ll be all right, Son. Just don’t fuck with her no more.”

“I’m not! That’s not even my girl.”

“So you cheated on your girl, huh?” He put his arm around me. “See what happens when you’re not faithful?” I was throwing up again and I think it was because of my fear and my anxiety for having something wrong with my dick. I was terrified.

We waited in the E.R. for about fifteen minutes before I was called to the back with my dad. I felt bad because my dad had to pay a hundred dollars out of his pocket for the visit. The doctor came in the room and I told him my symptoms and he asked me to strip out of my clothes and put on a gown. He left the office and I stripped down and put on the gown, feeling embarrassed and ashamed of myself. I could smell the odor coming from my dick and it was like a fishy smell. “Gotdamn!” I whispered. The doctor came back in and had some stuff in his hand with a cup. “What’s that?”

“I’m going to do a STD culture on you.”

“What?”

He laughed. “You’ve never had sex I take it until recently, huh?”

"Yeah."

"Okay, well, this is for sexually transmitted infections. It sounds like that's what you have, I just wanna make sure. Let's have a look here. Lie back for me and relax."

He stuck something in my dick and I screamed out. "Oh shit," I frowned.

"Yeah, looks like you have a mild case of gonorrhea. Let's get you treated for it. Now if you still have symptoms in the next seven days, I need you to come straight back here, okay?"

"Okay. Is this curable?"

"It is, you're lucky. Make sure you tell your partner so she can be treated, also. I'm going to give you a shot and give you some pills to take here, okay? Hang on," he said, taking off his gloves and washing his hands after he finished with the testing kit that he had. I was so fucked up. That bitch gave me gonorrhea. Uggh! That's some nasty shit! I knew exactly what it was and Rowena always told me that girls had diseases and I didn't believe her. She never gave me anything and she was molesting me. It was crazy. My dad came in the room and asked me if I was okay.

"Yeah, Dad, he said that I have gonorrhea."

"Wow…so that's what it was, huh?" He shook his head. "Stay away from that bitch, but make sure you let her know that she gave it to you, aiight?"

"I will, I'mma cuss her out."

"No, just tell her that she needs to go and get checked."

The nurse came in after I had my clothes back on. She gave me the shot and it burned and then she gave me ten pills to take. "Awww man," I sighed after taking the pills. The doctor wrote me another prescription and told me to give it to Megan. I wasn't giving her shit. She needed to go to the doctor on her own and get rid of it. I wasn't going to make it easy for her. As soon as we got outside, I ripped the prescription up and my dad shook his head and laughed.

"That's wrong, Son."

"Forget her! She gave me a disease, that's nasty."

"Well, make sure you tell her, okay?"

"I'm about to call her right now," I said, dialing her number.

"Hello?"

"Aye …"

"I'm in class, can I call you back?"

"Whatever," I ended the call.

The medication made me go to sleep and two hours later, my phone was ringing. I answered it, hoping for Alia, but it was this nasty bitch. "Yeah?"

"Hey, Cheetah, what's up?"

"What do you mean what's up? You gave me a disease. That's what's up."

"What? No I didn't."

"Yeah, you did, I just came back from the E.R. and he said that I had an STD and it came from you!"

"What about, Alia, ain't you sleeping with her?"

"UUUH NO! She's a virgin! I got this shit from you Megan and you need to go and get it checked out. Don't call me no more! Nasty ass!" I ended the call and my brother Steven came in the room looking like he was about to tell me something good.

"What's wrong with you?"

"Nothing man, what's up?" I asked.

"So I sent off your demo to G.B.. Let's see what he does with it … I just wanted you to know that. You sure you're okay?"

"Yeah, I'm good," I yawned and laid back on my bed, looking for anything from Alia. I hadn't heard from her in a few days. I really missed her and I felt like shit for cheating on her. This is what I get. She didn't deserve this. Megan is a nasty broad. That's one of the reasons why a pretty face and nice body ain't always cracked up to be what people think. The light skin bitches be the main ones with diseases! They get all the action so of course they're the ones with the worst diseases on the planet. I'm lucky that it wasn't HIV.

The next day, my mom and dad took me to PVA in Paradise Valley. The symptoms had gone but it was just a little bit of tingling that I felt when I used the bathroom; it wasn't anywhere near what it was the day before. I was so happy about that. Megan sent me a text apologizing, but I didn't respond to her. Maybe she went to the doctor to get the shit cleared up. I was happy to be going to PVA and I prayed that they accepted me. If they did, I was going to do right by Alia and stay faithful. All I wanted to do was make this vision come true and be a famous singer. G.B. called while we were in route to the school. "Hello?"

"Aye, young magic, what's good?"

"I'm on my way to PVA with my parents. We're scheduled for a meeting up there."

"Oooh, congratulations young blood, that's good. I got your demo and I love it, call me when you're done with that, okay?"

"Okay."

"Who was that," my dad asked.

"That was G.B., this guy that I know. He's in the music business, Dad, and Steven sent him my demo."

"Oh, well you should've let me talk to him."

"I can call him back."

"No, just wait until we're done," he said, pulling into Paradise Valley Performing Arts Academy. It was a lot of white kids that attended this school and it was clean outside and rich looking; the building looked like a university, with big white columns at the entrance holding up the red brick. It was luxury cars parked out in front of the school and a Greek statue of a naked piece of male art. It was dope.

"This is a nice school," my mom said. I was glad she was dressed nice and my dad was in his Air Force uniform. We looked like we had money. It was a nice first impression. I followed them in the school and the white girls were looking at me, smiling. I kept it pushing, trying to keep myself away from girls right now, especially after what I just went through with Megan. I threw away the boxer shorts that I wore yesterday. They had that fish smell and it was gross. I couldn't believe she burned me like that. Novi probably knew she had something and he pushed the bitch off on me. I looked at him as foul for that. It was my fault because I was the stupid one that fell for it. She sent me another text message and it was a picture of her in the E.R. Good. I still didn't reply to her. At least she did go to the doctor; I was glad to see that. The lady helped my parents and I sat quietly watching everything in the office. They were professional and it was different from my school. Students wore uniforms here. Tan khaki's and black polo shirts with the school logo of a lion on the front. It was nice. They had the shirts up in a glass cabinet for sale, with the pullover hoodies and coats. They were expensive. A white woman came out and met my parents, shaking hands with them and told them to follow her in the office. I had to go with them and the girls were checking me out and it made me feel good. "Hello, you must be Anthony Featherstone, huh?" the lady smiled.

"Yes, ma'am."

"Oooh and he's respectful, I like that … have a seat, Mr. Featherstone," she said and I sat down.

"My name is Mrs. Cochran and I'm the Assistant Principal here. Mr. Heath is not here today. He had to go out on an emergency, so I'm going to be stepping in for him and Mom and Dad, if you guys could just read over this paperwork and sign and date it, that will be great. We have all of his records already that were faxed here yesterday from Mr. Acorn, so all we need is for you guys to read over the school rules and I will go over everything with you. Anthony, do you like for people to call you Cheetah, or Anthony?"

"Cheetah is what I go by."

"I like that. It fits you. What tribe are you from?"

"Navajo and Apache," my mom cut in.

"Oh I see, how nice and you guys live on the reservation in Maricopa?"

"Yes," my dad replied.

"I see, okay … so Cheetah it is," she said, pulling her hair behind her ear. She had pretty blue eyes and she was a red color. "So, Cheetah, I'm not sure if you went over what PVA is like, so I'm going to let you know that this academy is based on performing arts. We range from a variety of music, drama, dance, theatre like Broadway and acting as well. We have ballet classes as well if you're interested in ballet; we have Jazz and tap dancing and in between we deal with academic studies also, but we are mainly focused on whatever your passion is. Now from what I see with your application your passion is music and songwriting."

"Yes and I also dance, not ballet tho." We all laughed.

"Okay, perfect, we teach hip hop here, too, if that's what your into. We have a fantastic dance team here and we do compete every year for championships. So I'm sure you'll be excited for that."

"Yes, absolutely."

"Now in order for you to attend here, Cheetah, it is a charge for our classes, but we got a scholarship from your aunt, Rowena Whitehawk. She paid for four years for you to attend here, so we're waiving the application fees."

"Wow," I whispered and my mom looked at me with a big smile.

"So if you don't mind me asking, how much is it annually for people not on scholarship?" my dad asked.

"Oh it ranges from five thousand to fifteen thousand a year."

"Wow."

"Oh yeah and we have placed some of the top students in film and a lot of them have gone on to have great careers in the Film and music industry. I dunno if you guys heard of Razzmatazz, the rapper."

"Yes, that's my friend's brother."

"Oh okay, yeah, he went here for a year and we also have a lottery program where we pick kids in the inner cities depending on their grades to go here as well. We teach so many students, but not everybody is as gifted to make it big in the industry. We can't promise everybody a spot in the starlight, but we can sure give it a big shot at it."

"My son will make it," Dad said proudly grinning.

"I'm sure he will, too, but Cheetah what I would like from you is a two-page essay on why you feel that you would be an asset to PVA; it will due on your first day of school here, which will start in January, since we are going on winter break and school will return after the new year, the new millennium, shall I say. You will turn it in to me. If I'm not here, you can give it to my assistant, Sherry. She will make sure that I get it and just give me a brief description of yourself and tell me what you feel would be a good reason to be a student here."

"Okay," I agreed.

"I'm going to give you this packet to read, Cheetah, and right here, I would like for you to sign and date, the no violence rules here and the zero tolerance for drugs, alcohol or weapons on the campus. We have absolutely no issues with violence gangs or any type of drama here. We're a drama-free zone; the only drama that we want is from our acting classes," she said making us laugh.

"I hear you," Mom said.

"Yeah, we like to keep everybody happy and we have a lot of upper-class moms and dads that send their kids here and we want to keep them coming if you know what I mean," she said winking at my mom. I knew what she meant. I wasn't going to bring drama at all. Just because I wasn't rich didn't mean that I was going to be a problem. I read over the packet and signed my name. I had neat handwriting and she complimented me on it when I gave her back the paperwork. "Do you guys have any questions for me?"

"Yeah, do we get a tour?" my dad asked.

"Yes! I was going to tell you that next but you beat me to it. The kids that go here also can stay in our dorms that we have set up for students who are 16 and up. Since Cheetah's only 13 right now he will be bussed and come here on a daily basis like the other students his age, but once he turns 16, he will have full access to the dorms here, which also are monitored by our campus police and there is a curfew."

"Good, I was going to ask that," my dad said.

"If you guys can follow me out this way," She said. I was excited to look around the school. I was anxious at seeing what it was like here. This was a dream come true and Rowena kept her word.

We had to get on a golf cart to ride around the campus because it was so big and the first building that caught my attention was the music hall. "Cheetah, that's where most of your classes will be," Mrs. Cochran pointed. "You'll be here 90 percent of the time. This is where all of the music majors attend."

It took us an hour to ride around the entire campus and I was impressed. I was so happy to be attending here, I almost forgot about being burned by Megan. I was excited enough to want to call Alia after we headed back to the car. When I called the number, Nicole answered.

"Wassup Nicole, this is Cheetah."

"I know who this is, what's up, Cheetah?"

"Nothing much, how are you?"

"I'm good, where's your brother?"

"He should be at home, you haven't talked to him?"

"I tried to call him twice and I got no answer."

"Oh, well I'm on my way home, I'll tell him to call you."

"That would be so nice of you. Do you wanna speak to my cousin?"

"Yes, please, can I talk to her?"

"Hold on."

"Hello," she answered but she didn't sound too happy.

"Hey, how are you?"

"I'm so pissed right now, I mean, really pissed."

"Why—

"I can't talk about it right now, but I want you to call me in an hour. Don't forget."

"Okay … is it about me?" she hung up the phone. Damn. She didn't hear me.

"Cheetah, I'm proud of you, Son," my dad said as we were riding back to the reservation. "Thank you, Dad. I'mma keep making you proud."

"I know you will … I have faith in you."

"Make sure you are serious about music, Cheetah, because this is going to be expensive as far as your uniform and your food," Mom said.

"Don't worry about that, Lora, I'll buy his uniforms, I already ordered them and paid for them. That's coming out of my check next pay period."

My mom sighed giving me dad a sideways look. She was always complaining about money and we had no rent to pay on the rez. The only thing that we needed money for was food and for our water and utilities. My mom actually had it good compared to people living off the rez. “I just want him to be okay, Raymond.”

“He will be,” Dad told her. “Stop worrying so much,” he said, trying to make the conversation light since I was in the car. I was wondering what Alia was upset about. My guilt started to eat at me and it made me wonder if she found out about me and Megan. I hoped not. I was scared to call her back.

We made it back to the rez and the first place I went was in the shed with Cochise to give him the good news. “OOOH SHIT! My brother is a PVA student now?”

“Yep,” I said, showing him my temporary student ID. He displayed all of his teeth and gave a quick chuckle. “I knew you would end up there, bro, I knew it. It’s going to be good for you. At least one person in our family can do something great you know,” he shouted over the music.

My alarm went off and I knew that I needed to call Alia. I gave my brother a hug and told him that I was going to use the phone. “Aiight, congrats Cheetah.”

“Thank you.”

I went out in the backyard and dialed her number. The phone rang three times and then she answered, “Hello?”

“Hey.”

“Yeah,” she said, but it was dry. “I’m so mad right now.”

“Why?”

"Did you have sex with Megan?"

"Who told you that?"

"Did you?"

I didn't want to lie to her. "One time," I admitted.

She started crying and I felt so bad. Maybe I should've lied but then I would've been looking like a sucker for lying. "I'm sorry, Alia, it just happened it wasn't something I planned."

"So she was telling the truth? Why would you?" she sobbed. "She accused me of giving her a disease and I never been with you like that, she came to fight me yesterday saying that I gave her an STD. She had everybody on the block looking at me crazy all of the guys and my aunt jumped on me and beat me up thinking that I was having sex. How could you do that to me? Oh my God," she sobbed. I didn't know what to say.

"Alia, let me explain."

"Explain what? That you cheated on me when you promised me that you would never hurt me? I thought you loved me?"

"I DO LOVE YOU, will you listen to me, please?"

"I'm listening!" she said and she was still crying. I felt so low.

"Novi gave her my phone number and she sent me some naked pictures of herself."

"And you fell for it?"

"Alia I—"

"No, Anthony … you got weak because she sent you pictures of her naked body and you couldn't hang up on her or delete the pictures and tell me?"

"I should've."

"YES, you should've did that, how can I be with you now when you were with her and did she give you an STD, huh? Don't lie to me, Anthony."

"Yeah, but I went and got medicine for it."

"Oh my God!" she squealed in the phone. Tears made it hard for me to see the ground. My brother Chepi and Marisol walked in the backyard and I turned my back.

"What's wrong, bro, who is that?" Chepi asked. I waved him off.

"Is that Alia?" he whispered. I nodded and kept my back turned.

"Who is that in the background? Everybody knows that you cheated on me. I feel so stupid," She said, "I can't be with you."

"Alia, WHY? I don't wanna break up!"

"Why do you wanna be with me if you can't be faithful?"

"Because I love you, that's why!"

She was crying in the phone. "Alia, please! I love you, I swear I do. I don't wanna lose you. Just let me make it up to you."

"You can't! You can't, do you know how many guys she's been with? Novi is one of them … she's a HOE! I don't feel right staying with you after you cheated on me with her! I don't want to."

"So just like that it's over? I can't come and see you so we can talk?"

"Talk about what, Anthony? You don't care about me."

"Man, YES I DO! I do care about you. I told you already how I felt about you, Alia, c'mon, why do you wanna make it so hard for me? I just got accepted at PVA and now I gotta go through a fucked up break up with my girl! Are you serious right now?"

"Yes, I can't be with you."

"YOU KNOW WHAT?"

"WHAT?"

"FUCK YOU! YOU DON'T WANNA BE WITH ME … I AINT ABOUT TO BEG YOU NO MORE … FUCK YOU! BITCH!" I yelled and she hung up on me. I threw my phone and it hit the doghouse but it didn't break. Chepi came back in the yard. "Bro, what's up man, you wanna go over there?"

"Nah, fuck it! She wanna break up, fuck it! I'mma dog bitches from now on! Fuck it!" I sat on the fence.

"Come here, bro, I know you're hurt," he hugged me and I cried a little bit and then sucked it up. "FUCK THESE BITCHES man … fuck 'em all!"

"Cheetah, calm down, bro … she might come around; she's just mad right now. Just let her cool off."

My phone started ringing and Chepi ran over and grabbed it. He flipped it open, "Hello? Oh yeah, wassup … yeah, he's right here."

"Who is that?"

"It's Flip."

"Oh." I turned away and he brought the phone to me. "Hello?"

"Aye Cheetah wassup man, are we practicing today and I heard you got accepted at PVA. Congrats."

"Yeah, who told you?"

"They were talking about it at school. Mrs Cochran told us all over the intercom that you were coming. I'm happy man."

"I am, too, but … she broke up with me."

'Whut? Wait a minute, Alia broke with you, why?"

"I did some stupid shit, man."

"Hold on, bro, my phone is beeping, stay on the phone."

"Aiight."

Flip came back on the line, "Man, guess who that was?"

"Who?"

"Novi … that nigga just told me yawl broke up. He said he told her that you fucked Megan. Did you hit that shit, dog? Please don't tell me you hit it?"

"Man, I did … stupid, I know."

"OH MY GOD … nigga, I fucked, you fucked, Novi fucked, everybody hit that shit, dog."

"Man … she burned me too."

"AWWWWW HELL NAH," he laughed. "I ain't trying to laugh, bro, but dayyyum, she burned you with an STD?"

"Yep, I got it cleared up tho. I just hate that Alia broke up with me, man, and Novi told her, huh?"

"Yep, I told him that I was on the other line, I'm not calling him back. He likes drama, man. I think he did that on purpose to get yawl to break up so he could get with her."

"Yeah, I'm on my way over there. Let's see how much drama he likes, faggot!"

He laughed. "Aiight I'll see you in a minute, bro."

"AYE, CHEPI!" I roared.

He came to the back, "Wassup, man? You aiight, did she call you?"

"Fuck no! Take me over there on the block, bro."

"For Alia?"

"Nah, I wanna see this fool, Novi, running his mouth about me. He's the one that told Alia in the first place."

"Whut? Awww, I told you not to trust him."

"You were right. Where's Marcus? Let me text him, I bet he's over there."

I sent my brother Marcus a text message asking where he was. I went in the house and changed into something comfortable that I didn't care about. I was irritated and frustrated, especially after breaking up with a girl that I really had feelings for. While I was getting dressed, I put on one of my dad's old school albums. Switch. I loved listening to Bobby DeBarge. He was one of my idols when it came to singing. His voice was amazing and I learned a lot from him when it came to doing falsetto tones. I learned how to hit those notes and because I'm young, I still had the octaves where I wanted them and I put on the song, "Friend in the Sky." It was like a church song, but I liked singing it and it helped me to stay calm. I had to learn how to channel my anger now. I can relate to Bobby in a lot of ways because he was molested as a kid, too, and yet he continued with his music. It saved him for a little while until the drugs caught a hold on him. I had to keep from doing drugs and keep my mind occupied. Now that me and Alia weren't together, what other reason did I have to be here outside of music. I sang along with Switch as they harmonized the hook. Chepi came in the bedroom doorway listening, I felt him listening and watching me and I turned towards the mirror, singing along with Bobby when he hit that long high note. Chepi started clapping. "You got it Cheetah. You're the new Bobby DeBarge with a new twist bro! You got it! C'mon man, you ready? Marisol's out front waiting for us."

"Yep, let's go," I turned off the music and we headed out. I was sad on the inside and I thought about Rowena's pregnancy. It was so much coming at me at one time. I'm too young for this shit, I thought. I was going to take it all out on Novi's face.

When we got close to the block, Marcus hit me back telling me that he was on the block with Nicole and Alia was with her. "Oh, she's on the block now since she broke up with me. I wonder if Novi's over there."

"He might be, bro. I mean if she's not meant for you, then oh well, she'll regret it later when you get famous."

"Fuck that bitch! If she is over there with him, I'mma beat his ass in front of her. See how she likes that."

"Calm down, Cheetah, I know how you are, bro, you're hurt right now."

"HELL YEAH! I have a right to be!"

"Yeah but remember, you fucked up, bro! You broke her heart first, dog! You can't be mad at nobody but yourself."

"I KNOW THAT! I know that Chepi! But he had no right to tell her NOTHING, bro, that was none of his business!"

"Okay, you're right. All I want you to do is try to stay calm. You're too mad and you're working with feelings right now, bro. If she's over there don't fight him."

Hmm. I stayed silent as we turned the corner and everybody was out. Sneaky was even over there. G.B. was there, too. I was surprised he was on the block. I spotted Alia right away standing with Nicole.

They never hung out like this before; why was she out now? I was pissed. Chepi had Marisol park the car down the block. "Cheetah, just stay calm, bro."

"Fuck that! I'mma beat his ass."

"Don't fight him over her, Cheetah," Marisol said. "She doesn't like him."

I climbed out of the backseat and headed up the block. "CHEETAHHHHH," Sneaky whistled again, trying to get a reaction out of me, but I didn't throw my arms up like I usually did. He knew that something was up. He started heading towards me. G.B. climbed out of his Mercedes, smoking on a Black and Mild. Flip was outside and it seemed like the whole block was out for some reason. "Wassup dog?" Sneaky hugged me and I moved around him.

"Aye aye aye, Cheetah, hold up, dog. What's wrong, bro?"

"I'm about to beat his ass."

"Who?"

"Novi."

"Awww shit … well, hold on, dog … let me make sure it's gone be fair, man."

"I don't give a fuck!" I said, ready to fight whoever. Novi turned around and saw the expression on my face as we walked up. "Wassup, Novi, you running about me to Alia?"

"What you talking about, nigga, I ain't say nothing to her about nothing."

"YES YOU did, nigga! You did!" I pointed in his face and he stepped back.

"I didn't say shit to her, dog, I dunno… you're mad at me because yawl broke up?"

"Nigga I need that, wassup," I shoved him and he squared up. I rushed his ass, serving him and he grabbed my braid.

"NIGGA, LET MY HAIR GO! LET MY HAIR GO, BITCH ASS, NIGGA," I started kneeing him and Chepi and Mitch separated us.

"C'mon, nigga, you wanna get at her anyway!" I looked at Alia. "You wanna be with him? I want you to see how tough your new man is."

"I don't wanna be with him," she shouted. He tried to rush me but I grabbed him and flipped him over and slammed him on the ground.

"HOLD UP, HOLD UP!" I heard Mitch.

"Don't grab my brother, dog."

"I just wanna break it up," I heard Mitch tell Marcus. I was on top of him. Novi was out of breath. "He got asthma man. Let him up, Cheetah."

I punched him in the face and Chepi snatched me off of him. "Bitch ass nigga!"

I snatched away from Chepi. Mitch was helping his brother up. Novi was talking shit.

"Wassup? Wassup then," I balled my fist ready to take off on him again. But Marcus blocked me. "Leave him alone, man. He's just talking shit because ole girl is out here. He don't wanna fight, he's trying to look tough."

"Fuck that nigga," I turned to Alia. "You want him now?"

"I don't want him!" she said, turning her back to walk away when Megan pulled up quickly in the Mercedes. She threw the car in park. I was yelling at Alia and she jumped out, talking shit to Alia and Alia ran towards her and they locked up fighting. OH shit! I didn't even break 'em up. Alia was getting her ass kicked and she got dropped on the ground and Chepi ended up going over to break them up. I was still hurt that she broke up with me, I didn't care. I grabbed Megan, to make Alia jealous. "You aiight?"

"Yeah babe, I'm good," she said, pulling her hair back. "He's MINE now bitch!" Megan roared.

"SO WHAT! YAWL CAN HAVE EACH OTHER!"

"YEP, gimmie my ring back bitch!" I said, hugging Megan to make Alia feel my pain. She snatched the ring off and threw it and I caught it. "Here," I put it on Megan's finger in front of her. Alia was crying and waved us off and started walking away and Nicole was yelling for her to come back. "Let that bitch go," I said.

"Cheetah, you wrong dog," Chepi said.

"So what! She broke up with me, remember? How am I wrong? Fuck her!"

"Man, let's go," Chepi said, grabbing his girl.

"Matter fact, I'll get a ride from Sneaky. Take me home, Sneaky."

"Aiight Cheetah, we need to clear the air."

"I'll take you," Megan offered and I went and got in her Mercedes.

"Gotdamn, everybody catchin ass kickings over here today," G.B. said, making the guys laugh.

"I didn't get my ass beat," I yelled from the car. "I'm out of here."

"You gone, Cheetah? G.B. asked. "Yo bad ass, you need to call me young blood, hit me up."

"I will, I promise."

I can't believe I was in the car with the bitch that burned me. I looked at her. "You're scandalous as fuck."

"Who?"

"YOU! Who you think I'm talking to?"

"Why babe, I didn't do nothing."

"We're not together now, thanks to you and Novi … now I'm single."

"Cheetah, you know I'll do anything for you. I love you. Forget her! You were made for me not her! I will DO ANYTHING for you."

"Anything, huh? You sure about that?"

"Anything."

As soon as she pulled up in front of my house, I looked at her. "If you're willing to do anything, I want the latest retro Jordans."

"Those five hundred dollars tennis? Okay! I'mma get 'em for you. Are we gone be together?"

"I dunno … we'll see." I climbed out of the car and closed the door.

"I'mma go get em, what size?"

"Ten and a half."

She was smiling as she drove off. Cochise came out of the shed. "Who was that? That wasn't Megan, was it?"

"Yep."

"Are you with her now?"

"Nah man, I'm just using these bitches now! There's no need for me to put my heart in nothing except the music."

"AYYYYYYYYEEEE," he slapped my hand in the air. I went in the lab and we worked on music. I had to do something positive to keep my mind focused. I couldn't stop thinking about Alia. I was trying to forget about her but each song that I wrote had her name all over it. I was doing some dope ballads and was thinking that I should go going solo, because I needed to set the world on fire with my voice. Maybe it wasn't meant for me to have a girl. The universe was talking to me in a strange way and I wasn't trying to listen. I had my mind set on doing what I wanted. It was meant for me to be involved in music. I let my heart take me with the melody.

The next morning, my mom was shaking me awake because someone was at the door for me. "Cheetah, it's a girl out there for you."

"Who? Alia?"

"Elina go see what this girl's name is," Mom said, turning the light on, waking up Marcus and Chepi.

"Mom turn the light off."

"No, it's time for you guys to get up anyway."

"Why? It's no school," Chepi said, jumping off his bed to turn the light off. He flicked it off and jumped over Marcus's bunk and back in the bed. I sat up, wondering who was there for me. Elina came to the door, "It's Megan for you."

"Oh." I got up and slipped on my sweats. It was chilly in the house. I heard thunder and rain coming down on the roof. "Is it raining?"

"Yep," Elina said, going in the kitchen with Mom; she was cooking.

"Is Dad still asleep?"

"Yep."

I opened the door and Megan was standing outside with shopping bags in her hand. I let her in. Fuck it! I couldn't believe she actually bought the stuff.

"Mom, c'mere," I said and my mom came from the kitchen, sizing Megan up with a grin.

"This is Megan, this is my mom … and that's my little sister, Elina."

"Hello, nice to meet you. I bought you guys something," she said.

"Nooo, you didn't have to do that," my mom said and to my surprise, she had bought my mom an expensive sweater and my sister some outfits.

"Wow! Thank you so much," Elina was happy about that. I sat on the sofa opening up my shoes. She bought the exact ones that I had my eye on. "Thank you."

"You got new shoes again. This boy has thousands of shoes," Elina told Megan.

"I'm sure."

"Thank you for this," I told her.

"You're welcome."

"So, Cheetah, is this your new girlfriend now?"

"I dunno yet, Mom."

"Yes, I am," Megan said. "He's trying to be hard."

"Okay, well good. At least someone can keep him in line. You're welcome to come over for Thanksgiving if you'd like."

"Wow, Mom," I laughed. She just invited her without my consent.

"I'll be glad to," Megan laughed and she got up and followed my mom to the kitchen asking if she needed anything or help with anything. I felt like Megan owed me since she burned me with that fucked up STD and now she was trying to worm her way into the family. She got on my mom's good side instantly when it came to the sweater. My mom was into shit like that, too, and she bought my sister some nice expensive outfits. I took my shoes to the room and Marcus was up. "Oooh shit, you got the retros, lemme see? Dayyyyum, Cheetah, you lucky ass! Who gotchu these, Alia?"

"Man you got jokes. Megan bought 'em."

"Oh so you messing with her now?"

I shrugged. "She wants to be with me, Alia dumped me."

"Wow bro. You get all the fine bitches!" He laughed. Chepi rolled over and looked at the shoes.

"Those are nice. Take care of them because they're going to be worth money later."

"Yep, I know. You ain't gotta tell me, bro. I take care of my shit! All of my shoes and when I get famous, I'mma have a place for my shoes to go in my walk-in closet."

"I believe you too, bro, just don't forget about us."

"Never! If I get rich, we all get rich!"

I got a text message. It was Rowena. *Cheetah, I really need to talk to you. Please call me.* I hoped this didn't have anything to do with her wanting me to be a father because I had forgot all about it until she hit me up. Damn. I went to the bathroom and dialed her number. I should've thanked her for the help she gave me to get in that school.

"Hey, Cheetah, what are you doing?"

"Nothing," I yawned. "I just woke up, what's up?"

"I have some bad news." I hoped she was going to tell me that she had a miscarriage but instead she told me that she had Stage 4 breast cancer. "Wow, what? How?"

"I dunno," she sobbed in the phone. "I don't wanna die."

"Can you take medicine or something to get rid of it?"

"They told me that it was already in my lymph nodes and I knew that something was wrong but I didn't want to take care of it."

"So you already knew this?" I frowned. "What about the baby?"

"I dunno," she sobbed. "The doctor told me that I'll be lucky to last three months … is your mom home?"

"Yeah, my father is here, too."

"He's still there? I thought he was leaving soon."

"He is, after Thanksgiving tomorrow. He's leaving on Tuesday."

"Can you tell your mom to call me?"

"Yeah, I'll tell her."

"Cheetah, I really need to see you. I have some things that I want to talk to you about."

"Okay. Do you want me to call you back or no?"

"I'm going to call your mom, but I would like for you to come over so we can talk. I don't wanna die and leave you in the dark about things that you should've known."

"Okay. I might stop by there later on today."

"Okay, come alone."

I was hesitant about that until she said. "I'm not going to try anything; I'm too sick."

"Okay. You want me to put my mom on the phone?"

"No, I'm going to call her."

After the phone call with her, it was like a shakeup. One thing after another after the good news. I was hoping to hear something good from G.B. instead of more bad news.

We had a nice Thanksgiving. My dad was spending time with us and we had a lot of laughter and just for today, I was in a great mood and feeling good about my accomplishments. G.B. had called me late that night and told me that a record label was interested in me but they hadn't gotten back to him. He said that he had a feeling they would reach out to him after the holidays. That was great news, outside of the breakup with Alia and I and me missing her. I still thought about her despite me having Megan around, when I didn't like Megan for a girlfriend. She seemed loyal and was right here. She kept me company to keep my mind off of Alia as best as she could but Alia still crept in my mind and I wondered how she was doing. We had a great meal. My mom made turkey, ham, dressing, mac and cheese, mashed potatoes and corn on the cob with a bunch of pies and cakes. Mom invited Rowena for dinner but she was too sick to come. I don't think she was able to face my dad after what she's been doing to me.

"Why are you sitting over here by yourself?" Megan came over and sat near me.

"I'm just chilling," I whispered. I had snuck a cup of my mom's Moscato. It was pretty good and I had a slight buzz. "What are you drinking?"

I put a finger to my lips. "My mom's wine. You want some?" I gave her some. She liked it.

"I want some."

"Hold on, I'mma wait until they're not looking and I'mma sneak some more. It's good, huh?"

"Yep," we laughed.

"You gotta nice family."

"Yeah, they're cool."

"My mom cooked but I didn't want to be at home. It was going to be boring dealing with my family. They're not really my blood."

"What? What do you mean?"

"I was adopted," she admitted.

"Where's your real parents?"

"My mom died when I was two and my dad is doing life in prison in Puerto Rico. I'm half Puerto Rican and black. My mom died of AIDS."

"Wow, no shit? You don't have it do you?"

"No silly! She caught it after I was born. She was using drugs and my grandparents got me taken away from her but then they died so I was put in the system and adopted by the family that I have now."

"Wow, that's deep. Are they nice?"

"Hell, yes! I'm spoiled. I have to admit, I get everything that I want. I just wish that I could've had my mom and my dad in my life."

"Do you talk to your dad at all?"

"No," She shakes her head. "I don't want to know him. At first I did but now I don't."

"Why is that?"

She shrugged at first and then said, "He's a loser. He couldn't even stay out of jail to raise me; he has other kids but I don't know them. I heard he's never getting out so what's there to know about him? I never knew my dad."

"Wow! That's deep."

I was on my way to see Rowena the day after Thanksgiving to give my mom and dad time to be together. They were having sex so loud that it woke us all up. We were all laughing at them. Elina was upset because she thought they should've gotten a hotel room, but shit, they're married. It wasn't no big deal to me; that's how we all got here. They're still in love and I'm happy for my parents. I wish I could've had that with Alia, but I had to get her out of my mind. I dialed her number last night and hung up before anybody answered. I dunno what I was thinking. The walk to Rowena's house wasn't as bad as I thought it would be. It was kind of cool outside, now that summer was finally gone. The leaves had all fallen to the ground and the rez looked more naked now. I had a few more blocks to go before I got to the ritzy area of the rez which was where all of the rich Native American people lived. We even had a casino on the rez and it wasn't popping like it could've been; people just didn't really come here to gamble because they were tight on the winnings. Rowena's got so much money that it didn't matter to her if people gambled or not. This side of the rez, didn't even look like it belonged here; the houses were mini mansions.

I made it to her door and I knocked and rang the doorbell. I'm sure she could see me through the cameras. She came over the loud-speaker. "Hey, Cheetah it's open, come on in."

I went in and her little dog came running to my feet; he didn't bark. He ran straight upstairs back to her room. This room I hated because this is where she started molesting me and the smell was even the same. I thought I would never come back here but here I was. Why? I don't know. One would've thought that I would be happy that she was going through this because I had wanted her dead once upon a time, but now that death was coming for her, it was different. I wanted it to be fast and violent, but this one wasn't anything of the sort. When I stopped at the doorway of her room, I looked at her and she looked different. Damn. She was skinny when she was well. She was shaped nice when she was well, but now she looked like a skeleton. Her eyes were sunken. Damn! I didn't realize she was this sick, but once I saw her reality settled in.

"Come in," she waved me on. "I know I look horrible." I wasn't expecting this so fast. The universe really took care of people that needed to be punished.

"How are you feeling," I asked as I came in and sat at the foot of her bed.

"I feel like shit! I'm in a lot of pain. I should've told you a while ago, Cheetah. I knew that something was wrong, but I didn't want to deal with it. I went into denial. Before I became pregnant the doctor found a lump on my left breast and so she had me take a mammo and I did and it came back positive for cancer. She called me and told me to come for a biopsy but I put it off and got pregnant. Then I told her that I couldn't come and I waited and it spread and now here I am."

"Why didn't you go?"

"Because I didn't want them to take my breast off; I didn't want to face the fact of me having cancer. I didn't want it. I've had so much bad shit happen to me in my life and to deal with this was like a slap in the face, Cheetah. I didn't want to deal with that."

I looked at her and thought to myself, the shit that she put me through, this serves her right. I stayed silent.

"Cheetah I wanted you to come up here because I wanted to personally apologize to you for putting you through so much pain. I know what we did was wrong!"

"So why did you do it?"

"Because it happened to me! Your mom and me have different fathers. We don't have the same dad. My dad was a rapist. He was the chief of this reservation—"

"Wait a minute. Chief Whitehawk was your father?"

"Yes! He raped your grandmother and she became pregnant with me. After I was born, she gave me to him and he raised me and then when I turned nine years old, he started molesting me."

"Wow!" I whispered.

"Yes, Cheetah, he was having sex with me up until the day that he died."

"How come you didn't tell nobody?"

"Who was I going to tell? He was the Chief and he had money. Nobody was going to believe me. My mom didn't tell anybody when he raped her. She kept quiet about it until I was born. She gave me to him and he put me through hell and then when he died, I moved back in with your grandmother and guess who treated me like shit?"

"Who?"

"Your mom; she hated me. She used to torment me until I got old enough to inherit his money and that's when she changed."

"Wow, I didn't know that. So you did this to me because it was done to you?"

"It wasn't just you, Cheetah. I was involved in so much stuff, child trafficking for people in high places. I was involved in sending young Indian girls to men old enough to be their dads. I did a lot of shit and I feel like this cancer is my payback."

Damn right! It was! I kept quiet.

"You don't know how sorry I am and I'm going to make sure that you're okay when I die."

"What do you mean?"

"You'll see. I'm going to make sure that you have what you deserve because you're a good kid and I'm not pregnant anymore; I had a miscarriage," she admitted and that was good news for me.

"When did this happen?"

"Last week. I knew it would happen, like it always happens. My father ruined me, I can't have children, every time I get pregnant, I lose the baby. He ruined my womb. I'm not sad about dying," she said. "I don't wanna die, but I'm not sad about leaving this world, Cheetah. The only person that I'm sad about leaving is you."

"Did you tell my mom?"

"Yeah, she knows. I told her. She thinks that I'm going to leave her my money but I'm not leaving her anything because she treated me so bad and the only reason why she changed was because of my money. It was all fake. She never gave a damn about me."

"Why?"

"Because she was jealous because my mom showed me a lot of attention because she was feeling guilty about giving me to my dad. I told her what he did to me and she felt guilty about it and—"

"That's why Nana's been around you so much and catering to you," I realized.

"Yes! I became her favorite and your mother hated me for it."

"Did my mom know about what Chief Whitehawk did to you?"

"She knew, but she didn't care. Do you know she let six girls jump me and cut off all of my hair?" My eyes grew wide. I was speechless with that. Damn, Mom was ruthless.

I went back home with a lot to think about. All of this stuff that Aunt Rowena dropped on me was like snatching all of my clothes off and sending me outside naked to be laughed at. I was confused and ashamed of a lot of things that I didn't understand. I had to grow up fast and take everything in like a man at thirteen. Now was the time that I really needed Alia. I wanted to call her so badly but my pride stepped in and wouldn't allow me to dial her number. I missed her so much. I dialed Megan instead.

"Hey boo, what are you doing?"

"Just sitting her with a lot on my mind. Do you have weed?"

"Yeah, I do, you want me to come over?"

"Yeah, can you?"

While I waited for Megan to show up in Alia's place, I went out to the shed where Cochise was and he had made a beat that he wanted me to hear. I ended up writing to it. *Without you … my heart is filled with stone … I don't know what to do … I buried myself in this song. When I think of you … I'm fighting to pick up the phone… I'm missing you … it's making weak and alone…* After I sang that to my brother, he was in love.

"THAT'S IT, CHEETAH! THAT'S IT BRO! That's a powerful hook. How do you do it?"

"I just do it! That's how I'm feeling right now. Give Alia thanks," I added and it made him laugh.

"Bro, finish that song. That's dope! I love it!" I grabbed my notepad and sat down and started writing to it. I poured out my heart on paper and created another beautiful timeless piece that I even liked. A lot of my songs I thought weren't as good as everybody else felt that they were. I really liked this one because it made so much sense and I felt that a lot of people could relate to it. Megan appeared in the lab. I was in the booth this time. I had the headphones over my ears indulging in my work. I started singing. *A melody to a song … an ageless beauty sharp as a thorn … and you want it to last … forever and ever … staying in love where that magic is us together…* Tears filled my eyes as I sang this song, picturing Alia in my head. Music really does make you emotional and it brings out the best in your abilities and gifts. I felt like Alia was making me be more creative and to dig deep inside of myself to create a masterpiece. I had a feeling that this song would end up bringing me out. After I was done in the booth, I came out to see Megan crying.

"That was beautiful, Cheetah, I never heard you sing like that. Wow! It was so pretty. I love this song; this is my favorite."

"Mine too, thank you." I said, looking at Cochise. He gave a thumbs up.

"You wanna go out and smoke," I asked her.

"Yeah," she said, in a daze. I was going to let my brother mix and master the track while I sat outside and tried to take my mind off of the girl that my heart was attached to. Maybe after a few months, I could be over her.

"That song was so pretty, Cheetah. What's the name of it?"

"Missing you."

"Is that for Alia?" she asked. Why did she ask me that? I wasn't going to lie to her.

"To be honest, yeah."

"Wow. Do you miss her?"

"I do. I'd be lying if I told you that I didn't miss her."

She looked down with a sad expression. I didn't want to lie to her and I know it made her feel some type of way but I was being real. "I hope one day you feel like that about me."

I stayed quiet. That wasn't going to happen. I felt that I would never open up my heart to another girl.

Christmas came and went and I had Chepi drive me back over to Rowena's house. My mom had been taking care of her for the last few weeks and here we were in the new millennium and I was thinking that everything would stop working because people were scared about Y2K saying that the computers won't recognize 00 but they did. People were buying all kinds of canned goods and water just in case stuff stopped working and it would be the end of the world. My mom was even doing it but nothing happened; we were still here and still moving around like normal. Rowena wasn't doing so great from what Mom said. I found it hard to go back and visit her after the first time we talked. This time, Chepi said he was going in with me so I wouldn't be alone. I wanted to tell Chepi what she had done to me, but I kept quiet. Something told me to keep it hush. When we arrived at the house, there were some attorneys there and they were in the room with her, so we sat downstairs in the den and watched television until they left.

I went up to see her. She was still in her right mind. "Hey sweetheart. How was your Christmas?"

"It was good. As well as can be expected. How are you feeling?"

She shook her hand. "The pain is not as bad, but I'm on Fentanyl now."

She lifted up her shirt and showed me the patch on her arm. "Wow, that's medicine?"

"Yep, I can't keep anything down. My stomach is shrinking and I can barely drink water."

"Oh."

"Did your mom give you the money that I sent you?"

"What money? No."

"I sent five thousand dollars to you for Christmas and you didn't get it?"

"No."

"Wow, okay, don't worry about it. My lawyers just left. It will all be straightened out once this is over with."

"I don't care about your money, Rowena. I just wanted to tell you that I forgive you."

When I said that, the look on her face changed and she frowned in tears. "Thank you so much, Cheetah. I never thought you would say that to me. Oh my God. Thank you. I can leave in peace now because I know that you don't hate me."

"No, I don't hate you. I hate what you did, but I can't hate you. You're still my family and I feel like you're really sorry about what happened. I don't want you to keep suffering. My conscience is clear and I just wanted to tell you that what happened to me hurt and I hated it, I hated what I went through, but maybe it was a reason why I went through it."

"No, it was me being a bitch and being selfish and spiteful. You had no reason to go through what I put you through," she said when my brother Chepi walked in and shut her down.

"I didn't know you were here. How are you?"

"I'm good, Auntie, how are you feeling?" He asked after he hugged her.

"I'm dying," she said. "It won't be long now. I'm in so much pain, I'm suffering. The cancer is all over my body now, look at my legs."

She removed the blanket and we saw the knots and bruises in her legs; it was crazy looking, I had never seen anything like it. It looked as if someone took a bat and hit her across the legs and put lumps on her thighs and lower legs. It grossed me out. I couldn't look at it any longer.

"Do you want me to give you more medicine?" Chepi asked.

She shook her head. "I have a patch right here, once it wears off, the nurse will be here to give me more. It wouldn't be so bad if I wasn't in so much pain," she admitted. I thought I could handle seeing her suffer, but after seeing this, I couldn't handle it. I was ready to go back and get in the truck. The way she was looking, I don't see her making it through the end of January. If she did, it would only prolong the suffering and nobody should suffer like that.

Chepi turned on some music for her. She fell asleep and we sat in the room with her until my mom showed up. As soon as she walked in, Rowena woke up and sat up, "Why didn't you give Cheetah the money that I gave you for him, Lora?"

"I had to use it for something; I'll give it back to him."

"You're a fucking liar! You didn't need it for anything. You have a husband with a job; you should've gave him the money. You've always been selfish and greedy," Rowena told her. I walked out of the room while they went back and forth, I didn't want her to talk crazy to my mom after what she put me through. It didn't matter, I didn't care about the money. Chepi came out of the room laughing.

"You ready to go?"

"Yeah let's go. I can't stay and watch her suffering, bro. Let's go."

"Yeah, bro, I don't think she's going to make it through next week."

More people were coming over. She had a lady helping with her guests. We went downstairs and passed some other folks that were coming to visit. It seemed like yesterday when she told me that she was sick and now she was on her way out; it was so fast. I never imagined that. We left her house quiet on the way back home. Flip called, interrupting the moment of silence. "Hey, bro, what's up?"

"Aye Cheetah, guess who just got arrested last night?"

"Who?"

"Mitch. They got him on gun charges and some mo shit bro. They said something about him killing a white girl."

"No shit?"

"Yep. They had Novi, too, but they let him go. I think he told on his brother."

"Whuut, damn, so where is he?"

"He's downtown in custody. I'll find out more later, but I just wanted you to know to not come around here because the cops are hot and from what Novi was telling me, the white boys that they robbed a few days ago ratted them out."

"They robbed some white boys?"

"Yep, took a lot of money from 'em and Novi was out here flossing and spending like he was rich and shit and Mitch went down for it. I think he ratted his brother out."

"Wow … okay, bro, I'mma hit you when I get home."

"Okay … hit me later."

I told Chepi what happened. "Oh shit … I wonder if they got that gun you let him use."

"I dunno, probably. That's crazy huh," I swallowed realizing that it was Rowena's gun and what if they trace that shit back to me, since it was on the rez? Fuck! This was all I needed. Things were going good and this fool had to go and use the same damn gun in another robbery. Dumb!

My first day of school was amazing. I got to meet a lot of nice people. The white girls were on me, just like Chepi explained that they would be. I was honored by the smothering of their presence. I'm not saying that I was attracted to them, but they rolled out the red carpet giving me what I needed and right there to assist me with my classes and just like Mrs. Cochran had said, I was in the music building most of the day which made things a lot easier for me. I met a guy name

Scott; he was a white boy, but he was into R&B music and he could play a lot of instruments, which was impressive. We hung out most of the day and I told him about the group Eleven. He asked for a copy of our CD and I promised to bring him one the next day. Steven picked me up from school with a somber look on his face. I already had a lot of books to carry and he added to it by telling me that Rowena had a priest at her house and everybody was over there. She had slipped into a coma. Instead of going home, we were heading straight to her house and there were many cars parked in her driveway. In the back of my mind I was worried about the gun charges that Mitch had. I wanted to call Novi, but he and I were at odds with each other after that fight. I was just hoping that he didn't run his mouth and tell the cops that the gun belonged to me. That was all I needed was for him to do that just to free his brother and I end up going down for charges that they committed with the damn gun. I didn't want to tell Steven.

"So did you hear from G.B. yet?" I asked to take my mind from the inevitable.

"Not yet. I'm sure it will be soon. They want you to go solo Cheetah. Oh and I might have a show coming up for yawl next weekend, but it's not set in stone yet."

"Okay, I'll let the guys know," I said as we entered the rez, my feelings became weary. I sent Flip a text message asking if he would be free next week because we might have a gig coming up. We needed the money; I sure did. He wrote back telling me that he would let David and Smoke know that they needed to be ready.

"Where is the gig going to be," he asked. I asked Steven.

"It might be at the Blue Lounge," I wrote to Flip and told him and then I asked him if he had heard anything about Mitch. He decided to call me. Damn. I didn't want to talk in front of Steven.

"Hello?"

"What's up, Cheetah, so far I haven't heard anything, but he ain't out. Novi's running around here like a loose cannon."

"What is he doing?"

"Just running his mouth, talking about someone better look out for his brother if he goes to jail and I know he ain't talking about nobody but you because he told us that yawl did a lick together and the gun is yours."

"What? He's lying, bro."

"I know, I don't believe that. He's on some hater shit. He got into it with Sneaky because Sneaky checked him about it and told him not to be running his mouth about you. I think he's pissed because he's still trying to get at Alia. She ain't giving him the time of day tho."

"Good. Fuck him. I'll beat his ass again if I have to."

"Nah, Cheetah you got too much to lose. How is your aunt?"

"Not good, I'm on the way over there right now."

"Aiight, I'll keep my ear to the ground, just call me if she passes, or do we need to come to your house now?"

"Nah, I'm good for now, bro, thanks, tho," I said. As I ended the call, we pulled up and Steven sighed and parked. "You ready?"

"Not really but yeah."

"I hear you. I ain't ready for this either," he said and we both climbed out of the truck at the same time. Just as I had expected, there were a lot of cars there. It was January 10th. Everybody was still leery about the year 2000 better known as the Y2K movement and here I am faced with yet another challenge. I just prayed to the creator to make things go smooth for Mitch. I hoped that nothing came out about him getting that gun from me because I was going to deny it. Chepi told me to do that. He said if the cops came on the rez asking me about it to deny it. That's what I was going to stick with, denial. I wasn't going to put myself in a cross and end up in jail. Mitch was over 18 so he went to a grown man's jail and Novi was out on the streets alone without his brother's protection. Perhaps this was time for me to get at him again.

We went inside Aunt Rowena's place and it was filled with folks. When my mom saw us come through the door, she waved me upstairs. "Hurry quick," she said. I bolted up the stairs with Steven and we went in the room. I thought Rowena was in a coma, but she looked at me and waved me over. I went to her and sat down beside her close this time. She wasn't talking; she was breathing weird. I saw her pulse beating through her neck and her neck was skin and bones. Her pulse was racing hard. The nurse was in the room with us. We locked eyes.

"What's going on with her?" I asked the nurse.

"She's dying, actively dying right now."

"Really?" I grabbed her hand and it was ice cold. Death was upon her and she looked at me without words and lay back on the pillow and let out a loud breathing noise; it sounded like she needed to clear her throat but the nurse said that it was the death rattle. She let out a loud breath and I saw her pupils grow big almost the size her entire eyeball. It was something that I had never seen before. DEATH!

She tried to take another breath but it cut off and her mouth and eyes remained open.

"She's gone!" my mom whimpered. "Oh my God she's gone," Mom cried.

"Come on, Mom," Steven grabbed her and I sat with her, staring at her. I looked at her body and there was no more life left in her. I thought I would get that opportunity to talk some more to her but I didn't. I wonder if she knew that I was there with her. She waved me over, so I think she did know that I was there. She was gone, January 10, 2000. I finally got up from the bed because the nurse wanted to come and take her vitals. She called the doctor and told him that she had expired. Damn! Expired? Why did she say that? This woman was what you call a hospice nurse and I didn't know what that meant, but she gave the doctor the time. 3:46 p.m. "Yes … okay, I'll let the family call the mortuary." The nurse said before she ended the call. Everything seemed louder now. She was gone, and I wasn't relieved like I thought that I would be. It happened so fast. I thought she would torment me for years to come but that didn't happen. At least I got answers as to why she did what she did.

My mom was crying downstairs as if they were close, but I knew the truth. Rowena told me how bad my mother treated her. I never watched anyone die before; this was going to be embedded in my mind. Gosh I needed to speak with Alia. Megan called me and I grabbed my phone and went downstairs after the nurse put the sheet over Rowena's body.

"Hello?"

"Hey boo, what you doing?"

"Nothing, I'm over at my aunt's house."

"How is she?"

"She just died."

"Oooh no, I'm so sorry, Cheetah! Do you need me?"

"I dunno what I need right now, but yeah, come over," I said before I ended the call. There was no reason for me to be in this house now. I told Steven that I was going to walk home. On my way outside, the sky had gotten dark. It was still early and it looked like it was going to rain. I wonder why it always rains when someone dies. I remembered when my uncle Danny was sick with cancer, when he died, it rained and my mom was crying because she was close to that brother. As I was walking the rain started coming down and the faster I walked, the harder it rained. So much went through my mind as I was walking and I made a vow to myself that I was going to go hard on the music. I was crying on my journey home and I heard a car behind me. I turned to see that cop that didn't like me. I stopped walking, wondering if he was going to harass me. He pulled up on the side of me. He lowered the window on the passenger's side.

"Nigger nigger! What are you going to do now that your aunt is gone?"

"Wow." I shook my head and started walking again, he drove on the side of me.

"Now that she's gone, I'm really going to have a reason to get your ass! I told you that I was going to kill you when you turned 18 … you'll be 14 this year … four more years and your ass is going to be out of here."

"Why do you hate me so much?"

"Because I don't like NIGGERS!" he said. This dude wasn't a Native American Indian; he was a white man!

"Now that your aunt is gone, you better not let me catch you doing anything or your ass is DEAD!" he said, speeding off and luckily Steven drove up behind that fool and picked me up.

When I climbed in the truck with Steven he asked me what the cop said. "He was just talking shit to me. He don't like me."

"Fuck him. He's always messing with people on the rez, fuck that white boy."

"Does he mess with you?"

"He used to, but he stopped after I went to his supervisor and told him that he was messing with me."

"Maybe I should do that," I uttered when Megan drove up. She had a big vase of flowers, which I don't know why she brought them to me. I climbed out of the truck and she met me.

"Here, give these to your mom."

"Oh, these are for my mom, thank you." I took them and invited her in. Steven spoke to her and went to his room and I put the flowers on the kitchen table and took Megan to my room. Nobody else was home right now. I wanted to relieve some stress so I asked her to give me some head. I made sure that my door was locked and nobody would walk in and catch us. It felt good and for a few moments I was able to escape the pressures of life. When I came, she was swallowing it; it was amazing. She backed up off of me and gazed at me. "Is that better?"

"Man, yep. Thank you," I said, pulling my pants up. I was ready for her to leave now, but I didn't want to be rude. I went to my drawer and grabbed some clean clothes and she said,

"When are we going to have sex again?"

I looked back at her. "Did you get rid of that STD?"

"Cheetah! Yes! I told you that I did, I don't have it anymore, it's gone."

"I dunno. I'm scared," I told her and she laughed.

"I'm not going to give you anything. We can use condoms if you want."

"I'm going to buy them, just gimme the money, I'll buy 'em myself."

"Fine," she said going in her purse. She pulled out five dollars and set it on the bed. I left her and went to take a shower. I cleaned myself, thinking about Alia. She was still on my mind and we had been broken up for over a month now. I thought I'd be okay but she was still heavily on my mind.

After my shower, I went out fully dressed and Marisol and Chepi were there.

"Hey Cheetah," Marisol smiled at me. "Sorry about your aunt."

"Thank you, I appreciate it. How have you been? How was your Christmas and New Year?"

"It was nice, what about yours?"

"It was aiight. How's your friend doing?" I asked and Megan got jealous. I didn't care.

"I'm going home, Cheetah, I'll call you later," she said.

"Aiight, bye," I said and she walked out of the house slamming the door. Marisol looked at me with a grin. "She doesn't like me."

"Oh well. So what's up with Alia? Is she doing all right?"

"Yeah … she still cries about you tho."

"What? For real. Does she talk about me?"

"All the time. She heard about you being accepted at PVA. She was happy for you about that."

"Yeah?"

"Yep. I think you guys will end up back together."

"She doesn't want me back. She probably hates me now."

"Are you and Megan together?"

"Nope, she's just a friend. She wants to be with me but I'm not into nobody right now."

"You still love Alia don't you," she said making me blush.

"I can't lie, I do miss her. But she broke up with me. I dunno if I wanna be with anybody right now. I'm just doing my music and staying focused on that."

"That's good. She's still going through the drama over there at the house with Nicole and her aunt."

"That's too bad. Is Novi still trying to get at her?"

"Of course, he's always trying to flirt with her at school, following her around campus but she doesn't like him."

I was irritated by hearing that, but I kept my cool. "Any other guys trying to talk to her?"

"Of course, but she's still in love with you, Cheetah. She cries all of the time about you."

"Wow, that's hard to believe."

"Believe it," she said when my brother Chepi came from the shower asking how I was doing.

"I'm good, bro, I'm going to go and make some music," I said, leaving them and going to the lab with Cochise. He was in there and I was glad about that. He had mixed down my song "Missing You" and it was dope. I loved it.

The New Dawn of Time

It's August 2001. It's a day after Anthony's birthday and a whole entire year has passed and I must admit that I still miss him tremendously. I finally got accepted at PVA before summer started but I asked Mrs. Cochran not to announce it over the intercom because I wanted to remain invisible since he was attending this school too. He turned 15 and he was scheduled to do a performance at PVA that evening and all of the tickets were sold out. I was lucky enough to buy one right before it happened. Marisol talked me into doing it because I wasn't going to go. He had so many girls on him now that he'd gotten older and his looks had changed. Gosh! Talk about FINE, that dude was the epitome of FINE. He should be arrested for being so handsome. His hair was down to his ass and he had developed a muscular body, not huge but cut up and he was rocking tattoos and he has these full beautiful cherry color lips, a nice neat goatee and peach fuzz around his top lip but more like a shadow to let you know that he wasn't a baby anymore. He was definitely being groomed for stardom because every girl at PVA had a crush on Cheetah. People were lining up just to come to PVA because of him. His name rang bells around the city.

He was like the new Michael Jackson in Maricopa. His Friendster page blew up so big; he had the maximum limit of 150 friends, which was all you could have on the site. I only had fifty friends but he exceeded his friends and people were in line waiting for folks to fall off of his Friendster page. His popularity grew with the guys, too; they liked the fact that he could dance and his fighting skills off campus, gave him a 'hood legend status. He'd been in so many fights on the block, that word got around he wasn't to be messed with because he would kick your ass. He put several dudes in the hospital and his brother Marcus was a known shooter on the block. Novi's brother Mitch got life in prison for robberies and a gun charge, which rumor had it that he got the gun from Cheetah. Novi was the one who started the rumor, so I wasn't sure what to believe because Novi lied so much about stuff.

It was hard for me today because it was summertime and I had a part-time job working at the liquor store. My aunt made me work because that was money that I could use for my uniforms and supplies at PVA. She was still keeping the money that the State was giving her for me. I was getting older and I needed the money but she refused to give me anything. She ended up buying Nicole a car and Nicole spent all of the free time that she had on the reservation with Marcus while Megan was with Cheetah. They had become a couple from what I heard. The bitch got lucky and ended up with the love of my life. I was jealous of Megan because she was one of Cheetah's friends on his Friendster page. He was posting pictures of them together and it hurt so badly, that it made it difficult for me to open his page. I had boring stuff on my page, because I was limited to the things that I could have. They were going places and doing fun things and here I was if I wasn't at work, I was stuck in the house. I hated my life now. I had to be at work at two and I had a feeling that the guys were going to be hanging out on the block. I had to walk to work, because my aunt was gone and so was Nicole. Cheetah has been frequenting the block because the group that he was in was doing more gigs. I heard that they would be practicing and Cheetah was going to be hanging out. I was nervous because the show was that night and if he was going to be on the block, that meant that I would see him on my way to work, that's if they were going to be outside. It was so hot, though, maybe not.

On my way to work, I pulled up my umbrella, had on my hat and shades, hoping that they wouldn't see me. I was moving fast down the block. As I'm walking I hear, "ALIIIIA!" It was Novi, but I pretended not to hear him. I kept walking and I crossed the street after the light changed and then a few moments later, I heard footsteps and turned to see Novi walking behind me grinning. He's cute but not my type. I wasn't into guys with freckles and Novi had a lot of them across his face. "Hey beautiful, you on your way to work?"

"Yes Novi, what's up?"

"Nothing but, I was just walking you to make sure you're okay. Cheetah's across the street. They're rehearsing for the show tonight."

"Good for him. I bet Megan is over there too, huh?"

"You already know she is. She don't let him go anywhere without her."

"Hmm."

"Are you going to the show tonight?"

"Yeah, Marisol talked me into going. I wasn't going to go at first."

"You can always sit with me. I'll keep you company." I looked at him and laughed. He was always trying his hardest to be with me but I didn't like Novi like that. "You know I always loved you, Alia."

"Why? You know where my heart is."

"Yeah but he's with someone else now. He's with the home-girl, Megan."

"Oh well. Once I'm over him then maybe I can move on with my life. Hopefully that will be soon."

"Yeah because you deserve better. Cheetah's a player, he's not even into her like that."

"Yeah right, I saw all of the images on Friendster."

"Alia, Cheetah has a ton of girls after him. He's about to blow up in the industry. He's not thinking about no females right now; he's having fun."

"How do you know all of this?"

"Because he told me."

"Did he now?"

"Yeah. He said he ain't got time for no serious relationship. He's married to his music."

"Well good for him," I said, going into the liquor store where the cool A.C. made me feel better. It relaxed me. "Well, Novi, thank you for walking me. I'll see you at the show tonight."

"Okay, love, have a beautiful day. What time do you get off?"

"Six."

"Okay, I'll see you," he waved and I went behind the counter and clocked in. The guy that owned the store was Asian and he was so cool; he was like a dad to me. He had bought me food.

"Thank you, Roy."

"You're welcome. Was that your boyfriend?"

"No, why do you always ask me that. He's just a friend, I don't like him."

"You still love Cheetah, huh," he smiled making me blush.

"Yes. I can't wait until I don't love him anymore."

Roy made me laugh. He was a funny Asian guy; he always had a lot of business in this store because he was doing so much for black people. He would let them buy gas with food stamps; he gave them cash for food stamps. He's the type of guy that saved a lot of people in this neighborhood and nobody ever thought about robbing him. He was even selling single cigarettes, which was against the law, but we made sure that he stayed under the radar. I was good at spotting undercovers and I saved his ass a few times. He had me cutting open boxes and stocking the shelves and people were coming in and out. I kept myself busy trying not to think about Cheetah. I found myself drifting off to him, wondering if he thought about me like Marisol claimed. Maybe she was just telling me that to make me feel good. I heard about his asking about me when his aunt died last year. Marisol said that he didn't really like Megan but why was he still with her? Why didn't he even try to come after me when I broke up with him. I wanted him to come and beat my door down and beg for me to be with him again and I would've but he didn't. Tears filled my eyes as I stocked the shelves. And the bell went off and I heard guys laughing and it sounded like Sneaky. My heart started racing and then I saw him! Oh my God. He was so handsome. I stood in the aisle looking at him as he was standing at the counter with his boys counting money. I turned my back quickly and then I heard, "Aye, Cheetah, there she go." I bent over and played busy and I felt him looking at me. I started grabbing the empty boxes and moved to the next aisle. My hands started sweating and Roy was making jokes with Sneaky at the front. Roy called me to come to the front. Why did he do this? Oh my God. I went to the front and then he said, “Ring them up.”

He grabbed his cordless phone and started dialing on it heading to the back. Shit! I looked at Cheetah; I was so nervous. Megan wasn't with him. He was alone with the guys. We locked eyes with each other and I broke the stare quickly and rang up the items they wanted. They were buying blunts when they weren't supposed to be because they were underage and that's why Roy wanted me to ring them up. I noticed he had turned the cameras away which was perfect. “Hi you doing, Alia? I didn't know you worked here,” Cal stated with a big grin.

“Yeah, I'm here only part time,” I said and Cheetah was all ears taking it all in.

“Are you coming to the show tonight? You know the homie Flip and them are performing.”

“Yeah, I heard.”

“You coming?”

“I think so.”

Cal looked at Cheetah and smiled. I looked at him again and he was staring me down with a look as if he wanted to say something to me but he didn't.

“You got a boyfriend yet, Alia?” Sneaky asked. I bet he told them to ask me that.

“Nope, no boyfriend too busy with school and work.”

“That's right, that's what's up … aiight, Alia.” he said after I gave him the change. He gave the money to Cheetah and they slowly walked out laughing and talking. Cheetah stopped at the doorway looking in his phone. I was checking him out. Damn he's FINE! Oh my God. He had my heart racing. He smelled good, too. He turned and glanced at me before he left. I turned and sighed when two girls walked in. "Wasn't that Cheetah?"

"Yep!"

"Dayuuuum, he's is CUUUUUTE," one of the Hispanic girls said.

"Yes! I'm going to that show tonight."

"Me too, bitch," they laughed as they walked by the cash register. Roy came back out and I went to the window watching as the guys made it across the street. Cheetah stood out among all of them. Damn, now he knew where I worked. Roy rang up the girls and I was in love again.

Marisol was right on time after I clocked out and Novi was walking across the street. "Girl, I was coming to get you, but you got a ride."

"Yep. I'll see you at the show, Novi, thank you," I said, getting in the car with Marisol. She took me to get food. "Girl, why did Anthony come up to my job today?"

"Really? Did he say anything to you?"

"No, he was just looking at me."

"He still loves you, Alia."

"I dunno, but Megan wasn't with him today. Novi told me that she was with him while they were rehearsing."

"I'm sure she was. She's always at the house when I go over there for Chepi. She stays underneath him and always puts hickeys on his neck."

"Hmm," I grunted feeling irritated by that. "I hate that he's with her. I wish he could find someone else."

"You need to get your man back."

"No, that's okay, I don't want her leftovers. She can have him."

"Uuuh excuse me but he's your leftovers. You broke up with him, remember?"

"Yeah, after she fucked him! I can't believe he slept with her and she gave him an STD."

"Really?" Marisol gasped.

"YES! I didn't tell you that, but she came to the house trying to blame me, saying that I gave her gonorrhea."

"Oh shit! NO way!"

"Girl, it was a nightmare and then when I confronted him he told me that she gave him an STD, so I know that he wasn't lying to me. That's one thing that I have to give him credit for; he didn't lie to me."

"You should've stayed with him."

"If I would've did that, it would've told him that it was okay for him to cheat on me. No, Marisol, I couldn't do it. I do miss him. I still think about him every day and I thought that I could get over him. He's so damn fine! Oh my God, he's looking better and better."

"Cheetah's always been cute."

"I know but, now … oh my God."

"Yeah with those tattoos and him getting older."

"YES … girl … I dunno, I might have to beat Megan's ass and take my man back."

"I would."

"He might not even like me anymore. He was acting all stuck up at the store. I'm sure he's got a lot of girls."

"Yeah …a lot of girls do like him," Marisol admitted.

Roy had given me a fifty-dollar advance on my paycheck and I had Marisol take me to the mall to get something to wear to the show that night. I wanted to look cute, just in case I saw him again. I'm sure Megan was going to be there and I wanted her to see me looking good. When I made it to the mall, I couldn't find anything, but then it dawned on me that I did have something to wear. I had the perfect thing. Marisol and I left the mall.

I felt like a celebrity when I was done getting dressed. My uncle came home and he gave me thirty dollars to have in my pocket and he told me to go and enjoy myself because my aunt was in Las Vegas for the weekend. I was glad to hear that. It was music to my ears. My uncle was always nice to me especially when she was gone. He made me feel normal. Nicole wasn't here so I felt like I had freedom for once in my life.

"How do I look uncle?"

"You look like a movie star. Enjoy yourself."

"Okay, thank you," I hugged him. I grabbed my overnight bags because I was going to spend the night at Marisol's house. I decided on wearing the dress that Anthony had bought me and I was rocking the Tiffany bracelet and the diamond earrings and I felt like I looked good. When Marisol pulled up, I was already on the porch waiting for her. Chepi was with her and he got out of the car and helped me with my bags.

"Hey, Alia, you look nice, girl. My brother is going to be happy to see you," he blushed.

"Yeah, he should. I'm wearing the dress that he bought me for my birthday."

"Oh wow, it looks nice on you."

He opened the back door for me and I climbed in, alone, instead of having Cheetah sitting on the opposite side. It was unbelievable that we weren't together; I always felt like we would be together forever. We talked about Always and Forever. He always said that to me whenever we talked on the phone or right before we hung up on the phone. Chepi interrupted my thoughts telling me that we had front row seats. He made sure that we had some good seats because the theatre at PVA was going to be packed. That was good to know.

The PVA theatre was packed. This school had a reputation for having the best performances. There were so many kids here that I felt like I was at a live concert with a real famous artist about to perform. Chepi led us to our seats. There were so many white people here. We had Grade A seats and I sat. "Do you want something to drink or a snack?" Chepi offered.

"Yes, please, do you need money?"

"NO, you good. Just relax," he said and Marisol went with him and I sat watching all of the students filling the building up. The stage was well lit and it was huge. It looked like a place where top performers did artwork. I spotted Nicole and I wanted to say something to her, just so she could see me there, but I changed my mind. She looked around but failed to see me. She was holding Marcus's arm. She was in love with that dude. I saw Native American people coming in; some had the feathers on their heads. I'm sure they were here for Cheetah.

I saw a woman come up to Marcus with the older people with the feathers on their heads. Marcus had them sitting in the front row, too. I guess this was Cheetah's family. A young girl sat with them; she looked over at me and gave a quick smile and turned her attention back to who I could've sworn was Cheetah's mom. I saw Megan; she went straight over to them and sat next to the woman whispering in her ear. She didn't see me, but she was all in good with them. Wow! That should've been me and I got so jealous of her having that spot. She got up from the chair and went in the same direction that Chepi and Marisol were headed. She disappeared into the crowd. Light skin people always had it better than dark skin people. I felt so out of place and a part of me wanted to leave but then here came Marisol with drinks and snacks. She sat next to me and the girl that was with Cheetah's family waved to Marisol.

"Who is that?"

"That's Cheetah's sister Elina."

"Oh, she's really pretty."

"Yeah, she's a sweetheart too."

"Is that his mom in the red dress?"

"Yeah, that's his mom and his grandparents … his grandfather is on the tribal counsel of the reservation now, since his aunt passed."

"Wow. That's pretty cool."

"Yep. They live in Rowena's house now, too. You should see her house; it's so friggin' nice. I didn't even think they had houses like that on the rez."

"That's cool," I said, watching the family. "Megan is cool with his mom, huh?"

"Oh yeah, she kisses her ass and buys her stuff. She's always over there, so yeah." I noticed Megan coming back with food and drinks for everybody and she finally saw me and her smile faded and she sat down whispering to Anthony's mother again and she looked my way with a serious face. I sat back and looked straight ahead. My feelings were all over the place.

"Maybe I should go."

"No, stay! He wanted you to be here! He knows you're here. Chepi told him backstage."

"Really?"

"Yes! Stay … don't leave."

"Megan is looking at me crazy," I whispered and then Nicole came and sat near us and she had the nerve to speak to Marisol but not me. "Maisol, I didn't know you were here, hey girl," she said but it was fake. She didn't want me to be here; she was putting on a front in front of Marcus to like Marisol.

The light dimmed and the crowd screamed. People were yelling out for Cheetah. I was ready to see why everybody was so crazy about him and why this place was so packed. Music started and screams filled the auditorium. A white woman walked on stage and stood behind the podium. "Good evening, ladies and gentlemen. I'm Mrs. Cochran, the assistant principal here at PVA and tonight we are proud to present a fantastic group of young men who also attend this school—"

The screams filled the auditorium and she had to fall silent until they were finished. "We are so proud to present tonight's end of the school year with a group called "ELEVEN" headed by Anthony Featherstone, aka CHEETAH." The screams went louder once she said his name. I folded my arms as she continued and when she walked off the stage, they were hollering and screaming again like we were in concert. The curtain lifted and I saw the guys in formation. The lights appeared and everybody screamed and went crazy as Flip, Smoke and David did a routine that I thought was dope. It brought a smile to my face. They got down, dressed alike and looking like real stars on stage in Hollywood.

"She's says I'm just a teeeeeease," Cheetah sang, and everybody went crazy as he came out on stage with the mic, hair down and he was without a shirt looking so fine. OH my God!

"Oh my!" I laughed, looking at Marisol. She was clapping and shouting for him. He sang the hell out of that song and I was blown away by how he held the audience with his beautiful sounding voice. That boy can SANG! He knew how to move across the stage and keep everybody's eyes on him. He was the star; the guys in the background were just that, background. Cheetah kept us all in awe with his voice. He went right into the next song and had the girls going crazy; they were trying to run on stage, but security had to stop them and it was just like a real concert, I mean, it was wild and I was very impressed by his performance. He put on a serious show, keeping us entertained throughout the whole time. He looked so professional and just then, I pictured him on a real stage in front of thousands of people. Yes. He's going to be famous…that's a given.

I had a new respect after tonight's show and people were smothering him and he was taking pictures with people, signing autographs like he was famous, and actually this was just the beginning for him. I stood to the side, watching and I felt someone staring at me when I looked over to my right; I saw Megan mean mugging me, she was talking shit but I didn't hear her. She made her way over to Cheetah and when she got near him, she looked at me and stuck her tongue out. I didn't respond, I just stood waiting for my friend. Marisol took a picture with him and he kissed Marisol and whispered something in her ear and then he looked over my way and smiled. My heart was racing and Megan blocked him and threw her arms around his neck, making it hard for him to see me. He saw me and that was all that mattered.

Marisol came to me. "He asked me where you were."

"I know I saw him whisper to you … he saw me. Did you see Megan acting jealous?"

"Yes, of course."

We were on our way out of the auditorium when Chepi called Marisol. He was standing by Cheetah and he looked at me. People were coming to him and he was busy staring me down. It made me feel good that he noticed me. He whispered something to Chepi and Chepi told Marisol to wait. "I'm going to be at the car," Marisol told him. We headed out of the building and Nicole was outside talking to Marcus and Cheetah's family. Marisol introduced me to Elina.

"Hi, nice to meet you."

"You too, you're so pretty," she said, making me feel good.

"Thank you, so are you."

"Thank you, did you enjoy the show?"

"YES! It was fantastic. Your brother is awesome."

"Yeah he is, I loved it!"

I heard white people talking about how awesome Cheetah was on stage tonight. A white man said, "He's going to be a star!" That stuck in my head when he said that. It stuck in my head right along with the song he sang, "*She says I'm just a tease and that I'll break her heart … but little does she knoooooow, she's the girl that stole my heart*." I never heard this song by him but it was my favorite after tonight's show. I loved it and so did the other girls that were there trying to run on stage and get him. I'm sure there were talent scouts at the show and A&R people from record labels looking at him. It took them a while to come to the car and people were leaving. There were only like ten cars left in the parking area. Finally Chepi was coming, but he was with Cheetah and six other guys. "Uh oh, there's Cheetah. Are you going to say something to him?"

"No. I'm shy," I said. "I'm going to stay in the car."

Chepi came to the car and Cheetah bent down looking at me. "Wassup Alia?" He spoke to me. "You look beautiful."

"Thank you," I said.

"Get out of the car," he told me. I was nervous but I got out and headed around the car to meet him. He looked so damn fine. "How have you been?"

"I'm good. You did a great show tonight; that was amazing. I didn't know you could perform like that. You're going to be big one day."

"You think so? That's what I'm aiming for."

"Oh yeah, you will be," I said and we laughed.

"I'm glad you liked the show … thank you for coming."

"You're welcome," I said when a white Mercedes pulled up fast and out jumped Megan running towards me to fight, but Cheetah blocked her.

"BITCH STAY AWAY FROM HIM!"

"GO TO HELL!" I yelled at her. "NOBODY'S SCARED OF YOU!"

"LET ME GO, CHEETAH!"

"NO get yo ass back in the car! Ain't nobody got time for this bullshit! Get in the car."

"STAY AWAY FROM MY MAN, BITCH, IF YOU KNOW WHAT'S GOOD FOR YOU!"

"NEWSFLASH, BITCH, HE WAS MINE FIRST," I yelled and she broke away from him and attacked me. Something told me not to fight her back because we were on campus and security drove up so fast and Anthony was trying to get her off of me, she had my hair. "LET HER GO, MEGAN! FUCK'S WRONG WITH YOU? LET HER HAIR GO!"

"NO! I'll KILL THIS BITCH!" She was trying to punch me but the cops grabbed her and shoved her away from me. Mrs. Cochran helped me up.

"Sorry about that, Alia, I'm sorry," Cheetah said.

"Cheetah, get her off of this campus before she's arrested," Mrs. Cochran said. I was glad that I didn't fight her. I made myself look like the victim. "Alia, are you okay? I'm so so sorry, are you okay honey?"

"Yeah, I'm okay," I said and I saw Cheetah looking my way like he was embarrassed. I was so hurt that I just cried and Mrs. Cochran asked if I wanted to see a doctor.

"No, I just wanna go home."

I cried on the way home and Chepi was mad. He called Cheetah and went off on him. I heard Cheetah yelling. "I didn't know she was going to pull that stunt bro, what the fuck you yelling at me for?"

"Bro, put your bitch on a leash!" Chepi hung up on him. He turned and looked at me.

"You okay, Alia?"

"No, I'm miserable. I just wanna get out of this town, everybody hates me." I cried. I was crying more about Cheetah being with her than the fight. I was crying because I couldn't fight her back like I wanted to. I was so hurt because he chose her over me. He was supposed to push her away and tell her that he wanted to be with me, but he went to her aid again and only served me with a stupid apology. Fuck him!

"Never again," I said. Chepi looked back at me. "Your brother is going to regret ever hurting me."

"He does now."

"No, but he will."

"Alia, trust me, he's not going to stay with Megan."

"He should've left with me tonight!" I cried. "He went with her instead of me. He should've left with me. I should've never come to that fucking concert," I sobbed.

Chepi sighed and turned back around in his seat looking at Marisol. "Fix this babe."

"What do you mean, how am I supposed to fix it? Cheetah should've come with us."

"I'll talk to him when I get home. I'm sorry, Alia."

I couldn't stop crying. I heard Chepi arguing with Cheetah on the phone in the backyard of Marisol's house. I couldn't stop crying. "I don't wanna live anymore."

"Don't say that. Don't say that, Alia, you're my best friend," she said and she started crying. "I love you. Don't ever let a guy take you to that level. Fuck him! Let him be with her. She's having sex with him, that's the only reason why he's probably with her anyway." It hurt when she told me that. "That's how guys are. She's probably sucking his dick. She's a slut."

"He wants a slut over me? He picked her over me? I can't believe he did that and he told me that I looked beautiful. I wore this fucking dress hoping that he would see that I still love him! I'm never giving my heart to nobody! I swear, Marisol, never again man, I swear," I cried.

"I don't know what it is, but it's so hard for me to stop loving him." I told Marisol. "I'm always thinking about him, I always do, every day. Since we broke up, I can't stop thinking about him. I need to die!" I sobbed.

"Nooo." Marisol hugged me and Chepi came upstairs. I turned to see what he had to say.

"What did he say?" Marisol asked.

"I dunno what's wrong with my brother, man. He's acting weird."

"He's not going to leave her," I told Marisol.

"He doesn't wanna be with her either. I think he's feeling himself now that the music stuff is getting big. He's got a record deal on the table now."

"Really?" Marisol whispered. "When did that happen?"

“I think yesterday. A label wants to sign him as a solo artist and they’re offering him a lot of money and now he’s got a big head.”

I sat on the bed and cried. “He doesn’t love me anymore Mari.” I wailed.

“Awww. Chepi you need to talk to him, look how hurt she is.”

“I know, I will. I’ll get through to him.”

Decisions

I have three record labels that want to sign me. My brother Steven and G.B. made it happen for me. I had a decision to make by Friday or else I was going to end up being independent. Steven though that me being independent would be better because I could do what I wanted, but we just needed the money to make it happen. You can't be an independent artist and not have money invested. I needed money for tours, promotions, videos. I was down to like fifty thousand from the shows that I was doing with the fellas. They all wanted me to be solo, too; they just wanted to be my backup dancers and after the show at PVA, it was meant for me to be a solo artist. I had a lot on my plate and I was in my bedroom with my head in the clouds. I broke up with Megan. I kicked that bitch to the curb. She jumped on Alia and that broke my heart, but at the same time, I was happy to see it because Alia hurt me. I still hadn't gotten over her; she still haunted my thoughts and my everyday way of life. I loved her, but I wasn't going to make it easy for her. I needed to keep my head in the music like Steven told me. If it was meant for us to be together, it was going to happen and nobody could stop it. Right then my dream was important.

Steven came in the room; he had his laptop with him. "I want you to see this shit," he said making me sit up. He sat beside me and showed me the plays that I had on my music. "You see that? Look at all these plays on Napster Bro, you're about to be a major deal in this business … you got almost a million fucking plays on this song right here."

"Yeah, everybody likes my ballads," I admitted. I looked at it again in disbelief. "Wow, almost a million."

"Yep and you see these plays …eight hundred thousand, bro, that's money."

"So are they going to send us a check?"

"Yeah, that's all I'm waiting for. I think you should really consider the record deal bro because you can move a lot of units, it will take longer if you go independent. That's money."

"So what do I need to do because I do need to be with a major label to get my name out there around the world at least."

"You can still get your name around the world; all you need to do is link up with a major artist and tour and you're going to make that happen. I mean I was looking at a P&D deal, which means that all the major label would have to do is publish and distribute your music. We can pay for all of the promotions on our own. That's if you decide to go independent. You won't be locked into a deal. I talked to an attorney who's schooled on what to do and my friend Ryan said that it's best to go that route, Cheetah. You're still underage so Mom and Dad will have to sign and Dad wants you to be independent, too."

"When did you talk to Dad?"

"Last night. He's going to be getting out of the military September 1."

"No shit? For good?"

"For good, bro; he's about to retire."

"Oooh yes! YES!" I laughed. "I need Dad, bro, I really need him," I said, covering my eyes with my arm because I was about to get emotional. I had so much on my plate that I wasn't sure which way to turn.

"I'mma let you sit in here and marinate on this a little more; your life is about to change, Cheetah."

"I know."

I sat in the room and thought about everybody and everything that had transpired in the last several months. I was doing well at PVA; the staff loved me and they all believed that I would make it big. I had that feeling, too, but at the same time, I was still caught up over a girl who made my heart heavy. She looked so beautiful that night. I hated that Megan destroyed my chance to be with her again. Chepi was mad at me and he was my favorite brother. Tears ran down my face and I should've just pushed Megan to the side and left with them. I would've been with her right now, talking and laughing and thinking about my future with her. Instead I was in my room thinking about signing over my soul to the devil. So many people talked about illuminati in the music industry and even Tupac talked about killing it, but in the back of my mind, I was wondering if it was real. All I ever wanted was to be famous and be loved for my music and now the opportunity was knocking. The universe removed everything out of my way to distract me so that I could move forward. What other choice did I have? I got up and turned on the light. The house was quiet because my mom took everybody out to eat after the show. I was supposed to be there but I came home with Steven. Megan was with them, but I didn't care; I wasn't trying to be with her. I made my way down the hall and I opened the door to Steven's room and got my wig blew back. What the fuck? I slammed the door quickly and went to the bathroom. I couldn't believe what the fuck I just saw! Damn! I turned on the faucet over the sink and splashed my face with cold water. I wasn't dreaming, I didn't even go to sleep but I wished that I had. My brother Steven had a white boy giving him head while he was lying on the bed. The white boy was naked; all I seen was his naked pale ass glowing in the darkness, not to mention his head bobbing up and down on my brother. Uggh! Oh my God! I couldn't even laugh. Why wasn't it a girl? Is my brother gay?

I heard a knock at the bathroom door. "Just a second!" I said.

"When you come out, I need to talk to you," Steven said.

"Sure, okay," I agreed. Of course, he wanted to talk to me. I walked in and saw him getting his dick sucked by another man. What the fuck was going on in the world? In my family especially. I get molested by my aunt and then I caught my brother getting sexually aroused by a man. A damn man! I took my time in the bathroom, I didn't even know how to face him after that. He didn't even give me a sign of him being gay. Damn. When I left the bathroom, Steven was standing in the hallway, dressed in a T-shirt and some basketball shorts and Nike slides with his arms folded. His facial expression told me that he was embarrassed that I caught him.

"We're going to my room, right?"

"Of course, yeah." he said, following me to my room. He closed the door and I sat on my bed and he stood. "I'm sorry I didn't lock the door, but you didn't even bother to knock."

"Yeah, that's my bad. Sorry about that," I said, with a slight grin.

"It's not funny, Anthony," he said, calling me by my real name. He was serious. Tears filled his eyes. "I didn't want you to find out about me like that, but I'm not ashamed of being who I am. I'm in love with him."

"Who is he?"

"Ryan."

"Ryan is your boyfriend?"

"YES! He's my boyfriend and I love him Cheetah. I'm not ready for the family to know about me just yet. I will tell them but when I'm ready. So please don't tell them what you saw tonight, okay?"

"I'm not going to do you like that Steven. You've been here for me and you're my brother and I love you. I don't care if you're gay, as long as he makes you happy. If he hurts you I'mma fuck him up!" Steven finally laughed. He wiped his eyes.

"I don't care about your sexual preference, bro, I fucking love you regardless and I will fuck anybody up that brings harm to you."

"I feel the same way about your crazy li'l ass with these damn girls. Thank you, Cheetah, for understanding. And next time nigga you better knock on my damn door. Oh and I don't take it up the ass if that's what you're wondering. But next time knock, okay?"

I laughed. "I will. My bad."

He left me and it wasn't as bad as I thought. Now I understood why he didn't have a girl in his life. He's gay and I'm okay with that, as long as my brother doesn't get HIV or AIDS, I'm good. He's still Steven and I still respect him as my big brother.

He came back to the room, "Oh I wanted to let you know that tomorrow you have a photoshoot and Paco Baca from Live 105 wants to interview you on the radio."

"WHUUT! When did you find this out?"

"Right before you came in the room and fucked up my nutt," he said making me laugh. He closed the door leaving me in giggles. After I got a good laugh off of my brother, I sent the homies a text message letting them all know that I'm going to be on LIVE 105 tomorrow.

"YES!"

I slept good until my sister came in the room with her big ass mouth waking me up asking about me being on the radio at six thirty in the fucking morning. "Yes Elina dayyyum, did you have to wake me up?"

"Sorry … ooops," she snickered and left the room. I lay there checking my phone. Everybody replied to the text asking what time I was going to be on the air. I didn't even ask Steven but I heard him in the room laughing with Cochise and Michael. They were up already. Marcus and Chepi were still asleep. I sat up in the bed and stretched, and Alia flashed through my mind. "Chepi? Chepi!" I called him. He was probably still mad at me. He turned over and looked down at me from his bunk. "You're still mad at me, bro?"

"No, nigga, but I should be, what you want?"

"I'mma be on the radio you wanna go with me?"

"Yeah, I'll go with you," he agreed and I was happy about that. "What time are we leaving?"

"I dunno, but I'm about to hit the shower just in case so I won't have to wait."

"Aiight," he said up grabbing his cell phone and checking his messages. I went to the closet and pulled out my gear that Megan bought me. I was going to wear all white today. I left the room with my white Levis and white polo shirt to match. "Elina, can you braid my hair for me when I get out the shower, just two braids?"

"Yes, brother, I will hook you up."

"Cool, thanks." I was getting ready to close the door when Steven called out to me tell me that we were going to be leaving in an hour.

"Okay."

Marcus, Chepi, Steven, Cochise and Mike decided to go with me to the radio interview. I was nervous as we rode on the freeway. I was going to be on the eight o'clock morning show and I hit Flip and told him to tell everybody that I was going to be on the morning wake up show. I always listened to this station and I loved Paco, finally I would get to meet him and D.J. Flame, who was always talking shit to people. He was hilarious and reminded me of Charlamane from the Breakfast Club. He was a trip; he was a hood and a character, I couldn't wait to meet him. They got the opportunity to meet a lot of celebrities in the industry and for them to finally get me on the show was an honor, which meant that they were going to play my music. "Which song did you give them, Steven?"

"'Missing you'. They like that one."

"I knew it, how come I knew that?" I laughed. "Aiight, that's what's up."

I let everybody know through a text message that "Missing You" was going to be on the radio. I was happy and Mike's phone went off; it was from his friend Wolf calling him from on the rez. Mike put him on speaker. "Aye, Cheetah, I'm proud of you, brother; you make me very proud, stay humble no matter what, okay?"

"I will, thanks Wolf. Let everybody know that I'm going to be on the radio and to tune in," I told him.

"No doubt I will. Love you, brother."

"Love you, too." I was glad that Wolf was going to let people on the rez know that I was going to be on the radio. It was a dream come true, finally, at fifteen. For most people it takes more than two years to make it. Like Wolf said, stay humble.

We arrived at the radio station and I was thinking it was going to be this dynamic building, but it was a normal size building that looked like an ordinary business; the only thing that stood out were the satellite dishes in the back that were surrounded by barbed wire fences and television towers. It was cool because the logo of the radio station was on the window and it was tinted. I was sure people walked by this place every day and didn't think nothing of it. We walked in and I was nervous as Steven greeted the white girl in the front.

"Oh yeah, perfect, Cheetah, where is he?" she looked at us and zoomed in on me. She smiled big, sticking her hand out.

"Nice to meet you Cheetah, I'm Amy. Come on guys, follow me."

The inside of the building was getting renovated. Amy had black lipstick on, black hair and black fingernails with piercing on her lip. She was cool looking and she was tatted up, dressed normal. She took us down a long hallway and was telling Steven that people were talking about me all through town so the D.J.'s were interested in the music that I had to offer.

“They love ‘Missing You’; I like that song and I’m not into R&B music but I love that song, it’s so relatable,” she said. “Did you write it, Cheetah?”

“I did.”

“Wow, that’s amazing talent you have.”

“Thank you,” I said and she opened the door to a room that was large enough to be like an apartment. There was a giant white table sitting in the center with microphone arm mounts sitting in sections of the table and headphones were hanging over the arms. Amy introduced us to Paco, who was actually Native American to my surprise. He was brown skinned like my brother Steven; he had a strong Native look to him and he was rocking a beaded headband and had on turquoise and silver jewelry.

“This is Cheetah, Paco.”

“Cheetah, finally get to put a face behind the name. Nice to meet you.”

“You too, I didn’t know you were Native.”

“Well now you do,” we laughed. He hugged me. “What tribe are you from?”

“Navajo and Apache,” I told him.

“I’m Blackfoot, from Canada.”

“Oh wow, okay, these are my brothers, Steven, Mike, Marcus, Chepi and Cochise.” I introduced and they all shook hands.

“Wow, I’m excited, I have a spiritual connection in here,” he said with a big bright smile. He’s a handsome dude and older. I thought he was young and a white boy but he wasn’t nothing of the sort. He had us all fooled on the radio.

"This is D.J. Flame," he said and D.J. Flame was a high yellow chunky baldhead dude who had light freckles on his face like Novi. He reached over the table shaking my hand and he greeted my brothers, too. "Are you nervous, Cheetah?"

"Man, yes, you can tell?"

He laughed, "I can tell, but don't be nervous, this is your special day today, just act like the mics and camera are not here. We're going to chop it up like regular folks, just feel comfortable."

"No cussing, tho," D.J. Flame said making us all laugh.

"At least not on this show. We do live steaming and you can curse as much as you want. Cheetah, I have a feeling that you will be here more than just today."

"Awww wow, it's an honor to be here that's for sure."

"It's an honor to have you finally. We're going to be going live shortly. You guys want water? Amy bring bottled water for these guys please."

"Sure," she said, disappearing out of the room. He told me that we would be going live in ten minutes.

Steven leaned over in my ear, "Don't be nervous, just relax and be yourself."

"Okay," I sighed and after Amy came back with the water, my phone started blowing up with the fellas on the block letting me know that they were tuning in.

"Okay, Cheetah, you guys put your headphones on, those that are going to speak, speak in the mic; if you don't want to talk, just relax and enjoy the show," Paco told us as they counted down from five to one.

"This is D.J. Flame with Paco Baca and we're back with the morning wake up show. Today we have a special guest live in the building this morning, a brand-new artist who's ringing bells all over the city and he's young gifted and talented and he goes by the name of Cheetah."

"What's good," I smiled as I greeted the outside world.

"Cheetah, man, we've been hearing your name every day for the past few months and last night you did a show at Paradise Valley Performing Arts Academy and got positive results. The girls are going crazy and you also have a favored song by fans called 'Missing You.' We've been dying to get our hands on a copy of that single and we will be playing it on the radio today for all of our thousands of listeners. How are you, Cheetah?"

"I'm good, I'm good, blessed to be here this morning, I appreciate the love and I'm just honored, what can I say."

"Well, Cheetah, you certainly are talented. I was at the show last night and I watched you guys perform. Now, how did you get started in music?"

"Oh well I've been a lover a music all of my life. I started singing when I was three years old. I would perform for my family and whenever I heard music I would stop what I was doing and go and run and stand right next to the speakers or wherever the music was coming from and I would sing."

"Yeah, he knew all of the songs that came on the radio. There was not one song that my brother didn't know," Steven added and we all laughed.

"Music is like fresh air to me and I wrote my first song when I turned 12 and I formed a group two years ago called Eleven and we

were doing gigs all around the city trying to make a name for ourselves and it was working out good but then people wanted to hear just me. Everybody that heard us would always say, you guys are good, but ... you are GREAT and we want to hear you solo but I didn't want to leave my boys. I guess it was because of me being so shy on stage, I didn't want to perform alone, but then they thought it was a great idea for me to be solo, so here I am, working on my first album actually and I'm calling it Eleven Eleven."

"Wow, Cheetah, and from what I was told earlier is that you have three record deals on the table, one from Prestige, one from Unicorn Records and another one from All Nations. Have you decided yet?"

"Uuuh, actually that's in the air and I have until Friday to decide, so I'm really not sure because I was thinking about staying independent."

"That's smart, very smart," D.J. Flame said. "I know a lot of cats that got these record deals and later on ended up broke with nothing."

"Exactly and I have a great team behind me, my brother Steven whose been my mentor and my advocate since I started doing music publicly."

"Wow, so you're from the Native American Indian reservation out here, Salt River, right, Cheetah?" Paco asked.

"That's right, I was born and raised and I wanna give a shout out to the tribe, send 'em my love, they're all listening and they're waiting to hear my music which I'm honored to have played today."

"And Cheetah we're honored to play it. So what have you been doing outside of the local gigs? Are you going to be doing any tours soon?"

"Actually, I can answer that," Steven cut in. "He's going to be opening up for Razzamatazz next month. He didn't know that as yawl can see the look on his face right now."

We all laughed.

"I am? Damn, I didn't know."

"Wow, Cheetah, that was a big surprise, huh?"

"Yeah, I'm happy to do that, tho," I laughed.

"But yes, he's going to be opening up for him and um, I'm working on getting more promotions for his new album and of course the single 'Missing You,'" Steven said.

"Are you guys all related? I see the resemblance. It's, what, five of yawl in here today?"

"Yes, we're all brothers," Steven said. "We're all standing behind Cheetah because he's destined for greatness. He always said he was going to be a star one day and here he is."

"I would say so, too. Cheetah, what was life like for you on the reservation? From my understanding you're mixed right?"

"Yes, I'm half black and half Native American and it was tough for me because I wasn't fully accepted being half black but most of my problems came from on and off the rez. On the rez, there were some issues but of course that's normal and everyday life but off the rez, I had more issues with blacks not really accepting me being biracial. And then there were some saying, 'Oh he's not Indian he's claiming to be something that he's not and he needs to just be black.'

"Wow," they all laughed.

"Yeah I mean it's tough and of course I have a tribal card that I have to carry around and racism does exist on the rez too, but not from the Native people, from law enforcement."

"What … really?"

"Yes! The cops kill more Native Americans than they kill blacks."

"Man, that's a new one on me, I know we have issues with the law but I didn't know it was going down like that on the rez."

"On and off the rez, not just the rez," Chepi added. "It's gang violence, drug issues and suicides on the rez as well."

"Exactly and I'm an avid reader and I want to also give a shout out to Elouise Cobell because she's been fighting for Native American people to get trust money that's been mismanaged for over a hundred years," my brother Mike added.

"Wow."

"Yeah I heard about that," Paco stated. "The Blackfeet tribe has oil on their land that our government has been using and mismanaging for over a hundred years."

"Yeah, I mean it's a lot to go through with racism issues and being biracial and then try to make it in this business has been pretty challenging," I added.

"So, Cheetah, tell us what you want to do and where you see yourself in the next few years?"

"I would like to be able to move my family into nice houses and um be successful with my music. I see myself being a worldwide name in the next few years; I'm working hard on that."

"I can see that for you, Cheetah; you got the look and I'm sure the girls are going crazy. Now we're going to drop your single, 'Missing You.'" What inspired you to write that song?"

"A girl that I have deep feelings for, let's just say that. If she's listening to this show right now, she knows that it's about her."

"Whoa! Okay ... you guys, we're going to take a break and listen to Cheetah's new single, 'Missing You' and then we'll be back. Stay tuned and callers if you're listening, get those fingers ready to start dialing."

My phone was blowing up. Flip was proud of me, he said that he was crying and he doesn't usually get emotional but he was crying. I wrote him back and told him that I wanted to keep them on my team forever and always. I told him that we were going to all grow big and for him to get ready because we were going to open up for Razz next month so we needed to come up with some fresh routines for the stage. Megan sent me a text message saying thank you. I wrote her back. "For what?"

"The song, it's for me, that's so sweet. You make feel special, boo."

It wasn't even about her but I didn't tell that it wasn't; I let her think what she wanted to think. Alia knew that I was talking about her and I prayed that she was listening.

Aye Cheetah, Marisol just sent a text, she and Alia are listening to the radio show bro, Chepi smiled.

"That's what's up ... aye, tell her to tell Alia that this song is about her."

He started typing in his phone. That's my baby, I can't lie about that. I got deep feelings for Alia Duarte and it wasn't going to change. I still couldn't believe that I was actually here on LIVE 105, one of the biggest radio stations in Arizona. Damn! Steven and Paco were talking heavy and Steven really impressed me with his business skills. He was on it, talking the language that the D.J.'s were listening to. They said that my song "Missing You" was going to be a hit and that it was timeless and very valuable to the music industry. I was honored to hear that and all I needed to do was keep my head from swelling up big. It was hard not to be feeling myself right now, but I didn't think this would happen so suddenly. Steven said that things were going to be changing for me and they were.

My dad called once we left the station. He called Steven's phone and wanted to talk to me. "Hey, Dad?"

"Hey, Son, I'm so proud of you. I heard you on the radio."

"How?"

"Your mom called me and put the phone to the radio and I heard you. I'm so proud of you, Son. How do you feel now? It's getting real, ain't it?"

"Yeah, it feels good, Dad. I can't wait until you come home."

"Yep, two more weeks, Son, and they're working the shit out of me right now. Just stay humble and don't let those girls get to you son, stay focused on the music, you hear me?"

"Yes sir. I hear you, Dad."

"Okay, I love you. Let me talk to your brother."

I gave the phone back to Steven and my phone was going off with text messages. Flip, Cal and Sneaky hit me up telling me that they were proud and they wanted me to come on the block, but I couldn't, I had to go straight to the studio and work on my album with Cochise. I didn't have time to be hanging out anymore, not like

I was before. Now I had something to prove and fans were calling in; these were people that were online that had heard my music on napster. They called in to give me props on the music and they wanted to see me in concert, so I had to smash and get on my grind. I couldn't do what I was doing before; it was all about working. Now that I was on summer break, I was going to have to spend most of my time in the studio working. We went straight to the photoshoot that Steven had set up. I needed layout cards and Steven paid for these out of his pocket. My phone went off ringing. It was Megan. I had a feeling she was going to call. I broke up with her, but she couldn't accept that and continued to call me. "Hello?"

"Hey, Cheetah. Where you guys at now?"

"On the way to a photoshoot. Why, wassup?"

"Novi's over here hating on you big time. He's telling people that he was supposed to be in the group but you didn't want him to."

"Oh well, let him lie if it makes him feel good."

"He's claiming that him and Alia are good friends now."

"Is that what you called to tell me? I don't feel like hearing that shit."

"I was just telling you and I wanna get back together, we need to talk."

"Well right now I'm busy. I'll call you later." I told her.

September 11, 2001

Everybody was elated and happy for Cheetah but then we got hit by two planes in New York City and that put everything to a screeching halt. It was crazy. Roy was watching the coverage on television in the store and it was unreal to see those people running for their lives away from the buildings as they collapsed. People were covered in a white powdery substance and blood. It was so damn scary and all we saw on television was desperate people crying and looking for lost family members in all of the rubble; it was crazy. I was at work early helping Roy clean out the freezer when it came over the airwaves about us being attacked by terrorists!

"Oh my God, now they got a plane going to the Pentagon!" Roy said, turning up the volume. He jumped on the phone and called someone in his family. He was talking in his language. Nobody came in the store that morning; there were usually people there early but nobody came in the store. This situation had me scared. I hoped that Cheetah was okay. I still thought about him every day despite the lies and bullshit that Novi was always trying to feed me about him and Megan being back together and into each other and all this blah,

blah, blah. Cheetah was still trying to communicate to me through his music and I was flattered the day that I heard him on the radio and he said that the song "Missing You," which is my jam, was written for a girl that he has deep feelings for. I knew that he was talking about me, and Marisol confirmed it when he told his brother Chepi to pass that message on to me. I wanted to call him but I was afraid that it would cause more problems so I left it alone. The song "Missing You" is beautiful and it has a nice melody and the music is beautiful, too. His brother Cochise was the bomb and they talked about him on the radio, too. He finally spoke about how he's always been into making beats and he never thought he would end up being a producer for his brother's first album. It all worked out the way that it was supposed to. A lot of people liked that song and Cheetah's voice made it even more powerful. Everybody loved his vocals and when I heard him sing live on the air doing a sample for Paco Baca and his fans to make his debut, I got chills all over my body. I knew after the interview on LIVE 105 that Cheetah was going to be a major star, despite what just happened in New York. It was crazy because all of a sudden, there were a lot of billboards with his picture up and his new album about to drop at the end of this month. His whole look changed; he had more tattoos on his arms and he just sprouted from a boy to a man in two years. I don't think I will ever stop loving him. I prayed about him every night before I shut my eyes for sleep. I asked God to bring him back to me. I wasn't going to talk to no other guy. I was going to save myself for him. If it's meant, only time will tell.

People finally came in the store and I helped them. They were all talking about the shit that happened in New York. People were scared to fly on airplanes and to be honest it put everybody on hush mode. I knew after seeing those planes run into those giant buildings like that, hell I was scared to fly too after that. They said that it was four planes that left different States and it was scary to even imagine myself being on one of those flights. I worked my little four hours and then I clocked out and said goodbye to Roy before I walked outside, watching my surroundings, when I saw Novi's crazy self-walking across the street. I have to admit, he was not giving up on trying to be with me and I appreciated the fact that a guy was coming to walk with me so that I wouldn't be alone. It was an angel on my side with this protection.

"How was your day?"

"It was good until the Trade Center attack."

"I know, huh, that shit was crazy! They're saying that people from the Middle East did that shit. Terrorists, but I'm just trying to figure out, how come they didn't shoot those fucking planes down? That don't make no damn sense."

"I know, that's true, I didn't think about that. Have you heard from your boy?"

He looked at me with jealous eyes. He hated when I brought up Anthony. "Who, Cheetah?"

"Yes, dummy, who else am I talking about?"

"Oh nah … that nigga's busy now. He's getting ready to go on tour next month I heard."

"Really?"

"Yep. They said that he's been opening up for that nigga Razz and turning shit up! They said the concert was lit. I heard Cheetah had Razz a little jealous about that shit. I think Cheetah was trying to steal Razz's shine."

I wanted to laugh because I know who Razz is and I've heard his music but Cheetah is far better looking and better performing, no doubt.

"Yeah, Flip, Black and the homie David they all dance with him. I ain't seen none of them fools since Cheetah blew up."

"Really?"

"Nope. The block's been quiet, even Sneaky's been hanging out with them now … I bet any kind of money Cheetah's going to change. He's not going to be the same."

"Why do you say that, Novi? I don't believe that."

"Because, money changes people. People think they're better when they have money and you know that nigga always been kind of stuck up anyway."

"Nooo, that's not true."

"Yeah he was. You know that nigga was stuck up Alia come on now, that was your boyfriend and all but, I heard he's even more stuck up and cocky now."

"I don't believe that. I think you're looking too much into it, Novi, that's not Cheetah at all."

"Well I do rap and he knows that I rap. Why hasn't he even thought about putting me on? My brother Mitch had that nigga'z back and always put him up on money whenever he was broke. Why wouldn't he put me on one of his tracks? He had Flip and them fools on and didn't even bother to add me to his team, but that's okay. I'mma come up on my own watch because I'm working on something right now underground and I'mma come out hard watch and see."

Novi could rap, I'd heard his freestyles and he is dope, but I don't think Cheetah wanted to add him on the squad.

"Just do your own thing."

"I am. You gone be my girl too."

I laughed. "Don't flatter yourself, Novi."

"You are; watch," he said trying to hug me until I shoved him back. He laughed.

We made it to my block and I told him that I couldn't be seen walking with him because my aunt would flip out.

"I know … I'll watch until you get inside."

"Thank you," I said, hurrying and going in the house. Nobody was home but I didn't want him to know that. I didn't trust Novi. He had a bad reputation for breaking in people's houses and robbing folks with his brother; his rep wasn't good at all. My biggest fear was to be at home alone and him breaking in and trying to rape me. That was my biggest fear of Novi. I picked up the phone and called Marisol.

"Hey, girl. You're home already?"

"Yeah, can you come over? Nobody is here."

"Okay, I have Chepi with me. Is that cool?"

"That's fine."

I fixed some lemonade because it was hot outside and I was sure they were going to be thirsty. I set up the den for company because I knew that my aunt wouldn't be back until Sunday. She had gone to Las Vegas again; she had been going out there a lot. I think she had a gambling problem. My uncle didn't care and Nicole wasn't here either; they left me alone and I didn't mind because I had this peace of mind.

I wanted to find out about Cheetah anyway and the only access that I had to him now was through my best friend's boyfriend. I really missed him so much and my heart ached for him. I felt like a part of me was missing, but yet I didn't have enough courage to call him and let him know that I was missing him so much. I wasn't sure how he felt about me but I still cried about him and Marisol knew this. She felt bad because she was in the middle and yet couldn't take sides. I didn't expect her to. All I needed was for her to understand.

They arrived and Chepi reminded me of Cheetah when they stepped inside. "Damn, it's hot out there," he complained and it was funny seeing the frown on his face. "It feels so good in here."

"You guys thirsty? I made lemonade."

"Hell yeah, let me get some of that," Chepi said and I brought the jug out and set it on the table before I got their glasses.

"How you been, girl?" Marisol asked, coming in the kitchen. I gave her that look like always. "I know, I know you miss him. You guys need to talk."

"I'm scared," I told her following her back to the den.

"She misses your brother, Chepi."

"I know she does. He misses her, too. He's just being stubborn right now but I know for sure that my brother still loves you, Alia."

"How is he?"

"He's been working his ass off on his album. He's almost finish with it."

"How is the album?"

"DOPE! It's a headbanger for sure. I gotta give my brother his props. He's got talent when it comes to his music. Cochise put some boss beats behind his vocals so yeah, I think this album will go platinum in no time."

"So did he sign?"

"Yeah he got signed with Prestige but they did a P&D deal, which doesn't tie him to the label, so he's still independent. He's hoping that this album goes platinum and if it does, he's going to launch his own record label."

"Wow. That's good. Tell him I said congratulations."

"Why don't you call him and tell him?"

"I dunno. I don't wanna deal with Megan and bullshit."

"Yeah, I feel you on that. He ain't into her like that."

"No?"

"Nah, hell nah. It's just one thing and my brother got music on his mind, he ain't trying to be serious with that girl. She's always on him."

"So is he going on tour?"

"After the album drops at the end of this month, yeah. He's been putting in like twelve- and thirteen-hour days in the studio."

"Wow, that's a lot of time."

"Yeah that's all they do now. He's been working at the label studio in Phoenix a lot but a majority of the album was done on the rez."

"Yeah, Novi's so jealous of him. He said that your brother knew that he could rap but he didn't want to put him on, so Novi's planning on doing his own underground stuff to make his own music."

"Fuck Novi. That nigga told on his own brother and got him that life sentence in jail."

"Really? He told on Mitch?"

“Yep. He ratted his own brother out. They both got caught by the cops and the gun was in the car under the seat and they asked whose gun it was and Novi was like, ‘That’s not my gun, officer.’”

“Ooooh, oh my God, he did that to his own brother and he was going around telling people that Cheetah gave him the gun.”

“Yeah but the police found Mitch’s fingerprints on the gun so he had to take the charges.”

“Awww wow.”

“Not to mention that they tied the gun to other robberies and murder cases. Those niggaz were wild and Novi is known to jack people so be careful around that nigga. Don’t let him in this house at all.”

“Oh I won’t. Trust me, I won’t. I know his reputation.”

“Yeah and he’s a hater. Don’t let him tell you nothing crazy about my brother because Cheetah will beat his ass and he knows it.”

“Damn, I can’t believe he snitched on Mitch like that, that’s crazy. How did you find out?”

“Mitch called Cheetah and told him what happened and my brother’s been looking out for Mitch. He sent him a care package and some money.”

“So is he rich now or what?”

“He’s doing good; I’m proud of my brother. He’s not hurting for money that’s for sure.”

I nodded, grinning and Marisol and I looked at each other. I was happy for him, I just hope he doesn’t stay with Megan. “I bet Megan will try to get pregnant.”

"Oh hell nah. He ain't having that. He's about to go on tour and he won't have her with him, I know that."

"Are you going with him?"

"Hell yeah. All of the bros are going; my dad is even going. Flip, Smoke, David, Sneaky and G.B. are going, too."

"Oh wow, that's pretty cool."

"Yeah, Sneaky's brother is Razz; you know that right?"

"Yeah. I heard that he opened for Razz—"

"Yeap and turned it out, too. Razz was happy, he made a lot of money that night. Razz looks out for my brother and I'm just glad that he's not hanging out over here no more."

"I know. Me, too. I do miss him."

"Alia, you need to talk to my brother. It's not like you don't know him. Both of you guys got these walls up and I think it's time to bring 'em down."

"Yeah, I think you're right, but I don't want to force myself on him. I think he needs to do his music and then when the time is right, maybe we might meet up in the middle. I just hate that he's with her."

"Yeah."

"When he goes on tour, what is he going to do about school?" Marisol asked Chepi.

"Oh, his teachers arranged for him to have a private tutor, so I think he's going to be taking some online classes or something like that while he's on the road. He's only going to tour in America."

"Just make sure he doesn't go to New York," I added and Marisol agreed.

"Yeah, that shit that happened in New York was crazy. Turn on the news, I wanna see what's going on," Chepi said.

I had the radio on but I turned it off and switched to the big screen. They were still covering the attack and now they were showing where the Pentagon had been hit but there was wreckage on the ground around the building.

"Dayyyyyum," Chepi sipped his juice. I didn't want to watch anymore. I was worried about Anthony, hoping that he would be safe on his tour. "Don't you think you guys should cancel his tour until this stuff is figured out?"

"Awww I don't think the label will do that. I'mma keep up with everything and let Marisol know and she can let you know. Don't worry."

"I'mma try not to," I added.

Press On

I toured seven cities: Houston, Las Vegas, Los Angeles, Miami, Kansas City, Atlanta, and D.C. So far everybody was elevated and I had every show lit. My boys made sure to keep everybody entertained and we had some dope dance moves to do on stage to keep the fans happy. I was pleased and so was the label. All of my shows were sold out so far. Even with the attack in New York, people were still coming to see the shows. Steven was keeping up with the billboard's top ten and "Missing You" was damn near at number 1. Not bad for a new solo artist.

"Cheetah, you keep this up, you're going to end up with a Music Award," Steven said as we rode to Louisiana. I was going to be doing another show in Baton Rouge. There were some fine ass females in Miami and L.A. I was like damn! They were coming at me hard, too. I fucked two and made sure that I had the jimmy on so that I wouldn't catch nothing else. I gave them bitches the business, too. It wasn't bad being an artist. I had pussy coming and going. Megan kept calling me but I was sending her straight to voicemail. I didn't want to be bothered while I was on tour, but don't get me wrong, I still had Alia heavily on the brain. I couldn't shake her for nothing. Chepi told me that she was asking about me and that made me feel great. He told me that Novi was hating on me. I didn't put it past him. I could've been an asshole and told the homies that he snitched on his own brother. I kept that to myself because Mitch asked me to. That's still his brother at the end of the day. I was worried about him trying to break in on Alia but she's strong enough to keep him at bay, hopefully. I just hope nobody else steps in and takes her attention from me. Believe me, there were days when I wanted to call her, but my pride got the best of me and I let it go.

"Aye, Cheetah, you want something from this burger spot?"

I looked out of the window and there were a lot of people in line. The place was a little hole in the wall burger spot. The line was long so it must be good. We were in a city in Louisiana. I wasn't sure which city we were in. "Yeah, get me a burger and some fries, no onions," I told Marcus. He had bitches on him, too; all of my brothers did. The only one that didn't come on tour with us was Mike. He stayed with my mom to make sure nobody fucked with our spot.

"Aye, Cheetah, you think it's some cute females out here," Sneaky asked, making me laugh.

"I dunno man, if it is, I'mma fuck!" I said making him laugh as we gave each other dap. "I've been a hoe ever since I've been on tour, dog."

"On me," Sneaky laughed. "I had to turn my phone off bro, my girl keeps calling."

"See, you should've broke up with her before we left," we laughed.

"Nigga, you crazy, Cheetah. I'm about to be a dad, bro."

"Serious? Silvia's pregnant?"

"Yep, I'm finna have a blaxican," he said making me laugh. His girl is Mexican and she's pretty; they had been together for a while and he said he wanted to marry her but he was being a hoe just like me on the road.

"What about you and Megan, man, you gone stick with her?"

"Hell nah, man, my heart is with Alia, dog! On God!"

He laughed. "I knew you were going to say that. I love Alia, man. She's solid and she's pretty as fuck! You should've never broke up with her."

"Man, she broke up with me."

"Well … shit … you should've been begging her ass, a female fine like that."

"Yeah, you're right, but my pride got the best of me. It's all good tho. I think I still might have a shot, I'm not sure," I said, watching as the line started moving. "I dunno, Sneaky. She might not wanna fuck with me after this shit. I mean, I'm enjoying fucking every day," we laughed.

"I'm serious. I'm getting more pussy than I deserve right now."

"Aye, Cheetah, you need to have fun bro … you earned it."

"Damn right I did."

"But get Alia back. You need to marry her."

"No shit." He was right about that. His phone went off and he held it up.

"Silvia," he snickered and answered his phone, going to the back of the tour bus. She was getting in his ass and I laughed and sat back thinking about Alia. I grabbed Steven's laptop and decided to pull up Friendster just to see if Alia had been online. I saw that she had visited my page more than once. It made me grin. I went to her page and was looking through her stuff. She had posted a poem about true love. It was nice and everything that I read in it was true. I pushed the star to let her know that I liked what she wrote. I wrote underneath, "*I miss you.*"

I wasn't expecting her to respond; I just wanted her to know that I did miss her and I hoped she acknowledged it at least. Sneaky was going at it with his girl and I was glad that I had my phone off so I didn't have to deal with Megan. I wasn't about to deal with her. It would be different if it had been Alia. Marcus came back on the tour bus with the food and everybody else stepped on the bus, too. I didn't get off because Steven thought it was best for me to stay on the bus whenever we stopped because people were crazy and especially at a time like this after the terrorist attack, I stayed put. My dad climbed back on with his food. Marcus gave me my burger and fries and everything looked delicious. "Damn, bro, this looks like a burger from home," I said, biting into it. "Mmmm, this is bomb."

"Yep." He passed me ketchup but I was cool without ketchup. I grubbed down on my food, glad that I decided to eat here. I looked at the name of the place as the driver was moving us out of the parking area. "Mama Mia Burger." Shit was delicious. Steven was grubbing on a burger and fries too and chopping it up with his boyfriend; they were acting normal around everybody else like regular friends but I knew better. After I ate, I went right to sleep.

When I woke up, we were in Baton Rouge and the city was well lit up with people and we were downtown from the looks of it. I overheard Steven telling someone on the phone that we were going to be staying at the Ritz Carlton hotel. This place looked so damn country; I wasn't used to this, I was used to the desert, but oh well, I was glad that we were away from that heat. I was hungry again by the time we got off the bus and headed into the hotel. It was girls outside, calling out to me. How the hell did they know I was going to be here? I waved at them, but I was blushing that they knew me and were calling out to me.

"CHEETAH, COME HERE BABY!" I stopped and one girl gave me a hug and some flowers.

"You are so fine, baby! Yes you are."

I laughed and gave her my autograph feeling famous. Her friend wanted to take pictures. These girls were older and country. The way they talked I could barely understand them. "I love you, Cheetah, baby."

"Thank you," I said, following my dad. We went up to the elevator as Steven was at the counter talking to the hotel manager. My dad already had our key cards. "Cheetah, you're going to be dealing with a lot of women, so be careful son, keep them condoms."

"Oh I am Dad, I learned my lesson," I told him.

I wasn't expecting what I was about to go through once I did my first show out here in Baton Rouge. We ate, I practiced with the fellas, we smoked and joked around and sat out on the patio enjoying the sun without it being so hot. I felt like I was already in the big time and when night fell, we headed to the concert hall and I got ready for the show while the guys did mic checks. We fell in line as if we were used to this and I thought I had everything down to a science. Time went quickly before I was out on stage, performing and blowing all of these southern folks away with my singing and dancing skills. They went crazy. I mean literally they were screaming and girls were trying to get on stage and it was tough because I had to step back a few times to keep from getting jumped on by these big black southern girls. I mean they were huge and I stood behind two big security guards, trying to sing at the same time; it was hilarious. I wasn't expecting this and we hadn't hired no security for me off stage, so of course when it was time for us to head to the tour bus to go back to the hotel, it was thousands of young females outside of the concert hall waiting for me. I looked at my brothers and my dad.

"Cheetah, this is it! This is what you gotta get used to." Heeeeelp! I'm thinking, damn, how the hell am I going to get out of here? It was funny to see. Sneaky, and the guys thought it was funny; they went outside and tried to distract the girls but it wasn't working; they were blocking the entrance for me to get out. I wasn't about to go out there and get smothered by all those women. A lot of them were gorgeous and it was just overwhelming. It really hit me that I was becoming famous. They were screaming for me and reaching their arms in the door; a few of them got past my dad and brothers and ran up to me and hugged me.

"OH MY GOD, YOU ARE SO CUTTTE!" they screamed, crying and hugging me so tight. I looked at my folks. "Yawl help me!" I laughed and security came finally and dispersed all of the crowds of girls. It was a big big help because after they were moved out of the way, I was able to make a beeline to the bus. I ran to get on the tour bus safely and Flip and the guys were laughing so hard at me.

"Were you scared, Cheetah?" Smoke teased in giggles. They were laughing so hard, I just sat in my seat exhausted, wiping lipstick off of my face from them kissing on me.

"Now I see what Michael Jackson went through. One girl almost tore my shirt," I explained.

"Yeah, we need to hire bodyguards," my dad said. We were making a lot of money at these shows and my father and Steven were the ones collecting everything. At the end of the tour they were going to pass out money in checks to everybody. My dad had to open up a bank account for me and he did that before we left Arizona. I went to the bus window and the girls were still outside, staring at the bus and waving and screaming out my name. I ended up taking pictures and Marcus let the window down, waving at them, making them scream harder. He was getting a kick out of all the attention. It was exciting but scary. I was scared, I'm not going to lie, I never seen that many girls together at the same time and all for me.

"Oooh, look at the girl in the yellow," Marcus whistled. "She's FINE!" I searched the crowd for her and saw her. She was cute, but not for me. I was checking them out and didn't see anything that struck my interest. None of those girls looked prettier than Alia and they were cute, but not as beautiful as my first girlfriend.

"Cheetah, let the window down and wave at them, show them some appreciation, because they're the reason why you're getting so popular," Steven informed me. I did what he told me and they were screaming so hard I could barely hear myself think. Damn! It was fun!

My album dropped on a Friday, the end of September. I was in Dallas this time and after the show, I went backstage and did a meet and greet with fans. I was so tired from all of the shows; in between the shows, I was doing schoolwork, so I was burnt out. I didn't think it was going to be this much work and once we got back from tour, we were going to be promoting the album, so a lot of the money that

I made was going to be going into promotions. I was going to be back at school once we left Texas and headed back to Arizona. I was going to be doing shows there, too. Most of my promotions went on this Eleven Eleven tour. We hit little cities with no streetlights and it was crazy; these people came up with the money to come and see me and the guys perform. I had more white fans than I had expected. It took me two hours to do the meet and greet and once I was done with the autographing and meeting fans, I was finally able to call it a night. I grabbed my bottled water ready to go. I started packing up my stuff when Steven busted in the dressing room.

"CHEETAH, guess what, bro?"

"What?"

"'Missing You' is number one on the singles chart!"

"You're lying! Seriously? It hit number 1?"

"YES, look!" Steven laughed showing me the *Billboard* magazine. My song was number one. Those bright red letters became a big blur. My pride moved to the side and I broke down crying!

"Awwww, don't cry, baby brother. You did it! You fucking did that!" Steven hugged and kissed me. "Now all we need is for your album to go platinum."

I nodded, buried in tears. My dad hugged me and told me that he was proud of me. I cried.

When we made it back to Arizona, the city was all in … and I saw my face on the billboards where my brother Mike had made it happen with the promotion of my new album cover. I couldn't believe it was me. I was happy.

"Look, Cheetah, another picture," Sneaky pointed out as we passed through the city of Phoenix looking at billboards.

"Wow!" I was shocked that it was finally happening for me. The bus driver turned up the music and I heard my song from my new album on the radio and we all cheered.

"You officially made it, dog, congratulations!" Flip said giving me a high five. I stood up. "I wanna thank all of you guys for believing in me. I really do appreciate all of the hard work and love. I'm so happy right now and I'm fighting back tears."

"We gotchu Cheetah, all we need to do now is go platinum! We need to light up the stage here at home for our people," Smoke added.

"Hell yeah, man, we got this!" Sneaky added and I gave them all love and sat back down, blown away by the success of my music career. It was unbelievable. I had my phone back on now and it was blowing up with calls from Cal, Novi, and other guys on the block. Megan had sent me a gang of text messages, but during the tour, I made sure to keep my phone off. I didn't need any distractions. I called her for the first time in weeks.

"Hello?"

"Wassup, I'm back in town."

"You asshole! I've been calling and calling, Cheetah, you never returned none of my calls or my text messages. That's fucked up. Did you forget that you had a girlfriend?"

"Will you shut up and meet me at my house, please? I'm on my way there."

“I’m already at your house. Hold on, your mom wants to talk to you,” she said and I laughed looking at G.B., who was snoring in his seat.

When I got home, everybody in the family was at my parents’ house. Nobody used to come and visit us like this but everybody in my mom’s family was here. Wow! I was amazed at the company in the house, and Mom had food on the table that she cooked. I didn’t really associate with my cousins but they were even here, staring at me like they had seen a star walk in the house. Literally.

“These are your cousins, Cheetah. This is Danny, Alex, Adrienne, Tyler, baby Wolf.” She introduced us and we all shook hands and gave each other hugs. My brothers greeted them as well.

“Congratulations, Cheetah on your music career. I heard the album it’s dope,” Alex said. “I’m into that type of music, dog.”

“Really. Wow, thank you.” I never got this type of support before I became popular.

We all gravitated to the den and Megan was on the sofa glaring at me with evil eyes. She was mad and yes, I had my share of females whenever my dad wasn’t in the hotel, I was getting my fuck on. I turned into a hoe, but I made sure that I kept a condom and that it never broke. I was fucking some fine females, too. All of the homies had their issue.

“What’s wrong with you, you’re mad?”

“Yes! I am! You go on tour and forget all about me!”

I leaned over and kissed her cheek. “You’ll be all right. The tour was fun by the way.”

“I’m sure it was. How many bitches did you fuck?”

“A lot,” I said and she snatched her hand from me. “I’m just playing, damn, stop being so mean. You ain’t glad to see me?”

“Yes I’m glad to see you, but damn, you changed since you been on the radio, all of a sudden, you’re big headed now.”

“Whatever. I’m about to go and say hi to my sister. I ain’t got time for this.”

“Fine, I’m going home.”

I grabbed her hand. I needed some head. I didn’t want her to leave. “Let’s go in my room,” I told her. Everybody was talking and enjoying themselves with food and I had her in my room. “I want some head,” I told her. “I miss that mouf.”

She laughed. “I bet you did, asshole,” She dropped her head down below and I closed my eyes, glad that I locked the door. Someone knocked. “HOLD ON!” I said, holding her head in place. “Awww man that feels good! Don’t stop.” I said. I was hard as concrete and it wasn’t long before I exploded in her mouth picturing Alia doing this to me. I almost called out her name, but I kept quiet. I didn’t push her away because after having all those girls on tour, I learned to take it when I got my dick sucked. It was so bomb. “Damn, that was bomb, thank you,” I said slipping up my pants. “You can go home now!”

“Are you serious? Uh uh, nigga you finna give me some of that good dick!” she said, trying to be forceful, but I stopped her. “Not right now, we got people here,” I said and someone knocked on the door again. She smacked her lips; she was hot! She went and opened the door and walked out while Marcus walked in.

“What’s wrong with her?”

“Nothing, she’s pissed; she’ll be all right.”

Marcus laughed, "Bro, you're stupid. Nicole is on her way over here; I need to use the room."

"Nigga, you better go get a room; you got some money now."

"I didn't cash the check yet, can I borrow a hundred and I'll give it back to you tomorrow?"

I gave him a hundred dollars. I didn't cash my check either, but I had money put away under my mattress from the last few shows we did before we left.

"Thanks bro, I gotchu tomorrow."

"Don't forget."

He grabbed some clothes and went to the bathroom. I wanted to call Alia so badly, but I know that she wasn't going to talk to me. Chepi came in the room, "Bro, Megan sped out of here like she was pissed. What you say to her?"

"Nothing, she sucked my dick and I didn't wanna fuck her, so she's mad."

He laughed. "Bro, you're cold! Did you call Alia yet?"

"Nah, she won't talk to me."

"How do you know?"

"I don't know. I'm so in love with her, that's crazy, huh?"

"No, it's not. That's your girl and you need to make amends with her and stop being so prideful."

"I'm not being prideful. I just wanna make sure that I get all of this fucking out of the way first before I go to her."

"Bro, will you stop? You'll love her no matter how many females you fuck."

"She's not going to talk to me. I just have that feeling."

"You won't know until you try," he said checking his phone. "Marisol is here, I'm about to leave and go and get me some pussy. Shit, I'm horny," he said making me laugh.

"Have fun. Find out what's up with Alia."

I thought that I would be over Alia by now, but my feelings stayed and they actually grew since I'd gotten older. She was even more beautiful than she was when we first met. I was looking at the images of her on Friendster and wow! I knew dudes were trying to get at her and as I sifted through her post, I found one where she was at PVA! What? She was going to my school now. I looked through her pictures and found one that made me fall deeper in love. It was so beautiful. I saved it and took a picture of it with my computer. We had new phones, better, upgrades but the picture quality sucked. "Damn!" I whispered amazed at her beauty. I can't believe she's at PVA now, that's crazy! Now I get to see her. I couldn't wait to go to school on Monday. Megan called me. I answered. "Wassup, you still mad?"

"You're dogging me out for no reason. I don't understand you, Cheetah. Now that you're becoming famous, you're changing and I hope this doesn't go to your head. You're acting so stuck up now."

"I didn't feel like having sex, I'm not in my own room and you know that everybody is here. Why can't you just wait?"

"I've been waiting all of this time to be with you. I missed you and you act like you don't miss me."

"I did miss you. You just started banging on me as soon as I got home. I've been working my ass off and you told me that you understood that I was going to be busy in this music stuff but now you're acting clingy and I don't like that. That's why I didn't want to have a girl in the first place. I need to be single."

"Noooo. I don't wanna break up."

"Well, I can't deal with you acting clingy. You need to chill if we're going to be together."

"Okay, okay, I'll chill. Just don't break up with me. When you want to see me just call me okay?"

"Yep. Can I call you back?" I said, looking through Alia's page.

"Yes, call me."

"Aiight." I ended the call and I saw where she put a heart next to the comment I wrote about missing her weeks ago. So she liked what I said but she never responded. That's cool; at least she did acknowledge me. I put another comment under her picture that I saved. *"You're so beautiful."* I noticed that a lot of guys were commenting on the image. She didn't talk to any of them, but when I saw a comment from Novi, it sparked up a fury that irritated me. Why was he on her Friendster page? I had no right to be upset; I was doing what I wanted and it wasn't like we were together but this fucker was all on her. I logged off and called him. The phone rang four times before he answered. He wasn't even at school I bet. "Hello?"

"Wassup Novi, you called?"

"Cheetah? Awwww shit man, what's up with you, dog? You getting famous and can't reach out no more I see."

"Man, I've been busy. I just got back from tour. I got a show tonight at the forum. I'm just chilling."

"So how was the tour?"

"It was great."

"Yeah, you didn't even invite me to go, I thought I was your boy."

"It was tight, Steven is the one in charge of all of the stage crew and you know I dance with Flip, Smoke and David."

"What about that nigga, Sneaky? I know he went with yawl."

"Yeah, that's my boy, of course and his brother is the reason why I got this tour schedule, so I couldn't leave him out."

"Awww that's messed up, Cheetah. You didn't include your boy."

"What's up with you and Alia? Yawl talking or what?"

He laughed, "She's just a cool friend, man. You broke her heart so she ain't trying to talk to nobody. I walk her home every day from work to make sure she's cool. Nobody else is gone do it. So I make sure that I'm there."

"Hmm. She ain't with nobody?"

"I dunno. You know she's at PVA now, so it's no telling, I'm sure the white boys are bidding."

"Yeah, right. So what's been up on the block, have you talked to Mitch?"

"He called and talked to my mom. She told him about you blowing up. You changed, Cheetah."

"Changed how, nigga? What you talking about? I'm still me. Matter fact, I'll be over there in a few days, just let me handle this shit first."

"Put me on, man."

"What you mean, I ain't got connections like that yet."

"At least help me with my demo; you know I rap."

"I'll see what I can do."

“Aiight, hit me up when you come on the block.”

I wasn’t thinking about Novi. I wasn’t going to hook him up with nothing since he told on Mitch and not to mention stabbed me in the back. I called Flip to see what time they wanted to meet at the forum that evening. “Bro, we can meet at four, that way we can rehearse, eat and do the mic check.”

“Okay that’s what’s up. Guess who I talked to?”

“Who?”

“Novi, he’s all on Alia.”

“Man she ain’t talking to him. I heard she’s at PVA now.”

“Yep I know, I hope I see her on Monday. She’s so beautiful.”

“Why you won’t get back with her?”

“I want to but I don’t think she wants to be with me, bro.”

“Dog, I heard she still loves you and guess what else I heard from a girl that kicks it with Megan?”

“What, don’t tell me that she got a man.”

“Nah bro, this ain’t even about Alia. I heard that Novi gave Megan an STD. She fucked that nigga!”

“When?”

“I think it was a while back, but I’m not sure. You should ask her.”

“Uggh, I’mma do that right now, if she fucked that nigga, I’mma really dog her ass out. I don’t really like her like that anyway. I’mma drop her and get back with Alia if she’ll take me back.”

“Megan is fine dog, but if she’s fucking all these niggaz, she ain’t no wife material like Alia.”

"That's real! Uggh, lemme call you back." I ended the call disgusted with Megan. I dialed her number quick.

"Hello?"

"Aye … did you fuck Novi and don't lie to me?"

"Yeah, I did a long time ago, way before we got together. He gave me that STD."

"I knew it! That's some nasty shit."

"Cheetah, I swear to God, I haven't been with nobody since I been with you. I'm not lying, you can ask anybody."

"You better not let me find out you have. That nigga Novi gave you that shit?"

"Yes! I told him that he did and he didn't fight with me; he went and got it cleared up because he said they gave him a shot in his ass and some pills."

She wasn't lying because that's what they did to me. So that nigga knew that he had it.

"He said he caught it from a girl that lived up the street. He knew that he had it; he had it cleared up before I found out that I had it."

"Uggh! That nigga wants me to put him on the music scene, fuck him!"

"Don't do it, Cheetah, he's a hater and he don't like you."

"How do you know, he told you that?"

"I've been hearing shit; he's jealous of you. He's trying to get with Alia now, he's scandalous." As far as I was concerned, they were both scandalous. I didn't trust either one of them but like they say, keep your friends close but your enemies closer and I had to do just that with these two.

"Do you want me to come over?"

"Nah, not yet, I'm about to leave and go and deal with this show tonight."

"Oh okay, well don't forget about me."

"I won't," I ended the call with her and lay in bed thinking about the fact of Novi passing that STD to her and giving it to me. He set that up, because he gave her my number and knew that she liked me, so of course sex went down with us and he knew he had that shit. That's a dirty ass dude. It just made me dislike him even more. I couldn't blame anyone but myself because I chose to sleep with her and lose the best thing that ever happened to me. I wasn't sure if I would ever get Alia back. I knew she didn't trust me to be with her anymore, so I was unsure. The only thing left for me to do was concentrate on my music and hopefully the universe would send her back to me.

My sister came in my room. "Now I got a lot of friends on the rez because of you," she smiled. "I never had this many friends before."

"Yeah? Just be careful."

"What do you mean?"

"They're only around you because of me, not because they wanna be your friend, so don't trust 'em."

"I don't. I only have one friend and you already know her."

"Good, keep it that way."

June 2004

Four years had gone by and now I was full time at the liquor store. Roy acted like it was my store. I worked so many hours there that I had enough to buy a car and get my own place. I wasn't giving Aunt Olivia my work money and she thought that I was still making the same amount of money that I was making when I first started there in 2001. I'd been there three years and I was making eleven dollars an hour. I was getting burnt out working here and especially dealing with the same faces every day. I had applied to work at the library which was in Paradise Valley and it was paying thirteen dollars an hour. My uncle James said if I got the job there that he would help me buy me a car. I was about to be eighteen and I already had my driver's license, thanks to Marisol teaching me how to drive in her car. If it wasn't for her, I would've still been waiting to learn how to drive. My aunt was still a bitch to me, but now I was standing up to her because I got tired of her trying to hit me without me protecting myself. Once I was older, she was more hesitant on putting her hands on me because one time she tried to jump on me and I grabbed her and held her hands and she couldn't break free, so she knew that I was stronger than her. I could've hurt her if I wanted to, but I chose to keep things cool until I had enough money to move out on my own. I couldn't wait until that day arrived, I was going to give her a piece of my mind and move out. As soon as I turned eighteen I was planning to move out. Nicole and I barely spoke to each other. She wasn't home at all; she was always on the rez dealing with Marcus and Cheetah's family with Megan. They were all in cahoots with each other and I wasn't cool with her being that close to the man that I loved. She would come home bragging about how she had backstage passes to his concerts and how he knew all of these rapper dudes. She bragged about how rich he was and of course I was envious. I still loved him.

Cheetah's first three albums went platinum and he became a superstar; he won two Grammy awards and had become a solidified member of the music industry. He did a European tour in 2003 and since the war on Iraq, things were looking up for him and his family. From what I heard from Marisol, he was having a house built on the rez for his mom and dad. She said it was a mini mansion. He wasn't home long enough to have his own place, but he was about to be eighteen himself and he was lucky that he had no more money issues. He launched his own record label and it was called Safari Records. Marisol worked there part time and I was thinking about applying there but I was nervous about Megan finding out and putting a monkey wrench in that for me, so I just settled for the library.

Novi was doing rap music and was well-known underground. He still hadn't gotten a record deal yet, but he put out a dis record on Cheetah and people were buying it and waiting for Cheetah to respond to him. I think Novi was using this to try to get notoriety and become an above ground artist. The dude had flows, but for him to dis

Cheetah was wrong. Yes, I still loved him and now I was following him on Facebook and Myspace, which had become popular. Cheetah had over a million Myspace followers and his music was getting so much notoriety that he was established as a top of the line entertainer even though he was so young. Now that he was older, his looks developed and he was attracting older females. I'm sure Megan had her hands full dealing with him and his handsome looks. He's gorgeous!!!! With a capital G. Novi came in the store again with Cal.

"Wassup, Alia!? You looking good, girl," Cal said making me laugh. He was always funny but he was never disrespectful.

"I'm doing well, Cal, how are you?"

"Good, can I get two swishers and a black and mild?"

"Sure, that's three fifty," I told him.

"Damn, yawl went up huh?"

"Yes, since the New Year."

"Damn," he said, handing me a five. Novi was in his phone until it was his turn. He asked for a pint of Hennessy and a black and mild.

"Hi you doing, sexy?"

"I'm good, Novi. I heard that dis record you did about Cheetah, you ain't right."

They both were laughing. "He went Hollywood on us sis," Cal said. "That nigga used to be the homie until he got famous, now he's all Hollywood."

"Well, Novi, I seen where he had you at his album release party last year."

"Yeah, but he still ain't put a nigga on and he got his own label now. He's signing these other fools from L.A. but he ain't signed me and my bars is way better than those niggaz he signed."

"I didn't know they signed anybody else. Ain't his brother responsible for that?"

"Yeah, Steven's a fag anyway," he said and Cal burst out in laughter. I shook my head. "

"You didn't know his brother was on booty?"

"What are you talking about, Novi?"

"Steven is a faggot! He's on dick."

"Wow, no. I didn't know that, I thought you were just being funny on your rap, but I didn't know he was really gay."

"Yeah, look at his Facebook page. That nigga's a straight flaming sissy."

"I heard he could fight, tho," Cal laughed. "You better leave that nigga alone, Novi, he might come over here and beat you down and put one of them gay pride flags on your head."

They laughed and I didn't think it was funny. I liked Steven actually; he was nice when I met him.

"Yeah, Alia, Cheetah ain't been over here in like two years since he blew up. That nigga G.B. be hanging with him now, Sneaky, too, they all chill around Cheetah; they don't even fuck with us no more. They do their own thing and we do ours."

"Sorry to hear that, Novi."

"Don't be sorry. When I blow up, that nigga gone wish he had fucked with me, cos people love my music."

"Yeah, I like your rap too, but you just gotta ignore the bullshit and do your own thing."

"Oh I am. Fuck, Sneaky and fuck all them traitor ass niggaz. Novi is about to be universal."

He pulled out a wad of money and was flossing it. "See, I ain't gotta worry about money no more, I stay papered up."

"Good for you. Don't get robbed," I teased.

"Aiight, Alia, talk to you later sweetie," he said and they left the store. I shook my head. He was so jealous of Cheetah. He changed and he had the nerve to say that Cheetah changed; he did. He had no business talking about that man's brother like that. From what I was hearing, Cheetah was still taking care of Mitch and if Novi had money, he should be looking out for his brother.

I went to school the next morning, tired because I did overtime at the job. I stayed until closing and Roy ended up bringing me home. I didn't sleep much of the night because I was up, looking at Cheetah's Facebook page and his Myspace page listening to his music and enjoying myself while everyone else slept. I hope Anthony comes to school today. He was missing a lot of school but from what Marisol told me, he was doing classes for PVA online since he had to tour and do his music. He did come to school but I was always hiding from him and for some reason, I didn't feel the need to hide anymore. I felt like four years was long enough. I still loved and missed him. I thought that I'd be over him after this many years but the love got stronger.

I met up with my friend Dawn. She was at the lockers. She's white and we met on the first day that I started at PVA. She showed me around and made me feel welcome there and we'd been dealing with each other ever since. I had a feeling she would be a lifelong friend.

She has long red hair, and I loved the fact that her eyebrows were the same color as her hair and she has freckles and long red eyelashes too. She's so pretty; girls were jealous of her. She's into ballet and an advanced ballet dancer. She's so good at what she does, it wouldn't be a surprise to see her in Switzerland on a professional ballet team. She liked black guys too and was also a big fan of Cheetah.

"Hey, girl, are you going straight to class?"

"Yeah, why what's up?"

"I wanna go to the music building and see if Cheetah's there."

"Oh yeah he's here, I saw him this morning."

"Really? Oh my God," she laughed at me and closed her locker.

"You need to reach out to him, Alia, stop being scared."

"No, I want him to reach out to me; he owes me that."

We walked in the music building and I was nervous now because we were going to be passing his class. "I hope we don't become tardy," Dawn whispered.

"I know, huh? Let's hurry," I said, moving towards his class and he walked out with a white boy. I stopped walking and grabbed Dawn's arm.

"Let go of my arm," Dawn laughed.

"HEY, CHEETAH," she said and I turned away quickly.

"Hey, wassup," I heard him say. He came over and spoke to Dawn giving her a hug. I finally looked at him and he was looking at me. "Wassup, Alia?"

"Hi," I said. I was so scared and nervous that I swallowed the lump in my throat.

"Where you guys headed off to?"

"She came over here to see if you were here," Dawn gave it away and I laughed.

"Is that right, so you wanted to see me finally after four years?"

I shrugged, "I guess. How have you been?"

"I've been good, let me get a pass real quick and walk you to class. You need a pass?"

"Yes please."

When he went back in the class, I looked at Dawn and thanked her. My heart was racing, I wasn't expecting to talk to him. Four years: damn that was a long time and we are both old enough now to know better and to do better. He's famous but yet he was still down to earth and it seemed like we were going to pick up where we left off. The look in his eyes told me that he was still interested. He came out with our passes.

"Oh thank you, Cheetah. Alia, I'll see you later."

"Okay, thank you Dawn," I said, walking with him and people were speaking to him as we walked down the hall and out of the building across the grass. I was in a class way across the way.

"So how have you been, Alia? I missed you."

"Yeah?"

"Yes, I told you that on your Friendster page and you were acting all stuck up like you couldn't talk to nobody."

"I was NOT acting stuck up; I was hurt."

"I know. It was my fault. I didn't mean to hurt you like that but you really made me think hard over the last few years. I mean, I never stopped thinking about you. It was crazy, when I found out that you were going here, I would come to school and look for you and never found you."

"I know because I would hide from you."

"Why?"

"Because I was scared and still mad at you. Are you still with that girl?"

"Who, Megan?"

"Yeah—"

"On and off, I'm not really into her like that."

"On and off huh, hmm."

"Aww c'mon, don't be acting like that."

"Acting like what? How am I supposed to act, Anthony? It's been four years; you're famous now, rich, and I guess I can't compete with all of the other girls."

"It ain't no other girls."

"Yeah, right," I said making him laugh. Oooh, his smile was magnetic and his teeth were perfect; he was so very handsome now, why would I believe that it wasn't other girls into him. I stared in his eyes, feeling those butterflies again and it made me tear up.

"What's wrong?" he asked.

"Wow, I can't believe I'm standing her talking to you. I thought you hated me. It's like damn, am I dreaming or what?" He cheeses again, melting my heart with his beautiful smile. That's one thing about Cheetah; he's perfectly handsome. He has dimples, pretty light brown eyes and the perfect cherry color lips that looked as if he was wearing a cool red matte lipstick. His tattooed skin is tanned; he's over six feet tall with hair down his back; he's the perfect definition of an indigenous king. He makes Native American men the hottest looking men on the planet. Maybe it's his mixed blood that brings out his most handsome features because his dad had to be attractive for him to be so beautiful. With his looks, he needed to be locked in a basement somewhere. I saw his mother at the show four years ago and she's beautiful, so I can imagine what his dad looks like.

"So can I take you out later on?"

"Serious?"

"Yes, I'm not playing. I have a car now, I can come and get you and hang out with you unlike before when we were limited in seeing and talking to each other. Are you still going through that drama with your auntie?"

"Yes! But now she's not hitting me like she used to because I'll hit her ass back, I'm not taking any more ass kicking's from no bitch."

"Aww no, don't hit her, she's still your elder."

"I don't care, I'm not allowing her or Nicole to hit on me anymore. I'm working full time now and I'm going to get my own place."

"Are you still at the liquor store?"

"Yes, how did you know I was there?"

"I came up there and saw you working remember," he said, looking at his watch and I noticed that it had diamonds in it; it was nice. I felt retarded because he did come and see me working.

"Can I see your watch?"

He lifted his arm, grinning. "I see you're still wearing the bracelet, and earrings that I got you."

"Yes. Is anything wrong with that? I wonder if Megan is still wearing the ring you took from me."

"That's because you hurt my feelings, that's what it was, I was hurt."

"Hmm, are you disappointed to see me wearing the stuff you bought?"

"Hell nah. I'm happy," he chuckled. "So you didn't answer me, can I take you out?"

"Yes … what time?"

"After school, we can meet outside in the front. Who's taking you home?"

"I was going to take the bus."

"Nah, I'll meet you in the front. I gotta get to class before they come looking for us. I'm glad this is my last year here."

"Me too. I applied for USC in California."

"What, serious? Awww wow. What if they accept you, are you going to move to California?" he looked in my eyes and I blushed.

"I dunno, it depends. I didn't just apply at USC, I applied for college out here, too."

"Oh okay, that's what's up."

I went to class elated now that I talked to him. I couldn't believe that we talked and I wrote to Marisol telling her that we talked finally and she sent back a bunch of happy faces. I had a cell phone now and I gave him my number. I just hoped that Megan didn't get it and start calling me because I had an ass kicking waiting for her this time. I wanted my man back and I wasn't going to stand down this time. I spent four years thinking about him and crying over him relentlessly and I knew that he was my one true love. There was no way I was going to back away and let him escape. It wasn't because of his fame and fortune; I truly loved Anthony and I knew it had to be true love for me to still feel the way that I did after all of those years had passed. I felt his energy and he still felt the same way about me, but I didn't want to jump the gun and think that without confirmation. He could be just like the rest of these guys, just trying to get me in bed and then be done with me. I'm sure he had a lot of girls on him during his tours and his climb up the ladder of success. I had a lot to compete with and he could have any girl that he wanted.

Once school ended, and it seemed to take forever, I was racing to the front entrance to meet him. I wasn't sure what type of car he was going to be in. When I stepped out on the front steps, I saw people standing around a red Lamborghini and the doors were up like butterfly wings. It was so nice and I saw Cheetah step out of the car waving me over.

"Oooh, bitch!" Dawn came up behind me. "You see his fucking car, oh my God!" The white boys were standing around him checking out the car and he was keeping a level head. I was so nervous; I slowly came down the stairs wondering if this was real. I guess those platinum albums put him in this type of car. Damn! It sunk in that he was actually rich. I was smiling from ear to ear,

"This is nice, Cheetah."

"Cheetah? Anthony, remember?"

"Oh yeah, I'm sorry," I laughed and he grabbed my backpack and put it in the back and I sat in the car, blown away by how the leather felt and looked. It had a new car smell. "This is soo nice," I told him.

"Thank you," he let the door down and continued to talk to the white boys. He gave them love with hugs and they were all cool with him. White boys didn't just talk to anybody, especially these rich white boys over here.

"Aye, Cheetah call me fool," one of the white boys said.

"Aiight, aye Scott," he yelled and went over and said something to the white boy and he nodded and shouted something back to him. "Aiight." He climbed in the car and I had noticed a note from someone that read, "I love you." They put hearts on it. He grabbed it and put it in the ashtray.

"Is that from Megan?" I asked, getting jealous.

"Yeah, she does shit like that."

My seatbelt moved towards me without me having to attach it. This car was so nifty, I couldn't do anything but smile as we moved down the block near PVA. "This is nice, I didn't know you were doing it like this."

"Yep … where you wanna go eat at? You want Sharkey's?"

"Sharkey's? That's expensive, hell yes."

"Aiight," he took his phone from his pocket and his phone was even bigger. It made mine look like the cheap prepaid it was. "Hello, yeah this is Cheetah. I wanted to make reservations … yeah for two … hahahahah, okay, thank you John … aiight." He ended the call and looked at me.

"So what's up, Alia? Finally you let me back into your life or are you just hanging out with me for today because you found out about my success?"

"Well, that depends."

"On what? I can't lie to you. I messed around with a lot of girls since we weren't together. I've been doing my thing."

"I'm sure you have."

"I have but none of them grabbed my heart."

"What about Megan? I don't want to get into nothing that is going to hurt me."

"Listen, Alia," he said stopping at the light. "I still love you! I dunno if you believe me but I do. I don't just love you but I'm still in love with you," he said making me get chills and tears filled my eyes. It was hard listening to him without getting emotional. "I don't want you to cry, baby, I do still love you, Alia. I never stopped loving you. I thought about you every single day and I prayed that you would come back into my life. I was hoping that. Even with me doing my thing with the other girls, I wasn't into them like how I feel about you."

I wiped my face. "I cried over you every single day, Anthony!"

"I believe you! Don't think I didn't cry over yo ass! I cried over you, too!"

I gave him a disbelieving look.

"I did! Ask Chepi. I cried over you when you broke up with me! You broke my fucking heart and had me dogging females ever since. You did that shit!"

"Oh now it's my fault when you cheated on me first?"

"I told you that I was weak. She sent me those naked pictures and I got weak, I was stupid at the time, Alia. You didn't even wanna give me a chance to straighten it out."

"No … especially after you caught something from her and I heard Novi gave her that shit."

“He did … and he gave her my phone number too.”

“But you’re still with her.”

“I won’t be if you get back with me!” he said catching me off guard. “I’m serious, Alia, I will dump her.”

I stayed silent looking out of the window at traffic. It was crazy. He was driving and I was sitting in the car with a celebrity now, not just a guy that I grew up with, but a household name and all of the females on the planet wanted this seat. He stopped at another light. “Why you get quiet on me. You don’t wanna make that happen?”

“I do. Yes I do, but I wanna get married, I don’t wanna be just your girlfriend, Anthony!”

He was smiling, just like he was when we talked at school, that same beautiful smile that melted my heart. It’s magic when a guy is gorgeous and has a nice smile.

“What, you think I’m wrong for feeling that way? I don’t want you to want me for sex and then dump me.”

“You think I’ll do you like that?” he said driving and looking around as he drove. He looked sexy with all of those tattoos on his skin; I was trying to read them; I was looking for Megan’s name and it wasn’t there. I hoped it wasn’t, he had tatts on his chest, too.

“Did you put her name on you?”

“Hell nah!” he said making me laugh.

“I’ll put yours on me. But you didn’t answer me. You think I just want you for sex?”

“I dunno. You can have any girl you want, Anthony. You’re a superstar now.”

"I couldn't care less about my fame. I love you and yes, I will marry you," he said, giving me a matter of fact stare until someone blew the horn behind us for us to go. The light was green and he sped up and maneuvered in between cars, showing off now. He could drive. I was a little nervous and Sharkey's was right up the street. I saw the big shark logo sign. He pulled up and turned in the parking lot. My stomach was growling and I was going to feel shy eating in front of him. It's like that around a cute guy, you don't wanna look like a savage eating good food.

He parked and turned off the engine and looked at me. He smiled. "What?"

"I can't believe that you're right here. It's crazy but I always wished for this day to happen. I'm not letting you slip away again, believe that. Stay put," he said climbing out of the car. I watched him walk around and then he opened the door for me. He held his hand out and I grabbed it, his touch was electrifying. He held on to my hand and wouldn't let it go. We locked fingers and I felt a little weird because he was still with that girl. Maybe I was just being overly jealous because I knew that he was mine. He held the door open for me and I walked in looking around, remembering how nice this place was. I hadn't been here in so long.

"Hey, Cheetah, wassup man," the white guy smiled, shaking his hand like they knew each other.

"Nothing much, Ralph, what's good?"

"Working hard, bro. Right this way," he said and he grabbed my hand again and this place stayed crowded. The food was so good and I'm a seafood lover. I was going to have to break out of my shyness and eat in front him this time. I didn't care, I was starving and this place was my SPOT. His phone went off and he grabbed it and looked at it and didn't answer. It had to be Megan calling him. It was ringing again. It was her; I felt her dark energy. I tried not to let it bother me. We were seated in the VIP section. I noticed people recognizing him and these two beautiful women were smiling at him as we passed them. Ralph pulled out my seat first and then Cheetah sat across from me.

"Do you drink?"

"No, I mean I like wine, but I don't drink liquor and stuff. It's nasty."

"Whuut, are you serious," he laughed. "Since I've been doing this music, I get what I want, even with me being underage, they don't trip about me drinking. I like to have a shot of Gin."

"Gin, huh, wow. They say gin makes you sin."

"It's true. It's not good for me. My aunt used to drink that stuff and it made her crazy and evil … by the way she passed away in 2000."

"Really, wait, I think I heard about that. Marisol told me that she died."

"Yeah, she had breast cancer, it was crazy because she died right in front of me. It messed me up for a minute. I was going through a lot after we broke up, Alia. You have no idea."

"I didn't know that, but I went through a lot, too. My aunt was constantly picking on me and now my uncle stands up to her too. It's like he's tired of her bullshit. Now that I'm older, she doesn't hit me like she used to."

"You're so beautiful," he said making me blush. "I was checking you out on Facebook and Myspace."

"Really? I was checking you out, too."

"You never said nothing to me."

"I was mad." I told him and the waitress came to the table and asked if she could start us off with something to drink. Anthony ordered strawberry lemonade and I asked for the same thing.

"You sure you don't want nothing else?"

"I'm sure," I said. "That's my favorite."

"Mine too," he chuckled. "So where's your mother at? You never explained why you were living with your aunt. I always wondered that."

"I did, remember? I told you that my mom was deported when I was baby."

"I slightly remember but not really. So she's in another country?"

"She's in Belize. From what my aunt told me, she didn't want any kids so she was happy to leave me, but I don't believe her. I think she's lying and when I turn eighteen, I'm going to move out of her house and go and find my mom."

"I'll help you."

I smiled and the lady came back with our drinks and Anthony was ready to order and so was I. I ordered the crab feast and he ordered the steak and lobster. After we ordered he looked at his phone after I heard it vibrate. "You should answer her."

"Why? I don't wanna talk to her. Are you serious? I'm with the girl that I've always loved and you want me to ruin my appetite and argue with her, I don't think so. I'm happy, Alia. I'm happy that I finally get to talk to you and I'm not about to mess that up."

"Why did you stay with her?"

He shrugged. "I stayed with her because she did what I wanted her to do and she was with me when my aunt died and when I was going through that heartbreak with you; she stayed with me through all of that. That's the reason why. I mean she's cool, but I'm not in love with her. I care about her but I'm not in love with her like how I feel about you."

I dropped my head in tears. He got up and slid over next to me hugging me. "Don't cry. I didn't mean to make you cry."

I buried my head in his chest and released the emotions that I had held for him. He lifted my face to his. "I do love you, Alia. I've always loved you. I want you back in my life, not just as my girl." I was trying to turn away but he held my face steady. "I do love you. I mean it from the bottom of my heart."

"Okay, prove it."

"All right! I will. I will, I promise you that. I'mma do that! I'll show you that I'm not just talking."

"We'll see. You just told me that you care about her. I'm sure you guys have been having sex, since we broke up right?"

"Yeah, we have. I can't lie, but my heart is not in it, Alia! I've cheated on her so many times."

"Who's to say that you won't cheat on me again if we get back together?"

"Just let me show you. I want you back in my life. I do, Alia. I swear to God, baby, just give me a chance and I promise you that I'mma make you happy."

"I don't care about your money and fame Anthony. I love you for YOU."

"I know that. I just want you to give me another chance to make you happy. I wanna move you out of that house with your crazy ass auntie and I'm sure your cousin Nicole is a thorn in your side."

He had that right. She was a thorn. The waitress brought our food. Oh my God everything looked so delicious. He took a picture of his plate. "Let me see," I leaned over looking at the image. It looked like a shot in a magazine. "I'mma put this on my Facebook," he said. He uploaded the image.

"What if she sees it?"

"To be honest I don't care."

His phone was ringing again and he answered it. "Wassup, my nigga, where yawl at? Is that right? I'm over here at Sharkey's, come over here, yeah, yeah, it's cool, come on … aiight, I'm in the VIP area … yeah … aiight." He hung up. "That was the homie Sneaky. He's with his girl."

"I haven't seen him in so long. How is his brother Razz?"

"He's good, still doing music. I'm about to do a collab with him for my fourth album. I got it in the car. I want you to hear it and tell me what you think."

"Okay. That's awesome you're doing well; my favorite song is 'Missing You.'"

"Yeah, everybody likes that. It went to number 1 when I first dropped it."

"Yeah, I've been listening to all of your music. I really like 'Slow Down.' I love that song."

"Yeah," he smiled. "I wrote that when I was drunk."

"Really? It's the bomb."

"Yeah, everybody likes that one too …" He cut into his lobster and passed some over to me to taste after he dipped it in butter.

"Mmmmmm, it's good," I said making him laugh. I dug into my food not being shy. I was so hungry. I closed my eyes and chewed, making him smile. He was laughing at me as I ate. "This is so bomb, I'm having a party in my mouth." HAHAHAHAHAHAHA. "That's a new one, I'mma use that."

Sneaky and a Latin girl came to the table. "ALIA? OOOH MY GOD," he laughed and I got up and hugged him.

"Hi you doing, Sneaky?" I laughed.

"I'm good, oh my God, I wasn't expecting to see you, wow!" he snickered. "This is my wife, Sylvia."

"Nice to meet you, I didn't know you were married, Sneaky, oh my God."

"Yeah, I got a son now, too. It's good to see you," he looked at Cheetah and gave him love, laughing. "Man, I know you're happy now, huh?"

"You already know, dog," he said as we all sat back down at the table. The waitress came over and Anthony told Sneaky to order what he wanted. "I got the tab, bro."

"Awww shit, good looking, I'm tapped right now, just paid my mortgage, shit," we all laughed.

"I like your earrings," Sylvia told me.

"Thank you, I love that dress you're rocking."

"Oh this is old," she said and we laughed. She was cool; I liked her energy.

“I can’t believe Alia’s here with my boy. Yawl just don’t know, Cheetah was going crazy about you, Alia. I kept trying to get him to reach out to you, but his pride got in the way.”

“I’m sure it did.”

“Aye … it’s on now,” he shook hands with Sneaky. “It’s on now, she ain’t going NO where, she’s here to stay.”

“I heard that Cheetah … aye, my boy loves you,” Sneaky said, making me feel emotional again.

We had a good time and Sylvia and I had a lot in common. She was into cake decorating and so was I. At first I thought I wanted to do music and theatre but I wanted to cook and be a chef. Sneaky and Cheetah had gotten really close, I could tell by the way they were talking and laughing and Sneaky was really a decent dude, unlike the other guys on the block. Sneaky wasn’t meant to be on the block, nor was Cheetah or Flip. They were all made to be around each other and they were.

“Aye, Alia, did Cheetah tell you about all of the places that we toured?”

“No, I bet it was nice, huh?”

“Man, we been all around the world. Germany is the bomb!” Sneaky added. “I might move out there.”

“No we’re not,” Sylvia said making us laugh. The waiter came with the check and Cheetah pulled out a credit card. It’s been so long since I’ve been around him, everything was so different and more adult like now. He matured a whole lot and I was impressed by his style and poise. He kept looking at me and it was starting all over, the love that I felt for him; it was like we picked up where we left off. His phone kept ringing and he was not answering and I knew that it was Megan calling. I'm sure she was suspicious of him being with another girl, but little did she know, it was his ex-girl that was about to be his wife! She got me fucked up if she thought that I was going to let him slip away and be with her. When he told me that he cared about her, that broke my heart, but it was my fault because I should've reached out to him.

"Yawl ready?"

"Yeah, aye Cheetah thank you, I got yawl next time."

"Aiight, I'mma hold you to that."

"Yeah, you guys need to come over and I'll cook," Sylvia offered.

We all walked outside and he grabbed my hand again and I clinched his hand tight this time and he squeezed mine, too, feeling my vibe. This is MY husband! I'm not allowing him to escape this time. It felt good being with him.

"Girl, gimmie your number," Sylvia said and I gave her my number and I reached in my purse and brought out my phone and put her number in my phone. "It was nice meeting you."

"You too, girl, we need to link up and do something."

"I know, huh, I don't really deal with too many people out here. I'm from Meza."

"Oh really?"

"Yeah, I moved out here when I got with Patrick. I want to move back, but since he's doing the stuff with Cheetah, we've ended up staying, so oh well."

"Right. I'll call you and we can link up."

"Okay, call me."

"I will chica," I said. "Sin preocupaciones."

"Oh shit, habla espanol?"

"Si, mucho…el español es mi primer idioma."

"Oh si…¿de donde eres?"

"Nací aquí pero mi familia es de Belice."

"Oh … es bueno saber que hablas español," we laughed.

"Yes."

"Hey, yawl need to cut that out. I don't speak Spanish, shit," Anthony said making us laugh.

"Aye, bro, I'm starting to understand now, being around her for so long."

"Yeah, Cheetah, you should learn it," Sylvia told him.

"Nah, I'm cool, I'm having a hard enough time remembering my own native language. I can speak Navajo and Apache tho."

"I'm going to teach him Spanish, too," I added and Sylvia laughed. Once she realized that I spoke Spanish our bond was sealed as friends.

"I'm glad my wife finally found a friend, tho," Sneaky shook Cheetah's hand and they hugged. "Aiight man, we're about to head out."

"Aiight dog, hit me up."

"Fa sho … aiight Alia, take care of my boy."

"I will," I hugged him and I hugged Sylvia again.

"Bye girl."

"Bye," I waved and Anthony let the car door up and I climbed in and he walked around I unlocked his door for him. "Thank you, sweetheart."

He climbed in with his phone buzzing again. He grabbed it and looked it. "She's hot now! Look," he said showing me the text message. "YOU ASSHOLE, YOU BETTER NOT BE WITH ALIA!"

I laughed. "How did she know you were with me?"

"Because she knows that I still love you. I never denied my feelings for you to her."

"Wow, oh well."

Headaches

I walked into Megan's room and she was on the computer looking through my Facebook. "I see you went out to fucking dinner, huh?"

"Yep, I did," I said, going to the bathroom. I should've gone home but I came here instead to talk to her to try to keep the peace.

"Who where you with?"

"My boy, Sneaky, you wanna call him and ask him?"

"No," she grunted and gave me a sideways stare with a jealous expression.

"Why you looking at me like that? You be tripping, that's why I told you before I didn't wanna be dealing with this clingy shit."

"Whatever, Cheetah, you're going to do what you wanna do anyway."

"Yep," I said, closing the bathroom door. I sent Alia a text message letting her know that I made it to the house. She didn't need to know that I was here with Megan. She probably already knew anyway. Now I was trying to figure out how to let Megan down easy. I used the bathroom and then washed my hands. I was tired and maybe I should go home, because I didn't feel comfortable being over here. I went back out into the room and she asked me,

"Were you with her?"

"Megan, don't start aiight?"

She started crying. "I know you were with her, I just have that feeling."

"Okay so you're psychic now?"

"No, but I know you were with her." She sat on the chair crying and it was getting on my nerve.

"You know what, I'mma go home."

"NOO!"

"Fuck yeah, because I don't feel like dealing with you right now. I didn't come here to argue with you."

"Just tell me the truth."

"I don't have to tell you shit! You act like I gotta explain my every move to you, like you're the fucking police or something." I frowned. She snatched my keys.

"I don't want you to leave."

I sat on the bed. "I'm trying to be better, Cheetah. I really am. We had some good times and I just feel like you're drifting away from me."

"Maybe I am."

"Why?"

"Because, I'm just tired of feeling like I gotta walk on eggshells around you. You know? I'm tired of that. Every time I go on tour, I'm arguing with you. Every fucking time man, and I'm so done with that shit!"

"What do you expect me to do, I know how fucking FINE you are, you got all these bitches rushing at you, what am I supposed to do? How am I supposed to feel? You can have any girl you want!"

"I can't handle this shit! Before you had confidence and you was able to handle it, now that we been back off tour, it's more problems."

"Because I know how you feel about Alia, Cheetah, I'm not stupid. I know you still love her. You told me."

"Okay … what does that have to do with me being right here right now?"

She was quiet. "Nothing to say, huh? You didn't have no problems breaking me and Alia up, it was cool then, now all of a sudden, you're insecure."

"You're STILL in LOVE with her!"

"MAYBE I AM! Gimmie my fucking keys!"

"Nooooo," she started crying. "I gotta show you something."

"Show me what? What you gotta show me, Megan? Gimmie my fucking keys, stop playing aiight?" I looked at her and she stormed to the bathroom and opened the drawer and came out with something in a sandwich bag. She threw it on the bed crying.

"What the fuck is that?"

"It's a pregnancy test!" she said, throwing my keys on the bed. I snatched them. I grabbed the sandwich bag and looked at it. It had a + sign in dark red ink in a display box on a stick like device. It looked like a dipstick of some sort and it was plastic and the words on the top of it read, "EPT."

"What does this mean, are you saying you're pregnant?"

She sat on the bed, “Yes, I am! I wanted to tell you this earlier but you wouldn’t answer the phone.”

“So what do you plan on doing because to be honest, I’m not ready for no kids right now! I’m only 17 years old, I just started my music career, I’m not trying to have no kids and I thought you were on the fucking pill.”

“I was, but my prescription ran out last month and I didn’t refill it.”

I wanted to grab her and choke her. “Are you fucking serious right now, Megan? HUH? Are you fucking serious?”

“I’m sorry, I didn’t mean for it to happen either, Cheetah!”

“You need to get rid of it then. I don’t want it!” I told her and she looked at me with big crocodile tears running down her face. “I don’t wanna kill my baby!”

“Oh my God! I can’t believe you’re doing this to me! I DON’T WANT NO KIDS!” I said, getting flashbacks of how Rowena did me. I wanted to slap the shit out of her, seriously.

“You can’t make me kill my baby Cheetah, that’s wrong, that’s murder!”

“So you’re going to force this baby on me when I’m not ready? You could’ve fucking told me that you needed the gotdamn birth control pills, I would’ve paid for ‘em!!!! That’s fucked up!” I yelled. I can’t tell Alia this shit. She was going to really not want to be with me now! Oh my God! I got up from the bed with my keys. “I’m outta here!”

“Wait, Cheetah!”

“No, move out my way Megan!” I looked in her eyes. “Please, just move before I hit you and I don’t hit females!”

She moved to the side and I walked out of the room. Her mother came downstairs. "Is everything okay, Cheetah?"

"No ma'am, I'm leaving," I said, walking out of the front door and I heard her crying to her mother. She tried to run outside behind me. "Cheetah, wait, please don't leave."

"Let go of me Megan, move! I need some space right now! Get off me. Don't touch me!" I said, pushing her back. She stood in the yard looking as I climbed in my car. I was so mad I could've beat that baby out of her. How the fuck did this happen? DAMN! GOTDAMMIT! I sped off, leaving smoke behind me and I could barely see the road from tears filling my eyes. It was as if Megan had Rowena's evil demon possessing her or something, trying to destroy me.

I rode back to the rez with a heavy heart. I was disgusted with myself because I should've never had unprotected sex with this girl. I couldn't trust her. She called but I wouldn't answer the phone. I didn't want to be bothered with her and she got pregnant on purpose to try to lock me in. Bitch! I hate some females, they got some fucked up ways. Chepi called me. He always seemed to call at the right time. This is why he was my favorite brother. "Hello?"

"Hey bro, where you at, you driving?"

"Yeah, I'm on my way home bro. This fucking bitch just pissed me off."

"What happened, or shall I ask what did she do now?"

"Man, she's fucking pregnant!"

"What, is it yours?"

"It's gotta be."

"Awww shit! She's trying to lock you in, huh?"

"Yep and I don't wanna be with her."

"I heard you were out with Alia today, you and Sneaky?"

"Yeah man, it was all good until I get to Megan's house and she dropped this news on me."

"Oh shit, bro! Damn. I'll see you when you get home so we can talk. I'm getting ready to walk Marisol to the car right now."

"Aiight." I ended the call. Megan was trying to call me again. I picked up.

"What?!"

"Why are you acting so mean now?"

"Stop calling me, Megan!"

"Why—"

"I don't wanna talk to you right now."

"Cheetah please—"

I ended the call. Oh man! I called Alia. I needed to hear her voice. I just needed to hear it so that I could be calm. "Hello?" she answered.

"Hey sweetheart. What you doing?"

"Laying here, listening to music. I love your album; it's bomb. I just keep playing it and my favorite song is 'Sexier than Thou.' I love that."

"I knew you would like that."

"Yes, my fav … your voice is so beautiful. I wish I could sing like that." She had me smiling.

"You miss me?"

"Yes, of course I miss you and I had a great time. Where are you?"

"Driving."

"Oh, okay. Is everything okay?"

"Somewhat. I wanna go and get you a ring."

"Awww … I like the one that you took from me and gave to HER…but nevermind."

"Nah … I want you in something saucy."

"Saucy," she laughed. "Okayyy … like what?"

"You'll see. I'mma marry you, Alia. It's going to happen. I wanna take you out of that situation that you're in and put you in a house. If you want, we can have a house built from the ground up. We can design it how you want it."

"I would love to live on the rez in a house like that."

"The rez, you don't wanna live off the rez?"

"No, I never got the opportunity to see the rez and I think it would be cool to have a nice home there."

"Oh so you want it built on the rez where I live?"

"Yes."

"Why?"

"Because it will be away from everybody in a beautiful house with a lot of land. I would like that. I always used to envision us being together in a beautiful house with green grass and pretty waterfalls all around us. I road by the reservation with Marisol and it's really pretty."

"Yeah, the rez has got some nice parts, especially for the rich Natives. Where my aunt used to live is nice and I had a house built for my parents near there too, so I think you would like it, but I thought you would wanna live off the rez."

"No, I'd rather live in a beautiful house on the rez; that way nobody can bother us."

"Okay … that makes sense and if that's what you want, we can make it happen."

"I hope you're not just talking."

"I'm not, Alia. I really want that. I do love you, I told you that," I said, turning on the rez. "I missed you so much and thought about you every single day. Most of my songs are about you."

"Yeah, I can tell."

"I'm sure you can. Can I see you tomorrow?"

"Yeah. I have to work tho. When I get off work?"

"What time do you get off work?"

"I get off at noon. I gotta be in early and then I get off at noon."

"Aiight, I'll be over there to pick you up."

"Okay, that will be nice. I won't have to walk home in the heat."

"Oh hell nah. I'mma be right there."

"Okay."

"Can I call you tomorrow," I asked as I pulled up at my parents' house.

"Yep … call me."

"I will. I love you, Alia." I told her and she was silent.

"I love you, too," she said and it gave me butterflies. I ended the call feeling emotional for a few moments before Chepi came and got in the Lamborghini. I was glad that my parents had a better house. I had my own room here. My mom was happy and she wasn't drinking like she used to. She had a reason not to be because my dad was finally home every day.

"Sup bro," he said, passing the blunt to me to light. I fired it up. As soon as I hit it, I was coughing.

"Damn," I coughed and blew out the smoke. "Where you get that from?"

"Daniel had the hook up. Him and Marcus be having the plug."

"That's some good shit right there," I wiped my watering eyes. I passed it to him. He hit it and started coughing, too.

"So, she's pregnant, huh?"

"Man. This bitch is trying to trap me, bro. I don't wanna be with her and I don't want no kids by her."

"What are you going to do? You can't make her get rid of it."

"I wish I could. I swear I do. I almost wanna pay her fifty thousand to get rid of it, but she ain't gone do it."

"Did you offer it to her?"

"Nah, you think I should?"

"Hell yeah, I would. I know you're not going to tell Alia are you?"

"I wanna tell her, I don't wanna lie to her but if she gets rid of it, there would be no need."

"Man I wouldn't tell Alia shit, bro."

"Why not?"

"Because remember when you told her that you fucked Megan and she left you?"

"Yeah."

"What if she does it again? I mean shit, being honest got your heart broke."

"That's true. But I can't lie to her, man. I love her too much. I told her tonight that I wanna marry her."

"You should marry her first before you tell her. Get her to sign prenup."

"Nah man … I don't wanna make her do that. Alia's a good girl, man. She's who I want my kids by. Now if she was pregnant that would be different."

"You really love her don't you?"

"I told you that I do."

"Well you know dad is going to make you get a prenup if you marry her."

"I'm not doing that with Alia. As soon as I turn eighteen in August, I'm gonna marry her. I'mma offer that bitch Megan money to get rid of the kid. I don't care if it's a million, I'mma see if she'll do it and I'mma go with her to make sure."

"She might not do it, bro. These bitches are fucked up like that."

"FUCK man … uggh, I hate that I fucked her raw. I really do! I know I was lit on the Gin bro, that's why I hit it raw."

"I know, you gotta leave that firewater alone. Just go try to make that offer and if she takes the money, take her and sit there with her ass until she comes out."

"Hold on," I said, calling Megan's number. She answered.

"Aye wassup?" I was high off the weed and it made me calm.

"Hey …"

"I was just thinking, if I gave you fifty thousand, would you have an abortion? I swear I would pay you."

"FUCK NO!" she yelled. "I'm not killing my fucking baby! Are you crazy?"

"I don't want no kids, Megan. Why are you trying to force me to be a dad?"

"You don't have to take care of my kid, I don't give a fuck, but I'm not getting rid of it, I don't care if you offered me a million dollars," she said and I hung up on her. I looked at Chepi, he shook his head. "You hear this bitch?"

"Yep. Damn, dog! Shit!"

"I fucking hate that bitch man! I swear to God, I fucking hate her dumb ass."

She called me back, I answered. "What!"

"You have the fucking audacity to offer me money to get rid of my baby? How dare you! Are you fucking around with Alia again?"

"Yes. I wanna be with her and I told you that I still love her! So I'm getting back with her since you wanna know so much."

"I KNEW IT...FUCK YOU, CHEETAH!" She hung on me this time.

"Damn bro, you got a lot on your plate."

"Fuck it, she wanted to know, there it is! I'm tired of her anyway. The only thing that she can do is suck dick; that's all she's good at. We don't get along, she's constantly up my ass about shit and she makes me miserable."

"I knew you weren't into her, bro. You don't have to tell me, all those bitches you were fucking on the road."

"Yep. I mean, she's cool as far as being a friend but I didn't want no kids by her and she's forcing me into being something that I'm not ready for … at least not with her. I loved Alia from day one, since I was 13, bro. My heart ached the whole time I was away from her."

"Yeah, you ain't gotta tell me, I know."

"Now this bitch wants to make my life miserable."

"Just calm down bro. Take it easy, maybe she might decide to do what you want. She knows that she's not going to be with you now, so who knows?"

Megan showed up at my parents' house at seven-thirty in the morning. My mom knew something was up when she popped up so early. I could hear them talking downstairs and my mom wouldn't let her come up to my room, which I was glad because I didn't want to be bothered with Megan. She called my phone. I just let it ring. "Megan, he's asleep, just come back later."

"I really need to talk to him, Lora, please."

"He's asleep, I don't wanna wake him up," I heard my mom.

She kept trying to call my phone. This bitch was crazy. Fuck it! I got up and slipped on my sliders and went to see what the hell she wanted. "What? Why are you over here bugging my mom? Go lay down, Mom, I'll deal with her."

"Cheetah, your dad is still asleep."

"I know, I'mma take her outside." I told my mom and we went out in the backyard.

"Wassup, Megan?"

"I wanna know why you're leaving me for her? Why now? You didn't want to break up until you found out that I was pregnant."

"No, that's not true, I came to break up with you last night before you told me about the pregnancy. Then you dropped this bomb on me and expect me to be happy with it. I'm not okay? I asked you to get an abortion, I even offered to give you money and I'm still willing to do it."

"I'M NOT KILLING MY BABY!" she yelled.

"Lower your damn voice, my parents are trying to sleep!"

"This is bullshit, Cheetah! You're so fucked up! You're selfish!"

"How am I selfish? I'm telling you what I don't want and you're trying to force me to take what I don't want! How is that selfish? I'm being honest with you."

"You should've thought about that when you were fucking without a condom, Cheetah! You didn't bother to pull out, did you?"

I sighed. "You lied about the birth control. If you would've kept it real I would've never had to worry about shit, right? You're the one that's selfish, like you always been. You forced yourself on me, when you knew that I had a girl and you sent me those naked pictures, throwing your pussy in my face. You burned me with a fucking STD after you fucked my homeboy and now you're telling me that I'm selfish. I should've fucked and dumped yo ass four years ago, but I let you stay in my life. Now you wanna try to force me to stay with you when I'm miserable?"

She started crying and it made me feel bad, especially to see girls cry. I felt sorry for her but I wasn't going to throw Alia away. This was my only chance. "All I tried to do was love you, Cheetah, and I stayed with you because you said that you needed me as a friend and I stayed down for you because I told you that I was willing to do anything for you. I tried to make you feel love again, but you only used me!"

"You used me too, so I guess we're even now!"

"I never used you!"

"You're older than me anyway. We should've never been together, Megan. I was only thirteen years old and you took advantage of me."

"Oh" She chuckled. "Now you wanna play the victim. All those bitches you were fucking on the road were way older than you too, yeah right Cheetah. You wanna get rich and famous and then drop me like a bad habit. You're going to pay for this kid. You're going to pay me child support asshole!" She said going to her car. She climbed in and slammed the door. She started the car and sped off at top speed and I looked up at my parents' bedroom window and saw my mom looking. I threw up my hands and went back in the house. My mom came downstairs with a coffee cup in her hand. "So is she pregnant?"

"Yep! I don't want it and she's forcing me to have it. She lied to me about the birth control pills, Mom."

"Cheetah, you can't do her like that. I love Megan, she's a sweetheart."

"Mom, I'm not happy with Megan. I'm not in love with her."

"She's such a sweet girl. Don't do her like that. If that baby is yours, that's going to be my first grandchild."

"You're only saying that because you know the sweet side. She's messy, Mom. She gave me an STD." My mom's face dropped. "Yeah, you didn't know that, but she gave me VD and I had Dad take me to the E.R. to clear it up. She slept around with a lot of dudes mom, you don't know the other side of her. I was really sick behind that STD, shit had me throwing up…and she's only manipulating you to be with me mom, don't fall for it. She burned me and then she went back and told Alia and that's why she broke up with me. I love Alia, Mom, and that's who I wanna be with. My heart has always been with Alia, ever since I was 13. That's who I'm in love with."

"Wow! Oh my God. So what are we going to do about this kid? She's going to sue you for child support and drag this thing into the media. You're famous now; you don't need this."

"I know, Mom, just let me handle it."

"You need to talk to your dad about this. I'm sure he can get you a good lawyer. This is so crazy. Why didn't you use protection?"

"Because she said she was still on the pill and I was drinking mom. I don't even know why I'm telling you my business but that's what happened aiight?"

"Oh God! These women lie and she knew that you were going to be making a ton of money so of course she's going to stick you with a kid. I just hope that I can see my grandchild."

My mom was flipping out and I had to calm her down. "Just let me handle it, Mom, don't start getting worked up about my life."

"Cheetah, you're so young," she said, washing her cup out. "You got plenty of time to be falling in love. You have your music career in front of you, that's all you need is a kid on top of it. She's still living at home with her parents. How is she going to raise a kid at home with her parents?"

"I know. I wanna be with Alia."

"You have to deal with this one first, right?"

"No! I don't have to deal with her. I wanna be with who I love and I'm not trying to hear nothing else, Mom. I wanna be with Alia."

"Okay, Cheetah. You're going to learn the hard way."

"What about you? Didn't you get with dad when you were my age?"

"It was different back then."

I smacked my lips and looked at my mom, what was the difference when she was the same age as me. "You were seventeen when you and dad got together; you got pregnant with Mike and you got married to Dad and did you listen to your mom?"

"Sweetheart, I know that you love this other girl; I wish I could meet her."

"I'll bring her over after she gets off work."

"How old is she?"

"She's my age, Mom; we're the same age. Megan was older than me."

"What? I thought Megan was your age. That's what she told me."

"She lied, she's almost twenty-one."

"Oh my God! Well shit, she can handle being a mom then."

"See … I'mma bring Alia over here."

"Well you better hope Megan doesn't show up because I don't need these problems with these girls fighting on my property."

"It won't happen. I'mma bring Alia so you can meet her. She's way different from Megan, she has a job and she's goes to PVA like me."

"Oh really?"

"Yeah, that's Nicole's cousin."

"Marcus's girlfriend, Nicole?"

"Yep."

"How long have you known her?"

"Since I was 13, Mom. I told you. I was with her first. That's my first love."

"She must be your first love with the way you're sounding."

"Yep … I never had sex with her tho. She's a virgin and she's a good girl."

"Oh good! I'm glad to hear that," my mom sighed and sipped her coffee. "She might not be for long dealing with you." My dad came out of the room. "You need to talk to your dad."

"I will … I'm going to take a shower."

After my shower, I went to the kitchen and my mom had breakfast on the table, and she expressed how glad she was that all of her kids were at home for once, since it had been a while. I was always gone or we were gone on tour and my brothers were with me. Everyone was at the table and it was a great feeling to be in a newly built home with my family and not having to worry about the cost of anything or stuff breaking down. It was nice to know what we had more than enough food to eat and my sister wasn't crying about being hungry.

"Mom, can my friend come over?" Elina asked.

"What friend, I hope it ain't a guy," I said and she grinned and looked at my mom.

"It is a guy."

"Who is it?"

"None of your business, Mom. Make Cheetah stay out of my business."

"That's all right, I'll see who it is when he shows up."

"Nooo, Mom."

"Cheetah, she's old enough to date."

"Oh my God are you serious, she's only sixteen."

"I'm about to be seventeen in September so stop hating."

"So what, who is it? Do I know him?"

"No … and he's a nice person."

My dad snickered and flipped over his newspaper. "Dad, I need to talk to you," I said, getting up from the table. My other brothers got up, too. We took our plates to the sink and each one of us washed our dish out. My mom kept this place spotless as she promised that she would once it was built. I wanted to get to a level where I could hire housekeepers for her to have help. I was going to get there.

"Aye, Cheetah you wanna work on some music, bro?"

"I can't today, I'm going to get Alia. She's about to be off in thirty minutes," I told Cochise.

"Aiight, well come and mess with me when you have the time. I have some more beats that I want you to hear for the album."

"OH for sure."

I met my dad in the den. "What's going on, Son?"

"Megan's pregnant and I don't want it. I wanna be with Alia. Do you think I should tell her?"

"Wow … uuuh, if you like her, yes, you should tell her. What about the other girl, are you going dump her?"

“It’s already done, Dad. I didn’t love her like that.”

“Is she planning on keeping the baby?”

“I can’t make her get rid of it. But I’m kind of scared to tell Alia because the last time that I was honest with her about cheating on her, she broke up with me.”

“Yeah, I remember that. Well son … you can’t lie to her if you love her.”

“I do love her, Dad, I wanna put a ring on this one.”

“Oh wow, that serious huh? … what about a prenup? I think you should put one in place. You know a lot of these girls only want to be with rich and famous men for the money.”

“Yeah but she’s not like that, Dad. I’ve been knowing her since she was 13 before I got into this music game; she’s nothing like Megan. Megan is a golddigger.”

“Well, you know I’ll stand by you with whatever you want to do, but you better be careful with Megan.”

“I wanted to tell you that I need a lawyer for her. She’s already talking about suing me for child support.”

“Well you need to establish paternity first. Make her give you a DNA.”

“Yeah. I just need an attorney on standby.”

“Okay, I’ll make it happen for you. Just be careful, Son.”

“So you think I should tell her?”

“Yes, tell her.”

“Aiight. I’mma bring her over so you and Mom can meet her. Tell me what you think.”

"Okay."

I left and headed out to pick Alia up and Megan called my phone. "Hello?"

"Wassup? I called your bitch!"

"What are you talking about?"

"I called Alia and I let that bitch know that I better not see her or I'm going to fuck her up!"

I hung up on Megan. Now she was talking stupid. I didn't want to be bothered with that. In fact, I blocked her number from my phone. I wanted to make today the last day that I talked to her. If she's going to have this kid, I wanted to wait until it was born before I said anything else to her. I was going to have to tell Alia and just pray that she would understand and still allow me to be in her life. If she really loved me then I was sure she'd understand that it's not the baby's fault. I was going to the doctor to get checked just to make sure that I was safe also because at this point, it was no telling what Megan was up to and I wanted Alia to be safe.

I made it to her job five minutes before she was about to get off work and unfortunately I saw Novi strolling across the street. That didn't sit well with me at all seeing him moving towards her job. I climbed out of the car and he saw me. He stopped walking and screamed out my name like an idiot. The car stood out as it was and here this fool was screaming out my name. I put a finger to my lips and he laughed, thinking that it was comical to put me out on the front line in a bad neighborhood. Alia stepped out of the store and her smile lit up the block. The first thing I did was put her in the passenger's seat and Novi's eyes grew wide as if he weren't expecting what he just saw.

"Wassup man," I shook his hand.

"Aww wow, I didn't expect to see you on the block bro … what's good?"

"Nothing much, just here to pick her up."

"Yawl cool again?"

"More than cool, we're back together."

"Really? Wow … that's what's up man congratulations, I knew you guys were meant for each other, that's cool."

"Yep, that's my baby, but what's been up with you, where you on your way to?"

"I was just on my way up there to make sure she got home safe bro, that's all."

"Right, it's cool," I patted his shoulder. "I got it from here on. Thank you."

"No problem, Cheetah, when are you going to put me on one of your tracks?"

"You made a dis record about me and now you want me to put you on," I laughed. "Man, you got jokes."

"It was just a fun song, bro, no hard feelings man."

"Hmm … hit me up tomorrow," I told him, not really about to deal with him at all because I didn't trust him, I just told him that to move him out of the way.

"Aiight, Cheetah you got the same number?"

"Yep," I lied. We shook and I moved around to the driver's side of my car.

"I love the lambo, Cheetah, that's you all day. That's FRESH."

"Yeah, thanks. Hit me up," I said and closed the door down. I looked at Alia.

"Sorry, I didn't know he was coming," she said.

"Don't worry about it. You're not going to be working here anymore."

"You're right. I got a call for an interview at the library in Paradise Valley. We did a phone interview and they hired me, I start on Monday."

"Wow, that's good. You really wanna work there?"

"Yes, I applied for that job almost a month ago and they finally called me. I wanna work there. That job is paying good money."

I drove off and Novi was watching with lowered eyes that didn't look as friendly as the fake side of him that I saw when I pulled up. He looked like he was pissed. "Are you hungry?"

"Yes. I'm starving."

"You wanna get something fast or sit down and eat?"

"We can get something fast, I have a taste for a burger anyway. Whataburger?"

"Yeah, aiight, they have a drive thru," I said and I drove her to the other side of town to the burger spot on Indian School Road. It was out of the way but I wanted to spend as much time with her as possible. "So have you thought about what I said to you yesterday?"

"Yeah I did. I'm just wondering about your situation."

"What do you mean?"

"You and Megan, are you planning to break that off?"

"I told her last night that I wanted to be with you. I broke it off with her and she's pissed off, but I told her that I wanted to get back with you."

She was smiling but tried to conceal it. "I wanna move slow, Anthony."

"I know and I'm okay with that, as long as we're together. I don't wanna lose you again, Alia."

She was silent as we moved through town and I wondered what she was thinking about. I was curious so I asked.

"I'm just taking it all in, kind of shocked that you broke up with her so fast."

"Actually I've wanted to break up with her for a while now. I wasn't happy. I told her that I wasn't happy."

"Well, you know she called me early this morning and Nicole brought the phone to me while I was getting dressed for work and she went off on me telling me that she was going to kick my ass if she saw me with you … I told her to bring it because I'm ready."

"Nah, I don't want you fighting and she called me and told me that she talked to you. I don't want you fighting with her, Alia. I'm going to be with you."

"Did you tell her that?"

"Listen," I said, turning into the parking lot of the burger spot. It was a lot of cars in the drive thru. I pulled behind a white Toyota Prius. I took out my phone. I dialed Megan's number after I unblocked it. I put the phone on speaker. "Just listen, okay? Don't say nothing."

"Okay," she said.

"Hello?"

"Megan?"

"Yeah, Cheetah, wassup? Did you finally come to your senses now?"

"Actually, I'm calling you to let you know that I'm with Alia right now and this is who I wanna be with. So all that calling her and making threats can stop."

She laughed, "You got me fucked up, Cheetah, you and her both, okay?"

"How is that, I'm keeping it real with you. She wanted to know if I was serious about leaving you alone and I wanted her to hear this firsthand with you on speaker."

"Oh so you got me on speaker so the bitch can hear our conversation?"

"Uh I'm not a bitch, Megan, and I'm not scared of you. I want my man back and I got him! So back the fuck off, okay?"

"BITCH, FUCK YOU did he tell you that I—"

I ended the call once she got loud and started cursing. "Why did you hang up on her?"

"Because I wanted to talk to you about something and I hope it doesn't change anything."

"What, she's pregnant?" The look Alia gave me made me feel like lying to her, but instead, I admitted it and told her the truth. She started breathing fast like she wanted to cry.

"I didn't mean for it to happen. She lied to me about her birth control pills."

"That's if she even took them. I don't believe she's pregnant, I think she's using this to keep you away from me."

"No, she's really pregnant, I saw the test. She took the test and I'm trying to get her to have an abortion."

"No, Anthony … don't make her do that."

"I don't wanna lose you again, Alia."

"You're not! I'm not going anywhere. I don't care if she is pregnant. I let her run me off the first time but I'm not going to lose you again either, Anthony! I'm hurt because I don't want her to have your first kid, but hey," she paused getting emotional and I reached over and hugged her.

"Please don't leave me, babe."

"I'm not leaving you. I love you and I wanna get married."

"We will. I already told my parents about you. They wanna meet you."

"Really?"

"Yep. After we leave here we can go on the rez, unless you have something to do."

"No, I can go."

"Okay, thank you for being understanding."

"Thank you for telling me the truth. When you told me the truth about sleeping with her, I should've accepted it and stayed with you. You're honest and I appreciate that. I guess I wanted you to lie to me but it would've did me more harm."

"Alia, I been through a lot and at that time, I was going through some fucked up changes in my life. Do you remember my aunt, that I told you about that died?"

"Yes."

"She started molesting me when I was nine years old."

She gasped, getting tears in her eyes. "Really, oh my God, Anthony."

"Yeah…" I said, wiping my own tears away. "She stole my innocence and I was angry, going through a lot of emotional stuff. I wanted to kill myself but Novi, Mitch and Marcus found me on my thirteenth birthday and brought me on the block and that's when I met you. Ever since then, I wanted to live and you made me so happy."

"Wow," she whispered.

"Nobody's ever made me feel the way that you make me feel and I feel like we have a lot in common. My aunt didn't molest me but she abused me."

"Yeah, your aunt was fucked up too. Damn babe."

"I'm so sorry. I had no idea you went through that, why didn't you tell me?"

"I didn't want to tell nobody. All I knew was music and I just wanted to escape and then here comes Megan, showing me the naked pictures and she's older than me and it was like I was being molested again by her. My aunt got pregnant by me, too, but she lost the baby when she became ill with cancer."

"Wow, oh my God. That's crazy, does anybody in your family know about this?"

"No! You're the only person that knows."

"Wow, Anthony! That's fucked up. That's so fucked up," she said crying. We made it to the window and I ordered us burger specials. I let the window up and drove behind the Toyota.

"I'm not going anywhere, I'm staying in your life this time. I wanna be with you."

"I wanna be with you, too. I feel like we're meant to be together."

"Me too. When we broke up, I couldn't stop thinking about you or crying, I felt like I had a hole in my heart. I cried everyday for four years over you, people thought I was crazy but I did."

"ME TOO. I did, too, I swear. It was like a big void in my heart. I cried through my music."

"Wow! I was so jealous when I saw the pictures of you and Megan."

"Yeah, I did that to make you jealous, I was hurt. I missed you so much and I asked Marisol about you all the time."

"I can't believe your aunt did that to you. I'm sitting here in shock, literally. Wow!"

"Yeah ... and when she was dying, she explained why she was the way that she was. She got molested too by her father, who was the chief on the rez. He had a lot of money and when he died, he left her all of his money. She was buying me stuff and having sex with me at the same time. She had me eating her pussy and having full-fledged sex with her. It was crazy."

"Oh my God, that's fucking SICK and disgusting. She should've gone to jail for that. You should've told someone."

"I know, but I wanted to kill myself until I met you. Once I met you, I started having stuff to look forward to. I had a rough life, Alia.

It's a cop on the rez that threatened to kill me when I turn eighteen. It's crazy cos I seen him last year and he was like, 'One more year, nigger.'"

"Oh my God. He's still a cop?"

"Yep … but I got money now, so I'm thinking about talking to my grandfather and have him removed off the force."

"YES, Anthony do that! He's racist, get him off the force. If you can do it!"

Alia makes me happy and I had to open up and tell her what happened to me because I wanted to let her in on everything about me. She accepted Megan being pregnant and it hurt her but she was still willing to stand by my side. After we ate our food, I drove her to the mall in Phoenix. I didn't waste no time. I wanted to spend the rest of my life with her and I knew that now. We went to the jewelry store and I let her pick out the ring that she wanted. I wouldn't let her get anything simple, I wanted her to have a nice size diamond. She is so sensitive and when she picked out the ring, she looked at me with tears in her eyes. "I can't believe this is happening, oh my God." She covered her face and I held her because I wanted her to know that it was real and very real at that. They sized the ring to fit her finger. I bought her a four-karat diamond.

"I'm going to upgrade it on our first-year anniversary," I told her and the jeweler and people in the store cheered us on. We left in a hurry because people were starting to recognize me and I learned after the first year of becoming famous that people will attack you, not in a bad way but in a fanatical way and I didn't want Alia going through that.

We drove back to the rez. She kept saying, "I don't believe this, it's a like a dream. You're going to be my husband."

"Yes and I want it to happen fast, I don't wanna wait. I'm going to be going on tour in two months so I want you to be my wife before then."

"So you're going on tour in August?"

"Yep … at the end of August."

"Oh wow, I won't be eighteen until October."

"I know, we'll have to get your aunt to sign for you to marry me. Do you think she'll do it?"

Alia's facial expression lead me to believe that she wasn't sure if her aunt would do it.

"Maybe I can be emancipated because I have a job and I will have to file the paperwork with the courts and see if they'll allow it."

"Let's just see if she says no first. I don't want you to have to go through all of that. If we have to, we'll wait until I get back from tour."

She didn't like that; she wanted to get married right away just like I did. I didn't put the ring on her finger yet. I wanted her to meet my parents first. It took us thirty minutes to get to the rez and when we got there, Alia was excited about seeing where I grew up. She liked everything that she set her eyes on and it was amazing to see her delight about being here on the reservation. It was nothing happy about this place but for her it was the best thing in the world. She appreciated little stuff and that's what makes her so amazing. She was happy and when we got to my parents' house she fell in love with the house and the land around it. "See, I told you, I want something like this, Anthony."

"Okay … after we get married, I'mma make it happen."

“Over here, I wanna be here. Oh my God, this is so peaceful looking and beautiful.”

“Yep, we probably won’t be right here; we might be down the road.” I helped her out of the car and we hugged. She laid her head on my chest and it was the best feeling in the world. I got chills and butterflies at the same time. When separated from each other’s arms we went inside and everybody was home to my surprise. Marcus was there with Alia’s cousin, who looked shocked when she saw us walk through the door hand in hand. Nicole’s smile faded because I wasn’t with her best buddy. I had my wifey on my arm.

“Mom?!” I yelled. “Where’s Mom?”

“In the den. Wassup, Alia? Long time no see,” Marcus said, hugging her.

“Heyyyy how are you Marcus?”

“I’m good, I’m good … are you guys back together?”

“That’s right,” I told my brother. “For good.” I felt the jealousy vibe from her cousin. She was best friends after all with Megan but I didn’t care. I took Alia in the den and my mom and dad were in there watching television. “Hey Mom, hey Dad, this is Alia. I wanted you guys to meet her.”

“Oh hello, I’m Lora and this is my husband Raymond.”

“Nice to meet you both ma’am,” Alia shook hands with them.

“Oh don’t call me ma’am; you make me feel old.”

“You are old, Mom.”

“Shut up, Cheetah,” she laughed. “Don’t listen to him. Would you like something to drink?”

“Oh no, thank you, I’m full. We ate before we came by.”

“I see. So where do you live?”

“Mom, this is Nicole’s cousin; she lives with her.”

“Oh, okay.”

“And she got another job at the library in Paradise Valley.”

“Oh how nice; that’s great. You go to PVA as well, huh?”

“Yes ma’am, although I’m not really into music like your son. I do love art, basically behind the scenes. I like to write.”

“That’s great,” Mom said and my dad gave me a thumbs up without her noticing it. That made me happy. I knew that they would like Alia; she’s like night and day to Megan. I pulled out the ring. “Mom, Dad, I wanted you guys to be witnesses to this,” I said opening the box and Alia covered her face and started crying. It almost made me cry seeing her beautiful face. “Alia, I wanted to ask you in front my parents if you would marry me.”

“YES! Oh my God YES!” she said, and I slid the ring on her finger and she hugged me, crying.

“Awww, you guys are going to make me cry,” my mom stood up, wiping her eyes. My dad had it on film from his camera phone.

“Did you get everything, Dad?”

“I did,” he laughed. “Congratulations, Son, I hope you stay happy.”

“Oh for sure, I know I will,” I said, hugging my fiancé.”

My brother Marcus and Nicole came in the den. “What did I miss?” Marcus looked at me and I held up Alia’s hand showing off the big diamond on her finger.

Nicole's mouth dropped open. "Oooh cousin, oh my God. Come here, girl," she grabbed Alia's arm and they stepped out of the den. This was the first time she said anything to Alia and they weren't on the best of terms, but she was talking now.

"Bro … are you sure you wanna do this?"

"Yes, Marcus. That's my love right there. Yes, I'm going to marry her."

"Wow, bro. You just dumped Megan."

"So what? You know my heart wasn't in it with her."

He nodded with his lips folded down as if he wanted me to stay with Megan, but fuck that. Megan forced herself on this family and I was about to change that.

"Cheetah, as long as you're happy I'm happy," Dad said. The rest of my brothers came in the den and my mom told them that Alia and I were engaged.

"What?" Steven looked with wide eyes. "Bring your ass here!" he said making me laugh. He already told my parents that he was gay and they accepted it. He thought they wouldn't but they did. "Cheetah what are you doing," he asked me after we moved to the kitchen.

"I'm going to marry her."

"Okay, when did yawl get back together because I thought you were with Megan?"

"No, brother. It's over between us; we broke up."

"When, last night?" he said making me laugh. "I mean c'mon now, I'm trying to wrap my head around all this."

“Bro, I’ve always loved Alia, you know that. We got back together and I’m about to marry her.”

“You know you need a prenup right? All of sudden yawl back together after you become rich and famous?”

“No, she’s the one that broke up with me bro, I messed up. I cheated on her and broke her heart. When I cheated on her with Megan, Megan gave me an STD and Alia found out about it.”

“Wait, wait, wait … what kind of fucking STD?”

“Nothing that couldn’t be cured, bro. I got it cleared up.”

“Oh my God … okay … you’re about to be eighteen; you’re young. I hope you know what you’re doing. Are you going to get a prenup? Does dad know about this?”

“Yes and we already talked about the prenup.”

“And she’s willing to sign one?”

“No, I’m not going to make her sign one. I love her.”

He sighed and looked at me sideways. “Bro, you really—”

“Steven, I love her, that’s it! I’m not making you do that with Ryan. You made your decision to be with him and love him and nobody sweated you for it.”

“Yes I’m not marrying him either. At least not yet, until it’s legal.”

“If it does become legal and when you do marry him, I’ll be supportive of your decision. I just wanna be happy; that’s it.”

“Okay … if you know what you’re doing, okay. Just don’t be coming up with no babies no time soon.”

“Megan is pregnant.”

“WHUT?!” he shouted and I laughed.

"Alia already knows."

"Okay I'm so done with you right now," he said leaving me and I went and peeped out in the backyard. Alia came to me. "Sorry, babe. We were talking."

"Don't be trying to put no crazy stuff in my girl's head, Nicole." I teased and she laughed. "We just made up, she was mad at me and that's my blood, I'm not going to be doing her like that."

"Okay, because once we get married she's gone have my last name."

"Congratulations, Cheetah, I'm glad you guys are back together."

"I am, too, thank you."

Yeah right! She was a hater just like Novi and Megan. She didn't want to see Alia happy. And she didn't want to see her and me together but I didn't care, I was happy and I pulled Alia inside with me and took her to meet Steven and my other brothers and sister. My sister said she remembered her from the show at PVA. "You were in the front row with us right?"

"Yes, you remember," Alia laughed. My sister received her well and I was happy about that.

I took Alia to the movies, on a triple date, Marisol and Chepi, and Sneaky and Sylvia. We all went to see "Kill Bill." It was the type of movie that kept you interested because Uma Thurman was smashing in the movie and I was into action movies like this. After the movie we went to the waterfalls and smoked weed and chilled out with each other. I hadn't had this much fun since I was younger. This was something that I had been dreaming of doing and here it was.

"I don't wanna go home," Alia said, leaning back in my arms as we sat on the cliff watching the waterfalls. It was the best scene in the world, especially to see the moon out so bright and all the stars in the sky; it was like a painting. Arizona has some beautiful scenery especially with the mountains as a backdrop.

"You don't have to go if you don't want to."

"I do and I wanna ask my aunt if she would be willing to sign the papers for us to get married."

"Well we have to go and get the marriage license first. I'm going to have my dad sign for me."

"Yeah, I don't know if she's going to do it," Alia whispered feeling the worry all of a sudden.

"Don't worry about it right now, babe, let's just enjoy tonight."

She kissed me, catching me off guard. We started kissing and I had butterflies that started in my stomach and ended up all over my body. My entire existence was electrified and I felt the hairs on my skin standing up and even on the back of my neck. No girl has ever made me feel like this. My stomach kept quivering and the way she made her lips touch mine was as if she knew how much pressure to apply against my lips. I got excited and my erection grew and I had to stop and hug her. It was throbbing like the beat of my heart. Oh my God. Nobody has ever made me feel like that and I thought I would have an orgasm. "I love you." I whispered in her ear.

"I love you too … you made my whole body tingle," she said and all I could do was smile because I was feeling the same way.

"Aye, Cheetah, we're going to get going; it's getting late," Sneaky told me and Marisol and Chepi were up right behind them. Alia and I weren't ready to leave; we wanted to chill and enjoy each other's company.

"Aiight, bro," I shook hands with both Sneaky and Chepi and gave the ladies hugs before they all left.

Alia sighed, smiling. "This is so beautiful. I want this to be our spot."

"Yeah? Okay, if you want it to be like that, we can make it our spot."

"Yes, I like this area. I've never been here before and I didn't know that this place existed. Thank you for bringing me here."

"You're welcome. Steven told me about this spot. I didn't know about it either until he brought me here and I've written a lot of songs over here."

"Wow, that's so cool. I wish I had your talent," she giggled and I kissed her again, since we were alone, I just wanted to take advantage of her kisses and the way she was making me feel. She had me throbbing again; I was right on the verge of coming, I swear; it was amazing.

I looked in her eyes. "I hope your aunt signs those papers."

"Me too."

We hung out for another hour before we headed back to her place for me to drop her off. I didn't want her to go home either; I wanted to spend the night with her, but that wasn't going to happen. When we got to her house, the lights were on and she said, "Nicole is home, that's a first."

"I don' t really care for your cousin. I don't like how they treated you."

"Yeah, she claimed that she wants to start a clean slate, and she apologized for the way that she treated me, but I think it's all a front. I don't trust her."

"I don't either and just be careful what you say to her because she might go back and tell her best friend."

"Oh trust me, I know better now. I'm not falling for the dumb stuff anymore. She was on the ring too, talking about how gorgeous it was and how she hopes that Marcus marries her."

"I can tell you right now that my brother is not gonna marry her."

"She thinks because she's light skinned that she can get whatever she wants."

"Please, skin color doesn't have anything to do with it. I'mma miss you tho," I whispered and looked in her beautiful gray eyes."

"I'mma miss you too."

"Can I have a———

She kissed me and I swear to god, her lips were like a vacuum seal on my tongue.

Unfuck Me.

By July 8 Anthony had the documents for us to get married and all my aunt needed to do was sign the papers. This was going to be a challenge because it seemed like since Anthony and I got back together, people didn't want to see us happy. His brother Steven wanted him to get a prenup for me to sign and I had no problem signing one, but Anthony didn't want to do that. I had issues with Nicole hating now and her best friend was always calling her, talking shit about me. I wanted to fight but she wouldn't come over to make it happen. I'm sure she wanted to protect that baby she had inside of her, which she'd better because at this point, my love for Anthony had deepened and I wasn't going to let Megan ruin it. I was going to show her how I got down this time and I think Nicole told her not to fight me because I had kicked Nicole's ass a few months ago and it changed her attitude towards me. I had to learn how to fight and it earned me my respect from her and her mama. I had started taking boxing classes since I had my job at the liquor store and Roy's brother was teaching me how to box and do some martial arts, so I knew how to defend myself quite well and I was going to demonstrate some of my moves on Megan if she came for me.

I waited until I was off work to present the marriage license paperwork to my aunt. Anthony was going to come over with a notary to get the documents signed. I just hoped everything went well. Nicole was acting funny ever since she saw that Cheetah and I were engaged to get married; she was jealous and she tried to hide it but it was seeping out. She felt that Marcus should've asked her to marry him since they had been together longer, but Marcus wasn't ready to get married. I don't know why she was comparing her life to mine anyway.

I clocked out of work at the library and Sylvia called right as I was going to the parking lot to meet Anthony. He was right there, on his phone. "Hey girl, you caught me just as I'm getting off work."

"Oh okay … call me when you get home, I wanted to show you some wedding dresses that I found online for cheap."

"Okay, cool, I'll do that."

"Okay."

Anthony was out of the car; we kissed and he opened the car door for me. People were walking by looking. They recognized him. We got the hell out of there quickly and he turned the music down. "I got the notary on standby, so let's hope that your aunt is willing to sign the papers."

"I know; I pray that she does."

"Me too … how was your day?"

"It was good; it was kind of busy so it made time go by fast."

“Yeah, I’m glad that we’re out of school now, it makes things a lot easier for me. I’ve been in the studio all day working on music. My album is almost finished.”

“Good. I’m glad of that.”

“And my dad hired the guy to do the draft work on the house. So pretty soon babe, we’ll be having our house built. I just wanna see the plans once he’s done. It cost me ten thousand just for him to do the plans.”

“Wow, that’s a lot of money.”

“It’s okay, because in the end it will all be worth it.”

All I wanted to do was get married first and that would be one less worry. He took me to get food and I had a taste for a hotdog. I wanted it all day and when we got it, we enjoyed them.

“These are bomb,” he chewed. “You always have had good taste in food.”

“You think so?”

“Yeah babe. This is the bomb. I didn’t even know they had these out here.”

“Mmm hmm,” I moaned finishing my hot dog. He was fun to be around and it felt so normal and I was afraid that something bad would happen and I had to stop thinking that way but I couldn’t help it. I hadn’t been this happy in a long time.

“You ready?”

“Yeah and no,” I said making him smile. I loved seeing him smile. He has such a beautiful smile and his album cover is bomb. I put it on my Facebook page and got a lot of likes. I added him as a friend, too, and he was going through all of my stuff, giving attention to it. I wanted him to have my virginity. We held hands on the way to my house and when we got there, Nicole was there again. I was glad that my uncle was there, too. I wouldn't get such a hard treatment from my aunt with him being there. I was taking Anthony inside this time. When we pulled in the driveway, Aunt Olivia looked out of the window. "I'm nervous," I whispered.

"Don't be."

We got out and Anthony sent a text to his notary person and gave them my address to come over. I wasn't sure if she would sign so hopefully this wouldn't be a busted trip. We walked in the house and Aunt Olivia was setting some water down in front of Uncle James. He looked at me and smiled, "Heyyyy, Alia."

"Hey Uncle, this is Anthony, my fiancé."

"Your fiancé," Aunt Olivia laughed like I was joking, trying to make me feel like a stupid person; she was good at always doing that. I was getting irritated. "Since when did you get engaged?"

Nicole came from the bedroom looking and being nosey. She waved at Cheetah with a slick grin.

"I've been engaged for almost a month now. I brought him here to see if you are willing to sign the marriage license application for us to get married."

"No! Absolutely NOT!"

"Why, Auntie? Don't you want me out of your house?"

"You being out of my house will still happen when you turn eighteen, honey! It's only a few months from now. You can wait until you turn eighteen and do it on your own. I'm not putting my signature on NOTHING!"

"OLIVIA!" my uncle James shouted. "Let the girl be happy for once, goddamn you!"

"James, you stay out of it. I'm her legal guardian and if I say no, that's what I mean."

I looked at Anthony with tears in my eyes. "Why won't you sign it? We love each other and I'll take her off your hands. If you want me to pay you I'll do that," he offered.

"No, Anthony! Don't give her a dime! We'll just wait until I turn eighteen. I know why she don't wanna sign. It's because she won't be getting any more money from the State if she does that."

"YOU SHUT UP! I don't need that damn money."

"He's not giving you any money either!"

"FINE! He could've paid me and it would've been a lot easier."

"How much?" Anthony asked.

"I want twenty thousand."

"TWENTY THOUSAND?" I frowned.

"YES, he wants to marry you, he can pay. I heard he's rich anyway; I see the car that he's driving out there!"

"You're just greedy! You don't wanna see me happy? He shouldn't have to pay you twenty thousand dollars!"

"IF HE WANNA MARRY YOU SO BAD HE WILL!" She looked at Anthony and stuck her hand out, "PAY UP!"

I moved around Anthony. "He don't have to pay you SHIT!" I smacked her hand down and she tried to swing on me but I grabbed her hand and bent it back, trying to break her fingers.

"JAMES, SHE'S HURTING ME!"

"YOU LET GO OF MY MAMA, BITCH!" Nicole came towards me and I kicked her back and pushed Aunt Olivia on the ground!

"I'M TIRED OF BOTH OF YOU BITCHES! C'MON!" I held up my fist and Anthony grabbed me. Nicole got up talking shit.

"HOLD IT! GODDAMMIT! I'll sign the papers!" Uncle James yelled over all of the commotion. Anthony blocked me from my aunt and Nicole.

"YAWL JUST DON'T WANNA SEE ME HAPPY. I CAN'T WAIT TO GET AWAY FROM THIS HOUSE AND ESPECIALLY YOU!" I pointed to Aunt Olivia.

"BITCH, YOU CAN LEAVE NOW! GET OUT!" she shouted.

"FINE, I"LL LEAVE, C'mon Anthony."

"HOLD ON! WAIT, where's the papers?"

"You better not sign SHIT, James. I'm her legal guardian; you can't do that."

"I'm HER FUCKING FATHER! OKAY!" he yelled and Nicole's eyes grew wide and I looked with wide eyes. Olivia started screaming.

"YOU ASSHOLE! YOU BETTER NOT SIGN THOSE GODDAMN PAPERS! I WILL DIVORCE YOU!"

"GOOD! Where's the papers?" he looked at Anthony and a car pulled up in the driveway.

"That's my notary; we need to go outside."

"GET THE FUCK OUT OF MY HOUSE!" Aunt Olivia yelled. We all went outside and she slammed the door behind us and Uncle James went to the driveway and a white man got out of the car and Anthony told him that he would sign for me to get married.

“Thank you,” I hugged him. He hugged me and apologized. When we separated, I looked in his eyes, “Were you telling the truth in the house?”

“YES! You’re my daughter. I’ll explain everything to you once we get this over with.”

“Oh my God,” I looked in shock.

Anthony and the white man stood near the hood of his car and James signed and showed his I.D. and the man took the I.D. and copied it in his book before he put his stamp on the paperwork that we needed signed. My heart was racing and I was overwhelmed with confusion. I had no idea that this man was my father. Holy shit! So many questions ran around in my head and I was at a loss for words. Once they got everything signed. I looked over and saw Nicole and Olivia looking out of the window. I flipped Olivia off and she flipped me off and started talking shit. “You better find somewhere to stay, bitch! Don’t come back here!”

“I WON’T, don’t worry!” I said, trying to keep my voice down. Anthony shook hands with the white man and James and he came to me.

“You got my cell phone number, make sure you call me okay? Where are you going to stay tonight?”

“She can stay at my house,” Anthony said, without hesitation.

“I need to get my clothes.”

“Don’t worry about that; I’ll pack your things for you. They won’t touch ‘em.”

“Thank you so much. Can you get my important stuff and keep that for me?”

"I will."

"I'll take you shopping right now, babe," Anthony offered. We went to his car and when I got in the front seat, I spilled over in tears. I didn't want to leave like this. I wanted to move and have all of my stuff, but this was so hard to deal with, knowing that I was living with my father the whole time without knowing anything and Nicole didn't know either. So is she my sister or what?

"Don't cry baby. I gotchu. Don't worry about nothing! Your aunt is a BITCH!"

"I told you."

"Man! She's fucking crazy, wanting to charge me just to sign some fucking paperwork."

The drive to the rez was long and quiet. I was still allowing it to sink in that my uncle wasn't who he portrayed to be this entire time. How was he my dad? Was he messing around with my mom and she got pregnant with me and Aunt Olivia found out? "You okay," Anthony asked.

"Yeah. I'm just trying to figure all this stuff out. My uncle being my dad, wow."

"Yeah that's deep." He whispered. "Don't worry babe, we're going to get this behind us. We got what we needed."

Anthony was in the living room arguing about me staying here. I knew it wasn't going to work with me being here.

"Anthony, what if that woman sends the cops over here? We can get in trouble for that; she's underage."

"Mom! We're going to be married soon."

"Well you need to make it happen asap because I don't need any problems."

"Don't worry, Mom, just let me handle it. If she leaves, I leave."

"No! I don't want you to leave. I just want you to be careful," I heard her say. I felt so bad. I didn't even want to come out of the bedroom. I sat looking at the shopping bags and crying. My life was so fucked up right now. I couldn't wait to turn 18 so that I could be free and not have this shit hanging over my head. My aunt Olivia would be a bitch and send the cops here because Nicole knew where they lived, so it was no telling and she was jealous. Anthony came in the room, looking frustrated. "We're going downtown to get married tomorrow. That way, we can go and find an apartment or something until this house is built. I don't wanna stay here and have you feeling uncomfortable."

"Maybe I should just go to Marisol's house, babe, until we get this stuff straightened out? I can call her."

"No, I want you with me, babe … I did this and it's up to me to be the man right now. I'm going to be your husband soon and I don't want everybody in our business."

"Okay," I settled and let him take care of stuff the way he wanted.

"You wanna go and get a room or stay here?"

"Let's just stay here tonight."

Tuesday July 9, we went downtown with his mom and dad, Chepi, Marisol and his sister Elina. We had an appointment to get married early. The place opened at 9 and we got the marriage license without a problem. I had bought him a band at the mall because I had this feeling that we would end up getting married in the courthouse. It didn't turn out like I wanted it. I wanted a nice wedding with food and celebration but nope, it didn't happen that way. He was dressed nice, in a suit and tie and I was wearing a simple white dress that looked ritzy enough to get married in. His sister helped me do my hair and she put it up in a nice updo and added baby's breath in my hair. She was good at doing hair. I was forever grateful and we were waiting for the place to open so that we could be the first to get married. It was other couples there waiting too; we were going to be first. He was sitting chewing on his thumbnail. "You nervous, babe?"

"A little bit. What about you?"

"Yes," I smiled and he leaned over kissing me. His mom and dad were serious and they were off to the side talking to each other. I wasn't sure if his mom approved of us but his dad was happy for us. Finally the doors opened and the lady came out calling our names from a paper that she had in her hand. We got up, heading inside. Marisol smiled at me and told me that she was happy for me.

"Thank you."

"Do we have any witnesses here today?"

"Yes, me and her," Chepi said about him and Marisol. Sneaky and Sylvia walked in.

"Sorry I'm late, bro."

"You're right on time," Anthony said giving him love. Sylvia gave me a beautiful bouquet of flowers to hold. They were white orchids and roses mixed together with beautiful green stems and it looked like it was bought out of a wedding store.

"I made this for you."

“Awww thank you, it’s beautiful,” I said, getting teary eyed. “Thank you so much.”

After Chepi and Marisol signed the paperwork, the judge put on her black robe and walked over to the chair and we had to stand under an arch that had flowers over it. It was nice for it to be a quick wedding. I had nobody there for me other than Marisol and Sylvia. I was still happy; it didn’t matter. I was marrying the man that I loved for so long. We stood and the judge did our ceremony and Anthony was nervously shaking his leg the entire time. It was funny but joyful. Once she told us to exchange rings, he looked at Chepi and he pulled out a box from his pocket. I had no idea that he had bought another ring for me. He pulled out a beautiful all-diamond band and put it on my finger. It was so pretty; it glistened with nice size diamonds all around it. I put his band on his finger. I made sure that I got him an all platinum and turquoise crush stone band, which he liked and it fit perfectly. I spent my entire savings on his ring, six thousand dollars. I was using that money to move but what the hell, it was worth it for him. The judge finished the ceremony and then she gave a powerful statement about the state of Arizona and Maricopa county saying that the power was vested in her as she pronounced us husband and wife. Tears filled my eyes as we kissed. I started crying like a big baby, kissing him over and over. “I love you.” I whispered to him.

“I love you so much Alia,” He said, looking in my eyes with big crocodile tears. We kissed again while everybody cheered for us. My heart was beating so fast. I’m married now. We turned to face everybody and he lifted my arm up in the air and they all cheered. Sylvia was crying.

“Awwww,” Marisol hugged me and she was crying. I hugged Sylvia.

“Congratulations girl, that was beautiful.”

“Thank you guys so much for coming,” I said, hugging Chepi and Sneaky and my new father-in-law, and Anthony’s mom hugged me. She whispered,” I really wish this could’ve been a big wedding.”

“I know. Me too.”

I hugged his sister and she whispered, “Congratulations, I’m so happy for you guys.” She was wiping under her eyes. It was an emotional moment for all of us. I just wished that we could’ve gotten married in a nice sized ceremony but I’ll settle for this.

“Thank you so much Elina, sister-in-law,” I said making her blush. She looked a lot like Cheetah, so beautiful.

We went outside of the courtroom and took pictures. It was too hot to take them outside, but we had gotten a few under the arch, kissing, and they came out nice. Marisol and Sylvia were taking the best shots.

“Send me that one,” Anthony said, smiling. He was happy and not nervous anymore. We were married now, finally! Oh my God! My husband!

“You guys wanna go to Sharkey’s on me?” Anthony asked. “That’s our reception hall right there,” Anthony said making us all laugh. We ended up heading to Sharkey’s and I was excited and staring at my wedding band and his on his finger as we were driven by his mom and dad to the restaurant. “My wife now,” He lifted my chin and kissed me.

“I know, huh, this is crazy,” I laughed, nervously. I knew what was next and as bad as I wanted him, I’m so terrified of the pain. He locked his fingers in mine. “You look so handsome.” I told him.

“Thank you baby, you look beautiful too bad you couldn’t walk down the aisle to me huh?”

The meal was delicious. Anthony’s mom and dad left us early and we decided that we would ride back home with Chepi and Marisol. We all chilled and ate and talked.

“So where yawl going for your honeymoon?”

“I wanna wait until I get back from tour to do a real honeymoon,” Anthony explained to Sneaky.

“Me and Sylvia went to Cancun … it’s nice out there.”

“I wanna go to Belize,” I added. He looked at me.

“That’s where you wanna go, babe?”

“Yes.”

“We need to get a passport for you; I already got one.”

“Yeah, I need one.”

“Don’t worry, we’re going to make that happen.”

It felt so cool being married and not having to worry about my aunt delivering anything harsh to me now. I was with Anthony legally now and I felt like a new person. I was happy and he kept staring at me, catching me off guard. “My wife,” he whispered, delivering nice kisses to me in front of everybody. After we ate, we went to his house and I noticed a lot of cars parked outside.

“Damn, who’s all over,” he said, looking around at the cars. “I see my aunties cars are here and my uncles,” he said and when Chepi turned off the engine, we heard a lot of laughter and music. We all went in the house and nobody was in the house, so we went to the back and he opened the sliding glass door and everybody was out there: his boy, Flip, Smoke, David, and other guys that I never met were back there.

"SURPRISE!" his mom shouted.

"Oh my God mom for real," Anthony laughed. His mom had set up a reception for us at her house and the backyard had a big huge tent in it where everybody was at. We went in and they all greeted us and we had wedding gifts sitting on the table. It made me emotional and I met his family and they were so nice to me. They made me feel welcome.

"Wow, I wasn't expecting this, babe."

"Yawl gotta dance," Steven said with his camera. He was taking pictures of us and I was surprised to see a real wedding cake sitting on the table.

"Wow, my mom went in huh," he laughed, kissing me as we moved to the middle of the tent to dance. The song "Long As I live," came on and it made me cry because I remember when I used to listen to this song and think about him and now here we were married and about to dance to it. This song was by Jahiem. He pulled me in his arms and we swayed from one side to the next, singing along and on beat. Anthony was singing and smiling. His voice, wow! Wow, when life makes changes for you, it's not always bad. It's beautiful, too.

Sneaky, Sylvia and Marisol and Chepi came in the tent with gifts and all smiles. After Anthony and I danced, Chepi grabbed the mic and gave a nice warm speech. It was emotional. He was blinking back tears and then G.B. showed up, with gifts with his wife. It was really nice. I wasn't expecting to have a beautiful turnout like this and the only person that was missing was my mom and dad. Nicole didn't come because she was jealous and hateful and I didn't want her there either way; Marcus was chilling and happy because he was here alone and still happy for his brother.

"Congratulations, Cheetah, I love you, bro, and I wish you and Alia many happy years together." CHEERS! We all clinked the glasses together and it was a beautiful day.

After everybody started leaving, he wanted to get a room and he had his brother Chepi reserve a room for us because he wasn't going to be 18 until next month, so we needed someone to get the room for us being under age. Anthony and I were still having fun and dancing to R. Kelly's "Step in the Name of Love" and he had both my hands dancing with me when in the corner of my eye I saw Megan standing in the doorway with two girls that I'd never seen before.

"Look, babe."

I turned him around and when he saw her, he said, "Awww hell nah, hold up."

I knew it just couldn't be perfect without some drama. Lora ran over and got in front of Megan and pointed outside and they backed up. Megan pointed at me and I slipped out of my heels ready. I removed my earrings, necklace, and bracelet.

"Don't go out there, Alia. You have more class than that," Marisol stopped me.

"I will beat her ass! I'm not going to let her punk me anymore like she did four years ago."

"Yeah, but she's pregnant; you can go to jail."

I heard Anthony yell at her and told her to get the fuck out of his backyard. Steven and Chepi went out of the tent, too. I sat down with Marisol, upset.

"She just came here and ruined my night. Everything was going so good."

"She's jealous; that's all. She's pissed because you guys got married, but you and Cheetah were meant to be together; she needs to get over it. She's just a bitter baby mama."

"You're right," I laughed. "You're absolutely right. A bitter baby mama." That calmed me down but I was still worried about what she might do to my husband, and I wanted to go out there but Chepi and the guys were blocking the door.

All you could hear was her saying, "Tell the bitch to come outside! She's a homewrecker." Marisol and I looked at each other. The whole tent was empty with the music playing and this bitch got all of the attention trying to make me look bad in front of Anthony's family. I heard Sneaky out there talking, trying to keep Anthony calm. "Come on dog, she's not even worth it! Go back in there with your wife, man. Let us handle this."

"Fuck that! Tell that bitch to come out of that fucking tent! She's SCARY!" she shouted. She was a joke and I would've mopped her up and dragged her all through this tent if she wasn't pregnant. I heard Lora pleading with her and telling her that she had to think about her baby.

"Fuck this baby! He doesn't want it no way! Tell your black bitch to come outside!

"Oh my God," Marisol shook her head. "Now everybody knows."

"Exactly," I shook my head. I started to get up but my best friend grabbed me.

"Please, don't go out there. Don't do it! She's not worth it, Alia!"

Tears filled my eyes. "Just let me go, Marisol. I wanna beat her fucking ass! I went through years of pain because of her."

"But you got him now! She's not worth it! You're better than she is. You got him! He's your husband and legally yours; she's just his baby's mother."

I sat back down; I was so pissed. Elina came in. "She's so stupid! She's out there making herself look stupid! She's crying over my brother! He doesn't want her. She should've never came here!"

"Who told her?"

"She just showed up, nobody told her anything; she showed up."

I saw flashing lights outside in the front. It was the cops. "The cops are here; I'll be back," Elina said and I was hoping they arrested that bitch. She needed to go to jail. I put my heels back on and my earrings.

"Girl, she's not fucking worth your freedom, just think if you had fought her and the cops are here right now."

"Yeah, you're right Marisol. Thank you for keeping me calm."

"You're my sister, I'm not going to let you get hurt anymore. Megan brought those two girls with her; they might've had knives or guns."

"I know."

Sneaky and Flip and the other guys came inside.

"The cops are making her leave?"

"Yeah, you okay, Alia?"

"Yeah I'm good, where's my husband?"

"He's out there talking to the cops! That bitch is crazy!" Sneaky sat down and Sylvia came in and sat beside her husband asking if I was okay.

"What's her problem?"

"She's sprung; he got her sprung or something," Marisol said making us laugh.

Anthony's dad came in. "They're leaving now. The cops are making them leave."

Anthony and I ended up leaving the rez and Chepi reserved us a room off of Camelback Mountain Drive. We had a beautiful view and I couldn't sleep. I was scared for one, because I wanted him to have my virginity but I heard that it was going to be painful and I didn't know if I was ready for that pain. He snuck up behind me and grabbed my wine and set it on the table that was out on the patio. It was still hot out at night.

"What's wrong? You okay?"

"I'm scared," I said, as he put his arms around me and pushed himself into me and I felt his big penis through his slacks.

"Why?"

"Because I know it's going to hurt."

"I'm not going to hurt you. I'mma try not to. I can't promise that it won't … but if you let me taste it first, I can make you feel relaxed," he said making me laugh.

"You wanna taste me?"

"Yes, I do. I've been thinking about that all day. C'mon." We went in the room and the cool air soothed me. When we got to the bed, I sat down and we kissed and the kisses were so good, I got wet on my own. I was extremely turned on by him and he let his hair down. Oh my God. How did I get so lucky to be with a guy so good looking? I mean he's GORGEOUS! He helped me out of my dress and I was shy.

"Move your hand," he whispered and leaned in sucking on my breast. Just the thought of a good-looking guy on me like this was a major turn on. I closed my eyes and allowed the feeling to consume me. I ran my fingers through his pretty long straight hair. He sat back and removed his shirt and I slid back on the bed and he pulled my panties off. I clamped my legs together.

"Oh my God, I'm scared."

"Don't be," he said, kissing my thighs. His lips were cool and they felt good. I watched as he moved his way in between my legs and when I felt his tongue, on my thighs it tickled, and I laughed until he rubbed on my legs and made me relax as he continued. "Open your legs, let me see."

"I'm scared babe, I dunno if I'm ready."

"You're ready for me, or do you wanna stop?"

"Ummm, no I don't wanna stop." We both laughed. "Okay, I need to drink this wine," I said, grabbing the glass and downing the rest of it. It made me relax. "Okay, I think I'm ready." I lay back and allowed him the opportunity to explore. He licked my thighs, my knees and opened my legs slow and kissed my muffin. Oh my God. I closed my eyes as it was tickling at first and I tried not to be silly and laugh. I allowed myself to get in tuned with him. It was the best feeling EVER. It was perfect because it was HIM. I wondered if he ever did this to Megan. For some reason, I didn't feel that he did; I hoped he didn't. It felt so good, that I felt tears filling my eyes and I grabbed his hair, grinding on his face until I had a big orgasm. "Oh my God … oh my

God," I cried out, silently crying because of the way that I felt about him and it felt so good.

"I love you baby, you taste so good," he said, going in again and making me relax more. God I could get used to this and he had me soaking wet. I was so wet that when he came up to lay between my legs, I just wrapped my legs around him, wanting to feel him. I felt him against me and he was BIG. I closed my eyes and he whispered, "I want you to look in my eyes." I opened my eyes.

"I'm scared, oh my God; it hurts."

"Kiss me," he whispered and as I was kissing him, he threw me off from the pain and we both moaned loudly and I felt a "POP!"

"What was that?"

"I'm inside of you. I'm in baby. I'm inside of you," he said. "Do you feel me?"

I concentrated as he moved and I did feel him. "Yes!" I cried wrapping my arms around him. He paused, kissing me and telling me how much he loved me. He started singing to me.

"Baby … you mean the world to me … my love for you … goooooeeees soooo deep … I will always feel this way … forever … forever … my loooooove," he sang in a high tone and it made me cry. We were kissing again and he moved around and I rubbed his back and he told me to grind with him and I did what he told me to do. "Ssssss … ooh shit yeah! Awwww damn, Alia! You got the best lovin; in the world, girl! Oh my GOD!" he moaned in my ear. "Awww shit, I'm cumin," he said and I felt him inside of me; it was throbbing. I could actually feel it. I felt the chillbumps on his back and arms. "Ssssss oooooh that's so bomb!" he said. He looked in my eyes and we laughed.

"I felt it."

"Did you feel it when I came?"

"Yes. I felt it."

When he pulled out of me, it was a relief and my cooch felt swollen. Marisol said that after a few times when you lose your virginity, it starts to feel good. I couldn't wait to get that feeling. He snuggled up behind me and kissed me, asking if I was okay. "Yeah, I'm just wet down there and I'm scared to get up."

"You want a wet towel?"

"Yes, please."

I started crying after he left me to get the towel. My virginity was gone. I couldn't claim that virtue anymore. It was gone for good never to return. My womb was open now. He went to the clinic and got checked before we got married and everything came back clean. I just pray that he doesn't cheat on me when he's on the road.

"What's wrong," he asked when he came back to the bed and saw my condition of emotions overwhelming me. "Huh? What's wrong baby, did I hurt you?"

I shook my head. "It just hit me that I'm not a virgin anymore," I said, wiping myself with the towel and I looked at it and saw blood. "OH MY GOD … is this normal?"

"Yeah, I think so."

OH my God! I got up and went to the bathroom and sat on the toilet. I was so sore. He came in the bathroom and when I looked at his penis, it was so big! My God, my husband was hung! No wonder I was bleeding like this. I looked in the toilet and there was no blood dripping. It was just there when I wiped myself. It had stopped. I was so sore down there tho. I ran some bath water.

He whispered, "Are you okay, babe?"

"Yeah, I'm just shocked. I dunno. It's crazy because I was a virgin all my life."

"Why do you think you're so special to me? What really made me fall deeper in love with you, Alia, is the fact that you didn't get with nobody else. You waited for me and that made me feel special. That's why you got a ring and these other girls didn't get that. You got my heart always and forever," he said making me feel good. I sat in the tub and he sat on the toilet and washed my back for me, giving me a massage. "I love you so much. I'm going to give you the world …"

"You are my world, Anthony. I just don't wanna lose you again."

"You won't. I'll never leave you. When I go on tour, I'm going to call you every day. I'mma make sure that you're not missing me so much."

"How long will you be gone?"

"For a few months?"

"A few months? Oh my God, Anthony!"

"Don't worry, baby, I'mma make sure that you're taken care of. We're going to go car shopping tomorrow. I'mma buy you a car so you can get back and forth to work. Once they finish the plans on the house, they should be getting started on it next month."

"Oh God, I'm going to miss you. I hope I can handle being around your family by myself."

"You'll be okay, you got Marisol, Sylvia and my sister to kick it around. I'll make sure you got money, too." He climbed in the tub with me and when he sat behind me, I leaned in on his chest and it felt perfect.

"I dunno if I can handle it, babe."

"Don't say that; you can. I'm going to be working, babe, bringing in the bread so you can shop and buy nice stuff and keep your hair and nails done and look beautiful. I can't do that without money."

"I know … I don't even care about all of that; I care about you being around me. I'm going to be lonely, but I know I'll be okay."

"You will. I'mma make sure I keep in touch with you, I'mma get you another phone, too. I just want you to do one thing for me, babe."

"What's that?"

"Stay away from the block; don't go over there at all, okay?"

"I won't babe, I'll just go to work and come home. That's it. I promise you that."

"Okay, cos I don't want you around them fools and I'm not out here, you know? I don't trust Novi at all; that nigga is scandalous and I really don't trust Cal either. I only deal with a select few that I know got my back. My brothers are my main comrades. I just want my wife safe at all times."

"You don't have to worry about me, babe."

"I'm going to worry about you, because I got a crazy ass ex that might try to bring harm to you. She was talking shit tonight about putting a bullet in you. I can't have that; I will come home and kill that bitch."

"I'm going to steer clear."

"Yeah cos she's psycho and jealous! She's not allowed on the rez no more. The police told her that if she gets caught on the rez, she's going to jail, so she can't come on the rez."

"Good. You know who I'm worried about telling her where I work? Nicole, babe; she knows where I work."

"You need to be careful. I don't know if I want you to be working there come to think of it. Maybe you need to just be a housewife."

"Babe, I'll be bored."

"Go shopping, find a hobby or something."

"Yeah, I guess I can take some cooking classes. I need to learn how to be a good cook for you and I can decorate cakes for fun."

"Exactly … you can do that and not have to be looking over your shoulders. Maybe once she gets further into her pregnancy, she'll realize how stupid she's been acting."

"I hope you establish paternity,"

"Oh I will, believe that. I hope it's not mine."

"Yeah, me too, but … what can we do about it? It's not the baby's fault."

"True. If it's yours then I guess we'll have to deal with it, I'm not leaving you."

"You mean the world to me; I'm not leaving you either."

He turned my face to his and kissed me. It felt different not being innocent and a virgin anymore. I felt wide open. I was more afraid of getting hurt by him now than ever because I'm vulnerable in love. He helped me out of the tub and wrapped a towel around me and we went to the bed again. The air made it cold for me, so he turned down the AC and we climbed in bed and he snuggled with me until we fell asleep.

The next morning he woke me up to the same feeling I had with him yesterday tasting me. Oh my God, the feeling was unbelievable. I loved how it felt and he was making my body feel out of this world. He entered me again, slowly, and I could see his face this time and I stared at him the whole time that he was inside of me, and every time we moved together, he was telling me that he loved me. Damn! Imagine that. His moans were like a song that he was singing and he wasn't shy about moaning and letting me know how I made him feel. This time I really felt him and it made me connect more with him. Our lovemaking was powerful and something that I can barely describe because he was pulling himself in and out and gyrating his hips and telling me that I had the best muffin in the world. What did he mean by that? "Oooh, it's so tight," he kept saying. "It's so tight baby … oh my God, Alia." I squeezed him with my muscles and he cried out my name again. I could get used to this because he kept calling my name, so I kept gripping him to hear it. "Oooooo, it's so tight and good baby …oh my God." He paused, kissing me and then I felt him throbbing and he moved again, moaning and calling out my name. "OOOOOH GOD, baby! It feels so bomb!"

"Are you coming?"

"Umm hmmm … yeah I am." He froze, his body got those chills again. I wrapped my legs around him and moved my hips and he frowned and buried his head in my neck. I waited for him to pull himself out of me. "Did you come?" he asked me.

"I did when you put your tongue on me."

"You didn't come when I was inside of you?"

"I think so … I don't know but it felt good; it felt better it wasn't hurting as much this time."

"It's going to get better; I'm going to make you come this way too," he said, kissing me. "I love you, Alia."

We left the room and went to eat. His phone was ringing off the hook when he turned it back on. Like he promised, we went and found me a car. I wanted something simple. He bought me a 2004 Honda Accord. It came fully loaded with electric windows and leather seats; it was so nice and it was silver. It took three hours to get the car then I followed him to the mall and we went to the Sprint store and he got me a new cell phone. It was nice. He added me to his account. I got to keep the same phone number. He kept his word on everything he said that he would do for me. It showed his nobility and I was very happy indeed. I didn't want to stay with his parents, but his mom had relaxed now that we were married. Nicole knew that we were married now, so there was nothing that my aunt could do. I followed Cheetah to the reservation and on the way, I got a call from Uncle James, or my father.

"How are you? Did you guys get married? I heard you did."

"We did. He bought me a new car and I'm driving it right now," I smiled.

"That's nice. What kind of car did you get?"

"I have a Honda Accord."

"Wow, that's nice of him to do that."

"Yeah and he got me a new phone, too. He's going to be going on tour pretty soon and he wanted me to have a car."

"Okay, that's nice, are you still working?"

"Yeah for now. He doesn't want me to work because the girl that he used to deal with is threatening me, so I'm staying safe."

"That's good, Alia. I'm glad to hear that. But I want to meet up with you so we can talk. I have some things that I want to show you."

"Okay. You can come to the reservation; this is where I'm living right now."

"Okay, when will be a good time?"

"I'll be there in ten minutes; I'm not far from it now," I said, merging off of the freeway right behind Anthony.

"Okay, which reservation is it?"

"Salt River."

"Oh okay, I'll find you."

"I'll text you the address."

"Okay … let him know that I'm coming so that the cops don't harass me," he said and I agreed to do that.

I called Anthony as we were moving through the rez. I told him that James was coming and he said he was okay with it.

"Is everything okay?"

"Yeah. He said he wanted to talk to me. I want you to be there."

"Okay, I will baby." I still couldn't believe that we were married and I was in a new car. It seemed like a dream and I was going to wake up. When we pulled in the driveway of his mom and dad's house, his sister was sitting on the porch with her friends. She was looking at the car with shock in her eyes. When I got out of the car she asked, "Did my brother buy you a new car?"

"Yeah I did, why?"

"Where's my car?"

"Let me see your grades improve this year and you'll get a car."

She smacked her lips and sat pouting.

"Now she's mad. Is Mom and Dad in the house?"

"Yeah," she whispered. I felt bad because maybe she did deserve a car, too. We went inside and I went to the room while he went and greeted his parents. I felt kind of shy now. I started messing with my new phone and then I sent James a text telling him that I was here. I heard my husband laughing in the den with his parents. He sounded so happy. I wondered if he laughed like this before we got back together. I laid in his bed. I was still kind of sore; it was hard for me to walk normal after the sex. I sent Marisol a text message telling her that I wasn't a virgin anymore. She wrote me back saying, "I'm sure you're not, after getting married … did it hurt?"

"Fuck yeah!" I wrote back and she sent a bunch of laughing faces with tears coming down; it was funny to see those icons. She wrote me back telling me that it would get better with time, but shit, I dunno. He has a huge dick. I never seen a dick that big and I've seen them in magazines but none as big as his. She asked where I was and I told her that I was at the house on the rez and she told me that she would be by later.

Anthony came in the room and asked if I was okay.

"Yeah, I'm good babe … I'm just waiting for James."

"Okay, is he coming right now?"

"Yeah."

"Cool, I wish he would've come to the wedding."

"I know. I wanted a big wedding." He sat on the bed next to me.

“We can have one when I come back from tour.”

“It too late; we’re already married.”

“We can get married again and have what you want. I want you to be happy. I’m happy,” He smiled and kissed me.

“I’m happy, too. I’m going to miss you. I think I’m going to cry when you leave for tour.”

“Don’t say that. You’re going to make me feel bad.”

“I’m just being honest, but I’ll be okay.” He got up and looked out of the window.

“I think that’s him right now.”

I got up and we went out to the living room and to the front door and Anthony opened it.

“Hi you doing,” they shook hands.

“I’m well and you?”

“I’m good, come on in.” Anthony said and I hugged him and we took him in the den to meet Cheetah’s parents. I’m sure his mom was wondering why he didn’t come to the wedding, but after we introduced them, I took him to Cheetah’s room and he was with me. He had a briefcase with him. I sat on the bed and he sat on the chair.

“So I have pictures to show you,” he said. He pulled the images from the briefcase and I saw so many pictures, all different shapes and sizes of a beautiful woman.

“Wow, who is this, she’s really pretty?”

“That’s your mother. Her name is Sedahji.” It was pronounced, “Se-da-yee.”

"Really? She's beautiful and so is her name, this is my mom? Wow." I was staggered and I gave Cheetah the images as I looked through them.

"Wow," he mumbled sitting beside me. I started crying.

"She's so pretty. I didn't know if she was alive. Olivia kept telling me that she didn't want me."

"She's a big fat liar! First of all, your mother asks about you every time we talk and I talk to her quite often."

"Really? Where is she?"

"She's living in Belize. She's a singer and a very popular singer down there. She's been doing music and traveling for many years. Your mother is very popular in Central America and Europe."

"Wow! My mom sings," I looked at Anthony and he looked at me in surprise.

"That's great. So where is she living in Belize?"

"She's in France now, but she will be coming back to Belize next month."

"So did Aunt Olivia get her deported?"

"Yes! She got her deported because me and your mom fell in love. I was dealing with Olivia as a date and then I met your mom and my heart was with her. Olivia told me that she was pregnant and at the time, I didn't want to leave her with a child, so we got married but I wasn't happy. I was still seeing your mother and she became pregnant with you. Olivia found out and she got your mom deported after you were born.. Your mother was very angry with her because it was right after she had you; you were only two years old and she took you but I wanted you to be with me, so I thought that it was best for Olivia and

I to keep you and we did. We didn't want you going into foster care, I didn't! Olivia didn't care, she didn't want you, but I did and that was the only way that I would stay with her."

"Can I ask a question," Anthony cut in.

"Sure——

"Why did you keep this secret from my wife for so long?"

"Good question. I did because I didn't want to make things worse you know. Olivia already was jealous of you Alia. She hated that your mother and I were in love and she didn't want me to tell you that I was your father because she threatened to make things hard and I didn't want her doing that to you while I was in medical school trying to keep you okay and taken care of."

"She didn't want you telling me?"

"No and I didn't want to make things worse than they were, so I waited until you got older."

"What about my mom, did she really want me?"

"Yes very much so and she's dying to see you."

"I want to see my mom," I said and broke down crying again. Anthony pulled me in his arms. "I don't like for my wife to be hurting like this, I'm sure there's something that she can do to see her mother right?"

"Oh yes, it is."

He pulled out videos and said, "These are videos of her music and her shows. She sent them to me for you to see."

"Oh my God, thank you. I'm going to watch all of these."

"Here is her phone number. You can call her. She wants to talk to you. I told her that you were doing well and now it's up to you to talk to her and build a relationship with her without interference from Olivia. I still love your mom and she still loves me. As soon as I am done with school next month, I am leaving Olivia for good."

"What about Nicole?"

"She's not my daughter. I found that out last year and she tried to lie to me, but I met her father; he's Hispanic. He's from Paradise Valley; he has a wife and family. She was messing around on me the whole time."

"Oh my God," I looked at Anthony.

"Son, I'm glad that you came into Alia's life. She's so happy with you. I wished that I had been at the wedding to give her away, but you guys know how things have been going. Olivia is a very greedy and dangerous woman and she's very hateful. I am glad that you came and took her away, thank you."

"Thank you for allowing her to marry me. I'm going to do my best to make her happy."

"Yes, please, she deserves it."

"I know she does and right now I'm in the process of having our house built. I'm going to take good care of her and I will take her to see her mom, too."

"Thank you." He said, he started crying and it made me cry because I know he meant well. I was relieved when he told me that Nicole wasn't his daughter. I didn't want her as a sister. It worked out great in the long run and my mom was a singer, just like Cheetah. This was something to be grateful for.

Tapping In

I was getting ready for another interview with LIVE 105 right before my tour schedule started. It's my 18th birthday and it didn't seem like it because I was so busy working. Alia fixed me a nice breakfast and I was wishing to be with her today but it was work, work, work. I hadn't been down to the station since I first started my music career so I was happy to see everybody. I had been so busy, I hadn't had time to see D.J. Flame and Paco Baca. My new album was finished and due to drop that week and I was looking forward to the tour. Alia and I had been going strong. They started working on our house and finally Megan had calmed down since her pregnancy was making her so sick. It kept her in the house mostly which was a good thing for me, but she was still playing on my phone and sending harassing text messages since she couldn't come on the rez to mess with Alia. I made Alia quit her job so she could be safe. I wasn't taking any chances on her working at that library and ending up shot.

We made it to the station and the fans were outside waiting for me, which I didn't expect, but they were out there thick, waving and screaming my name which felt good because I appreciated the love energy that I got from my fans. I'd been so busy this week, doing guest appearances on talk shows in L.A. and now I was headed into the radio station.

"Cheetah, how are you Happy Birthday." Amy got up and hugged me.

"Thank you Amy, how are you?"

"I'm fine, still here," she laughed, walking us to the back. I hadn't seen her in a while and she had picked up a little weight and had her hair a regular color with regular lipstick on now, not gothic like the first time I had seen her. Paco and D.J. Flame were on the air when I walked in with my brothers Steven and Chepi. Paco waved with that magic smile and I waved and gave Flame a firm handshake before we sat. Amy gave us water before she left us and closed the door.

"*I'm D.J. Flame with D.J. Paco Baca and we're LIVE 105 where you hear the latest and the greatest R&B and Hip Hop on your favorite radio station. We're here with one of our favorite young superstars, Cheetah! He's here in the building today. CHEETAAAAAH, what's good man?*"

"*Happy Birthday*," Paco remembered.

"Thank you so much. What's going on around here?" I laughed.

"*Same ole same ole … blessed to be alive and still working. You made it another year huh Cheetah?* "

"Yessir … and I'm happy about it."

"*About to go on tour soon and the album is about to drop as well. Tell us about this new album.*"

"Well, I got a lot of collabs on my new album. It's entitled 'Native Anthem Volume 1.' I've worked with some big names, Razzmatazz, Yukon Tha Great—"

"*Oh wow!*"

"Oh yeah … Kamakazee. This album is about to be number one also. I'm very pleased with the production thanks to my brother Cochise and all of the executive staff at the new label."

"*You have your own label now. How is that working out for you? I remember when you first started, you had three deals on the table.*"

"Yes, I ended up signing with Prestige with a publish and distribution deal. Once Eleven Eleven did well, I happily took off in flight and launched Safari."

"*That's amazing, Cheetah. I'm hearing good things about Safari. You guys also signed other artists as well, that's dope man.*"

"Oh yeah, my brother Steven and my dad are doing great with the label. They're keeping me working and we have some new artists coming out, Doughboy, Cali Wiz and a female artist so I'm happy about that."

"*That's great, Cheetah. Now you're going to be doing a national tour this month as well right?*"

"Yes, yes, I'll be traveling across America again, promoting 'Native Anthem' and I'm also going to be working on a biopic about my life as well. I got some juicy stuff in there that I'm going to tell the world, which will probably have everybody's mouth dropped like," we laughed.

"*Oh wow, give us some peeks into it, man.*"

"Nah, not yet. When I come back from tour, I'm going to be starting on that."

"Awwwww wow, now he wants to tease———

"*Now Cheetah, I wanted to ask you how you felt about a dis record that's been made by an underground artist that calls himself Napol.*"

"Oh yeah … that was actually a childhood friend that I grew up with. He's not happy with the fact that the label didn't sign him—"

"*Why didn't yawl sign him?*"

"Well, his material is not what the label is looking for," Steven added. "We want R&B and Hip Hop mainstream artists with positive influence and we do like rap but we want it to be encouraging and not adding to the violent content that a majority of rappers have been doing."

"*That's a good reason not to sign him, but do yawl have a personal beef, Cheetah? Because I was listening to his lyrics and he was saying something about you taking his girl and never being a friend and going Hollywood on everybody.*"

"Nah, hahah … the girl he's talking about didn't like him. She chose me."

"*Oh so it's some truth to that?*"

"Oh yeah … he's not lying about the girl but, he's lying about me taking her from him. That's if we're talking about the same girl. It's two girls."

"*OOOH snaps,*" they all laughed. I looked at Steven and shrugged.

"*That's what this is all about. Yawl beefing over females.*"

"HE's beefing, not me! As far as me being Hollywood on everybody, I've always been the same person since you guys met me; nothing's changed. I've only been to Hollywood a few times since I got into this business, I'm not impressed by it to start acting like that's my life. I'm grateful to be successful and—"

"*You've earned everything that came to you, Cheetah. You're a fantastically talented artist and we appreciate your voice, man. I know you deal with a lot of haters out there. Keep being you,*" D.J. Flame said. "*I never met Napol. I've heard his music and he's got lyrical skills, maybe if he can change some of the content, he might get picked up as a great rap artist.*"

"Exactly, I'm on something far greater than worrying about the deception."

"*Now back to this biopic that you mentioned earlier what made you decide to do that?*"

"Well I'm not sure if you guys knew about this but I just got married in July on the 9th."

"*Nah, aww man, and we didn't get an invite.*"

"It was a small ceremony; we didn't do anything big."

"*Congratulations Cheetah, that's amazing. Is this the girl that Napol is talking about*?"

We all laughed. "I think so, but she's been in my life for years; this isn't someone that I just met. She's here to stay."

"*Congratulations, brother.*"

"Thank you, but she inspired me to do the biopic. We did some talking about it and she thought that it would be a great idea for me to come out with it."

"*I can't wait to see the trailer; you got me curious now,*" Flame said making us laugh.

"*Cheetah, how is the response from people on the rez now since you've been doing your thing?*"

"It's amazing and I have big plans for my people because I want to do something for them to make them feel like they've accomplished something, too. It's always been a dream of mine to fix up the rez and create jobs and make it look better than how it was when I grew up."

"*Okay, tell us what you have planned?*"

"I would like to put money into fixing up the school, setting up medical clinics there and also making thc housing a lot better. I have big plans."

"*Wow, Cheetah that's amazing. Most celebrities get rich and move out of where they came from but you're still there right?*"

"I'm still on the rez, building my own house as we speak. My wife wanted to stay and I decided to do that instead of walk away from my people and where I first started."

"*That's amazing," Paco said. "We're going to drop a track from Cheetah's new album 'Native Anthem.' We'll be right back with more from Cheetah. You're listening to LIVE105 FM where you hear the latest and the greatest R&B and HIP HOP. Stay tuned,*" Paco said, dropping my track called, "Addicted to Money!"

"I like this track, Cheetah; this is my joint right here," D.J. Flame cheesed. "I'mma drop that every hour. I can totally relate to this and the beat is slamming. Why didn't yawl bring Cochise? That's my BOY," Flame grinned.

"He had a meeting at the label with Cali Wiz, he's from the bay area; they want him to produce his album."

"Oh snaps, he's doing his thing too, huh? Yeah we need to get him in here."

"Exactly. He's dope. He's been doing his thing for years," I added. "He taught me a lot about music."

"I'mma ask you about him when we get back on air," D.J. Flame said.

"Aiight, fa sho," I sipped my water as my song got into the hook real nice. We bobbed our heads listening as I was spitting. "Cheetah I didn't know you could rap."

"Yeah, I like to flow, too."

"This li'l nigga been doing it all," Chepi teased and we all laughed.

"Yawl going on tour with him?"

"Yes, for sure, I always go on tour with my baby bro. He needs someone to keep him in line.

"How's married life, Cheetah?"

"It's good, great actually, I'm very happy. She's a beautiful woman, inside and out."

"Why you didn't bring her man?"

"She wanted to hang out with her friends; she had other plans, didn't wanna hang with me today."

"Maybe she's buying you a birthday present."

"Maybe," we laughed.

We were back on the air and D.J. Flame asked me about my brother Cochise.

"Cochise has been one of the dopest producers since I got started in this business. He's always been into making fantastic beats and he's self-taught. Don't get me wrong, he had major engineers teaching him hands on, but as far as him having the ear for good music, that's always been his thing and he taught me a lot."

"*Wow, yeah I mean he did great work on your albums and got music awards for it. He's a well-respected producer. Props to Cochise.*"

"Yeah, right now he's going to be working with some dope artists in Cali and um, he's going to be busy just like me."

"*Now, Cheetah you went to Paradise Valley Performing Arts Academy. What was that like for you?*"

"It was amazing! When I first started going there, I was kind of nervous because I was around a lot of kids that weren't the same as me. They were white of course and I was the only ethnic or shall I say indigenous and ethnic person that was there."

"*How did they treat you*?"

"They treated me with open arms, especially after I did a few shows. They were like, whoa, this dude is serious and they started taking me serious after they heard me sing and saw me dance."

"*Man, I have to admit, when I came to the show you did last year, I was blown away. You guys really kept me entertained. You do great shows, Cheetah.*"

"Thank you, I try my best to please everyone."

"*Do you plan on doing some acting in your biopic*?"

"Now that I dunno. Stay tuned," I said making them all laugh.

After the radio show, I was on my way back to the house. Alia sent me a text to see where I was. I told her that I was on my way back home.

"Okay babe."

I had a feeling that something was going on. My mom called. It was like my phone never stopped ringing. "Hey Mom?"

"Cheetah, two lawyers are here for you. They say something about they need to speak to you regarding a business matter about Rowena."

"Really? What's that about? They didn't tell you?"

"No. I have to call your dad too, because I think this is serious."

"Okay Mom, I'll be there." I said, looking at Steven as I ended the call. "Mom said something about lawyers at the house for me and it's got something to do with Rowena."

"Really? She's dead!"

"I know, I dunno what it's about. Why they want me."

"Yeah that's deep Cheetah. Maybe Mom got it confused."

"Maybe."

We stopped at the taco spot and got some food before we headed back to the rez.

"Aye, that's Cheetah!" I heard one of the guys say as we were heading back to the car.

"HEY CHEETAH! WASSUP MAN?" I turned and waved and we got back in the Porsche truck that Steven bought for himself. Girls were coming out of the taco spot looking and waving.

I waved at them and Steven laughed, "Pretty soon you won't be able to go nowhere."

"I know."

We made it home and my dad's Range Rover was in the yard and I saw a black Hummer sitting behind my dad's truck. This had to belong to the lawyers that my mom was speaking about. Alia's car was gone. My wife wasn't home. I sent her a text message asking where she was. She called me.

"Hey babe? Where are you?"

"On the way home right now. I had a lot to do. Happy birthday, babe."

"Thank you … you're coming home now?"

"Yes my love."

"Okay good, it's some lawyers here for me. I don't know what it's about," I said walking to the house. My dad was laughing and talking with them.

"Cheetah is that you?"

"Yeah … aye babe, lemme call you back."

"Okay, I'll be right there," she said.

I went in the den and saw the two white lawyers dressed in suits and ties. They greeted me with handshakes. They had open briefcases on the table. "I'm sure you're wondering why we're here, Cheetah."

"Yes, am I in some kind of trouble or what?"

"No … actually we're here because your aunt had set up a living trust with us and she wanted us to come to you when you turned eighteen. Happy Birthday by the way."

"Thanks."

"Yes, she wanted us to inform you of the money that she left for you and also an estate property in Texas and on that property there is oil."

"Really?" I gasped, looking at my dad and my mom walked out of the den.

"What do you mean oil, active oil?" my dad asked.

"Yes, there's a Well on there also that's being used and the money has been put into the trust account and it's quite a bit of money but it can't be touched by you Cheetah until you turn twenty-five."

"Oh I see, how much money is it?"

"It's a substantial amount," The lawyer said. I looked at my dad.

"So did she just leave this to my son or did she split this up among her family?"

"She left everything to your son. She made sure that she solidified these documents and had them filed in probate court; she wanted everything of value liquidated and not liquidated to go to your son."

"Wow! I wonder why she did that."

"Hey … don't look a gift horse in the mouth. I just represent her; I don't ask why."

"I understand," Dad said. "So, what is he entitled to now?"

"She's left him fifty million dollars of which he's entitled to the entire amount, but I would recommend he get a portfolio account set up so he could live off of the interest."

"I'm well aware, that's my background in finance with the Air Force."

"Oh well great; you're in good hands, Cheetah. Having a dad like you have, you will not have to worry about losing money."

"Fifty million? I whispered and my wife walked in the room wondering if she should've entered the room. I waved her in. "This is my wife, Alia."

"Hello Alia," the lawyers shook her hand. She sat beside me and I had to sign documents stating that I received the money that Rowena left for me and I signed the documents that held the amount of money that was owed to me from the land in Texas. It was held in a trust account and when I saw the amount, I almost passed out. I had never seen that much money before in my life. This is what she meant when she said that she was going to have it all straightened out before she died. Damn! She left everything to me and I don't know why she did that. Did she do it to spite my mom or did she do it as a way of an apology? I was only worth six million from my album sales and that was after the IRS took a big chunk and me giving the record label money for services, not to mention the overhead for my label, promotions, tour schedules, videos and me paying the guys and my brother and agent. I was only worth six million but now you could add fifty million to that. I could really do what I wanna do now. I was spending two million on the house that Alia and I wanted. It was as if the universe replaced the money that I spent and then some. After I signed the paperwork. "What do I do now?" I asked.

"Well, that's it, Cheetah."

"We need copies please," my dad explained.

"Oh yeah, thanks for reminding me."

I sat back in shock and my wife grabbed my hand. "Are you okay?"

"Yeah, what a helluva birthday gift, huh," I said, showing her the check. Her eyes grew wide.

"Wow, that's a lot of money babe." I gave the check to my dad.

"Can you put this in my account, Dad."

"Yes, I sure will. I'll do that right now, Son. Did you want me to transfer any funds?"

"Just two to my other account so I can pay for the house."

"Okay … will do."

I was reading over the documents after the lawyers left and my mom was in the kitchen talking to my dad asking why my aunt left me all of that money and didn't leave her mom anything.

"I dunno Lora, it was her sound decision."

"I don't think she was in her right mind, Raymond," my mom said. I shook my head, because I knew that my mom wanted that money.

"Babe, this is a lot of money, look at this," Alia whispered. "That's one point two billion dollars from that oil land. That's crazy."

"Yeah, I can't touch it until I turn twenty-five; that is crazy."

"That's a lot of money babe; you're a billionaire."

I put a finger to my lips. "That's between us, okay?"

"Yes, okay, I understand. Don't make plans for later."

"Why?"

"Because, I have something planned for us for your birthday. Please don't plan anything."

"Okay, babe."

My sister came in the den with a cake that had lit candles on it singing happy birthday to me with my brothers and mom and dad.

I stood up smiling and Alia stood beside me. "*Happy birthday dear Cheetah, happy birthday to youuuuuuuu.*"

"Make a wish, bro."

I closed my eyes and wished for me and Alia to be together for life. I blew out the candles and everybody cheered. "What kind of cake is this?"

"Chocolate, it's your favorite," Alia exclaimed. She had made the cake for me and it was nice, she made it into a Wolf. It was nicely detailed and looked like she bought it out of a store.

"Thank you, babe, you are so creative and sweet. You were doing this the whole time that I was gone?"

"Yes," She smiled.

"She's good at that cake decorating son," My mom said.

"I love you babe," I kissed her and she fed me some cake.

"I want a slice," Steven smiled and we all gravitated to the den.

"I'll be back, you guys," Dad said. He left and my mom said she needed to talk to me.

"Okay, Mom, here I come."

I went to the den with her. "Are you going to give your brothers some money. It's only fair."

"Yeah, Mom, I'll give them all money, I was going to do it on Christmas."

"Okay, that's fair."

"Exactly, I'll be back from tour and I can make them all millionaires."

"Good, what about me?" she said and she laughed.

I kissed her cheek and told her, "You'll never want for nothing."

"Awww, thank you son … I love you."

I went back to the dining room and sat with my bros and my sister to eat cake.

Marcus laughed, "Bro, I never thought we would end up living like this. I'm happy."

"Yeah, me too," Steven admitted. "We got what we deserve and this tour is going to make a shitload of money!"

"To US!" Chepi held up a glass of water making us all laugh.

My wife gave me some good love making before we left for the evening. She had plans for my birthday and I was happy with just spending time with her. She had me feeling so good, I felt like I was high on her love. The sex was BOMB! She was learning how to make me feel and she even went down on me; I was teaching her everything that she knows. She had some work to do on the head but I was patient with her. She was scared of my size and choking. With me teaching her it was making it all the better for me to have the best sex ever. She's a great student and once she learned how to please me at 100 percent, I was probably going to be the insecure one.

We made it to the Blue Lounge; this club was for 18 and over. "Oh wow! It's crowded up here tonight, huh? But babe, how are you going to get in here and you're not 18?"

"I got that covered!" she smiled, pulling into the VIP parking area. "We're going in through the back," she said. "They told me that since it was you, they were going to make an exception but they want us to come in through the back."

"Oh okay, I see you worked it out, that's cool."

I was going by what she wanted and if she wanted to hang out tonight, I was cool with that. We were both looking good and I was feeling fantastic, especially after finding out that I'm going to be loaded with money especially at twenty-five. My whole life changed. We walked in the back door and the bouncers checked the guest list. "Oh shit, Happy Birthday, Cheetah, come on in, sir."

I shook hands with them and they spoke to my wife. We were escorted up to the VIP section of the club and all of my folks were there. "SURPRIIIIISE!"

"OH shit!" I laughed when I saw everybody. Sneaky, GB, my brothers, and other folks from the industry, rappers that I hadn't seen in almost a year had flown in from Cali to celebrate my birthday, my boys from the Cali Swag district. It was LIT! "Babe, you got me," I told Alia.

She laughed and said, "Happy Birthday, I wanted to surprise you. Enjoy yourself, my love."

"Cheetah, my nigga, happy birthday," my boy Loaf hugged me. I was getting mad love, Razz was up here, with Kamakazee.

"Awww man," I laughed overwhelmed by all of the love up here tonight.

Wifey was doing her thing with her friends and I was getting faded with the fellas, having a few drinks and smoking some bomb cush. The music was going and the club was getting packed with people and of course we had extra tight security up on the VIP floor so anybody just couldn't walk in.

Flip came to me and said, "Aye bro, I'm looking forward to the tour ... now that you're married, it's going to be harder."

"Don't remind me, but I'm looking forward to the shows, too, and making money," We laughed and shook hands. Sneaky came and brought a fat blunt to me; it was lit.

"Damn my nigga, this is huge," I laughed, hitting it before I passed it to Flip. Smoke joined us. Flip was choking with me and I was faded already. They had crab boils on the table loaded with crab legs, crawfish, corn on the cob, red skin potatoes, quail eggs and mussels. Talk about delicious, everybody was getting it in and I think my wife was the one who came up with the food entrée. It was all good because the fellas ate well.

We had it popping and Sneaky looked at his phone,

"Man, I'll be back ... I'mma go see what this nigga want."

He disappeared from the VIP area and we continued to party. I didn't realize what time it was; it was late, almost two o'clock and we were having so much fun, I wasn't ready to go.

I was enjoying myself and the D.J. shouted, "LAST CALL FOR ALCOHOL!" We had our own liquor upstairs anyway; it was all the way live. I went over to Alia's table and she was laughing and talking with her friends when I thought I heard gunshots outside.

"Did you hear that babe?"

"Hear what? I didn't hear nothing but this loud ass music," she shouted over the music.

I paused for a few seconds and then kissed her. "I love this, thank you."

"Happy birthday boo ... muah," she kissed me until I heard loud screaming and people running from the back area of the VIP section.

"SNEAKY YAWL! SNEAKY GOT SHOT!" Sylvia jumped up quick and so did I. We all ran out of the back door. The police were pulling up with the ambulance. I saw Sneaky and tried to run over to him when the cop stopped me.

"That's my boy!"

"Let the paramedics deal with him right now sir. Stand back."

Sylvia was going crazy; they wouldn't let her near him and they put him in the back of the ambulance.

"Is he okay?" I asked the cop.

"I dunno, just hang out right here, sir."

"FUCK MAN!" I turned and saw Alia standing with her hands over her face. I hugged her, praying that my boy was okay. Damn! I remember him saying, let me go out here and meet this nigga! I wonder who he was talking about.

"Sylvia! You going to the hospital?"

"YES! He's going to ST LUKE!" she yelled and Alia and I rushed to the car.

"Aye, Cheetah, yawl going over there?"

"Hell yeah!"

"Where's RAZZ?"

"He's in the back of the ambulance already!" Marcus shouted. G.B. came up to me.

"Man, yawl going up to the hospital?"

"Yeah, follow us!" FUCK! This was a fucked up way to end my birthday! I hoped he was all right. I jumped in the car with Alia, Chepi and my brother Marcus and we hightailed behind the ambulance on the way to St.Luke's.